FELIX K

THE KERSTEN
MEMOIRS
1940–1945

With an Introduction by
H. R. TREVOR-ROPER

Translated from the German by
CONSTANTINE FITZGIBBON
and
JAMES OLIVER

ISHI PRESS
INTERNATIONAL

The Kersten Memoirs: 1940-1945

by Felix Kersten
with an Introduction by Hugh Trevor-Roper

Translated from German into English by
Constantine Fitzgibbon and James Oliver

First Published in 1957

Copyright © 1956 by Felix Kersten

This Printing in September, 2011
by Ishi Press in New York and Tokyo

with a new foreword by Sam Sloan

Copyright © 2011 by Sam Sloan

ISBN 4-87187-912-7
978-4-87187-912-5

Ishi Press International
1664 Davidson Avenue, Suite 1B
Bronx NY 10453-7877
USA

1-917-507-7226

Printed in the United States of America

The Kersten Memoirs: 1940-1945
by Felix Kersten

Introduction by Sam Sloan

A problem historians have in dealing with the Hitler Era is the lack of any written order signed by Hitler directing the extermination of the Jews. It is true that Hitler often said bad things about the Jews, frequently speaking of a "World Jewish Conspiracy". Hitler often said that the Jews had started World War II, whereas just about everybody else said that Hitler himself had started World War II.

In spite of all this, proof has been lacking that Hitler planned to kill them all. There is an alternate theory. Hitler believed that the Governments of the World, with the exception of his own, were controlled by the Jews. This belief that almost all other governments in the world were controlled by the "World Jewish Conspiracy" was aided by the fact that Karl Marx was a Jew, the Prime Minister of England, Benjamin Disraeli, was a Jew and there suspicions that President Roosevelt was a Jew. Even the Pope was a Jew, according to Hitler.

At least Hitler could feel confident that the Emperor of Japan, Hirohito, was not a Jew and that Benito Mussolini, Ruler of Italy, was not a Jew either.

This led Hitler to believe that if he threatened the Jews, they would tell the governments they controlled to be nice to Hitler.

While Hitler at first merely wanted to threaten the Jews so that they would direct the governments they controlled to be nice to him (especially since this policy seemed to be working such as with Neville Chamberlain and his ridiculous "Peace For Our Time" letter), Hitler's subordinate Heinrich Himmler did not see the need to waste any time over this and wanted to kill all the Jews immediately, as this book makes clear.

It was not only the Jews that Himmler wanted to kill. He wanted to kill all the lawyers too (some good points in that), all the tax-consultants and all the homosexuals.

Introduction by Sam Sloan

Himmler's hatred of homosexuals is especially strange because most (normal) men are quite happy to have lots of homosexuals around. For example, here in San Francisco, it is a paradise for those few very rare men here who like women, because most of the men here like each other.

Himmler did not agree with this idea of "The More Homosexuals the Better". He wanted to kill all of them immediately, as soon as they could be found out.

Himmler also wanted to set up special academies for "Chosen Women". These must be women of high intelligence and gifted in the arts. Of course, they must also be blond haired and blue eyed women, as only women with blond hair and blue eyes possess these traits. Himmler said:

> "These Chosen Women will receive the best possible education. They will have a good-grounding in history; they will learn languages and receive the same training as officials in the foreign service; they must be quick witted and know how to think and act swiftly in delicate situations. Daily games of chess will be part of the curriculum to develop their minds." (Page 75)

Naturally, we agree with these "daily games of chess" that these blue-eyed women will be required to play, as they will have to play with us, as who else is there for them to play? Certainly not with each other, a bunch of patzers?

Himmler did not seem to have a good solution regarding what to do with all these blond-haired blue-eyed chess-playing women once they had completed their training at age 26. It would seem that they should be put into Baby Farms where they would be assigned the task of producing more blond-haired blue-eyed children. (Did this really happen? It has long been rumored.)

Kersten was especially perplexed at Himmler's insistence on exterminating the homosexuals. When Himmler said that they should be rounded up because of their "Abnormal Sexual Behavior", Kersten replied, "From your point of view, Herr Himmler, but not from the homosexual's. According to his psychology, he is normal and we are abnormal."

Introduction by Sam Sloan

Himmler discussed with Kersten the case of a man who had risen to a high rank in the SS. When it was discovered that he had engaged in homosexual activity, he was demoted. Later, on his promise not to do it again, he had been reinstated and risen even higher, but then had been caught committing homosexual acts again. This time he had been imprisoned and sent to a concentration camp.

> "We can't permit such a danger to the country; the homosexuals must be entirely eliminated. The homosexual is a traitor to his own people and must be rooted out."

> *And if he has children?" I objected. "There are a number of men who have both sexual tendencies, live a normal married life and have quantities of children."

> "So much the worse," was Himmler's answer, "for then the homosexual tendency will be inherited. I have long been considering whether it would not be to the point to castrate every homosexual at once. That would help him and us."

We can plainly see from this book that Heinrich Himmler was a dangerous lunatic. We can be thankful that he ultimately killed himself in 1945. However, his words must be studied. We cannot think that World War II ended the matter. Right here in the United States of America there are prominent politicians, some who are holding or have held high elective office, whose views coincide with those of Heinrich Himmler, but they are diplomatic enough not to reveal their true thoughts.

This is especially true of politicians on the so-called "Religious Right" including one presidential candidate. It is often believed that politicians on the Religious Right support Israel and the right of the Jews to return to Israel.

What they really believe in is a literal interpretation of the Bible in **Revelation 16:18**, which states that all the Jews will gather together in the place that in Hebrew is called Armageddon, where they will all be killed in an Earthquake.

Introduction by Sam Sloan

So, our Religious Right USA politicians who say they are supporting the right of the Jewish people to return to Israel are actually trying to get them to go there so that they will all be killed.

There are a number of controversies involving The Kersten Memoirs: 1940-1945 by Felix Kersten. Mostly, they concern whether Kersten exaggerated his role in saving thousands of Jews and others from the Gas Chambers. He wrote this book years later with the benefit of history.

Kersten's claims of being instrumental in saving Finland's Jews from German hands may be exaggerated, but the Finnish government did use his services in the hope of influencing Himmler.

A documentary has been produced in Finland entitled *"Who Was Felix Kersten? Satan's Doctor documentary"* (directed by Emmanuel Amara, produced by Sunset Presse).

Woody Allen wrote a parody of Kersten entitled "The Schmeed Memoirs", in which a fictional barber in wartime Germany describes his time as a hair stylist for Adolf Hitler.

Felix Kersten was born on 30 September 1898 in a Baltic German family in Estonia when the country was still a part of Imperial Russia. During World War II he was the personal masseur of Heinrich Himmler. Kersten used his position to aid people persecuted by Nazi Germany, although whether his actions were as decisive as Kersten claimed in his memoirs is not readily verifiable from other sources.

During World War I he fought in the German Army and arrived in Finland in April 1918 with the German forces that intervened in the Finnish Civil War. Kersten served for a while in Suojeluskunta, was granted Finnish citizenship in 1920 and commissioned 2nd Lieutenant (vänrikki) in the Finnish Army in September 1921.

Kersten began his studies in Helsinki where he studied with the specialist Dr Colander. After two years' study he was awarded his degree in scientific massage.

Kersten had a number of very influential customers, among them Prince Hendrik of the Netherlands (after 1928) and Benito

Introduction by Sam Sloan

Mussolini's son-in-law and Foreign Minister Galeazzo Ciano. Kersten accepted Heinrich Himmler's request to become his personal masseur, writing later that he feared for his safety if he refused.

He was able to alleviate Himmler's severe stomach pains with his skills and gained his trust. Kersten used this trust to obtain pardons and releases of several prisoners.

During the War, Kersten also provided information to the OSS (predecessor of the CIA).

Towards the end of the War, Kersten arranged a meeting with Himmler and Norbert Masur, a member of the Swedish branch of the World Jewish Congress, in Harztwalde, a few miles from Ravensbruck concentration camp. As a result Himmler agreed to spare the lives of the remaining 60,000 Jews left in Nazi concentration camps days before their liberation by the Allies.

In December 1945, the World Jewish Congress presented Kersten with a letter thanking him for helping to save Jewish concentration-camp victims.

In his post-war memoirs, Kersten takes credit for saving, among others, the whole Dutch people from forced deportation to the Nazi-occupied East. In 1953 the Dutch government nominated him for the Nobel Peace Prize on this account.

However, a later official Dutch investigation concluded that no such plan had ever existed and that some of Kersten's documents were fabricated. The Swedish archives testify that Kersten was intermediary between Himmler and Count Folke Bernadotte in the negotiations that led to the rescue operation 'The White Buses', saving hundreds of Norwegians and Danes from certain death in the last days of the Third Reich.

After the War, Kersten lived in West Germany and Sweden, taking Swedish citizenship in 1953. He died on 16 April 1960 in Stockholm, Sweden.

Sam Sloan
San Rafael, California
September 24, 2011

Kersten - Original Back Cover and Flaps

During the dying days of the Third Reich, Felix Kersten held a most incredible position at Heinrich Himmler's court. As his personal manual therapist, Kersten was the only man capable of relieving Himmler's crippling stomach pains, and as such, his influence over the inhuman tyrant was extraordinary.

Becoming more and more dependent on his "good Dr. Kersten," the German Grand Inquisitor allowed his confessor great liberties and granted his outrageous, almost unbelievable requests. Kersten used his powers to render outstanding services to humanity. Thousands of Dutchmen, Germans, Jews and others owe their survival to his intercession. Almost daily he was responsible for the saving of some European's life until Himmler was prompted to say, "Kersten massages a life out of me with every rub."

The core of this fascinating book is the conversations held between the two men over a period of five years. Heinrich Himmler's pathetic, pedantic monologues reveal the principles on which a Post-war Europe was to be rebuilt. Himmler discourses on such varied subjects as Freemasonry, the Jew's, medicine, law, religion, and homosexuality. Discussions on bigamy, the chosen women, the superiority of blue-eyed blondes bring Himmler's character into sharper focus than ever before.

This picture of Himmler will jar many people - the picture of a man who, in the same breath, could be a philosopher and a butcher, a man who could not differentiate between right and wrong, a man who was responsible for filling German gas chambers with millions of bodies and yet was revolted by the killing of a pheasant for sport. The Kersten story is highly charged.

H. R. Trevor-Roper's Introduction explores the background of Dr. Kersten, removes many of the claims of the late Count Bernadotte, and records the final acknowledgment Dr. Kersten received for his great work. He states: "Since historical accident drew me into this controversy, and human interest prevented me from dropping it till I had satisfied myself on every point, I may claim an intimate knowledge of the matter, and it gives me great pleasure to be able to publish the facts in the form of an introduction to this book. . . .

Kersten - Original Back Cover and Flaps

As far as honesty of purpose and authenticity of documentation are concerned I am pleased to support with such authority as I possess the accuracy of these memoirs of Felix Kersten."

AN EXCERPT FROM "THE KERSTEN MEMOIRS"

19th July, 1942

Yesterday evening I was with Himmler to give him the treatment which had once more been postponed. He began talking about the Wehrbauern (villages to be inhabited by soldier-peasants) again.
"There is one question I should like to ask you", I said. "which is much on my mind. I don't see any churches in your peasant settlements. Yet a church is a part of any village - or at least several villages should have one between them. Do you intend to set up parishes?

"What are you thinking of, Herr Kersten?', answered Himmler. "spending our good money on churches! We aren't mad yet. Our military peasantry will need no churches."

"How about churches and clergy which care for the peasants now, and what will happen when they want their children baptized? What will you do then?", I argued. "Then the clergy should find the money themselves and build themselves a church at their own expense. We won't stop them, and apart from that these buildings will later come in useful for us. The more our training takes root and men become infused with our spirit, the less will they depend on the churches - and one day they will be empty. Then we will see to it that the churches remain the property of the permanent farming community. It will be a particular satisfaction to me when we take over these churches and turn them into Germanic holy places. our training will beat the clergy. You may be sure of that."

The Kersten Memoirs 1940-1945
Introduction by H. R. Trevor-Roper
Translated from the German by Constantine FitzGibbon
and James Oliver

Did any real ideas lie behind National Socialism? Such purposeful material power must have indicated, one might suppose, a corresponding power within. If anyone still credits the movement of Adolf Hitler with a serious ideology, that person's duty is to read Heinrich Himmler's pathetic, pedantic monologues on the principles on which the post-war New Europe was to be rebuilt. Felix Kersten, Himmler's personal manual therapist, has recorded their conversations between 1940 and 1945 as his dreaded patient lay, relaxed and grateful, under his soothing hands.

But there is another side to this astounding document. Holding as he did the keys of Himmler's physical salvation, Kersten became the all-powerful confessor who could manipulate at will the conscience as well as the stomach of that terrible, impersonal, inhuman, but naive mystical credulous tyrant of the New Order. How did Kersten use these extra-ordinary opportunities? Thousands of Dutchmen, Germans. Jews and indeed others owe their survival to his intercession. The Finnish Legation used him to rescue Norwegian and Danish prisoners; the World Jewish Congress credits him with the rescue of 60,000 Jews; he particularly devoted himself to the interests of Holland. Himmler himself .saw perfectly well what was happening, but could do nothing. "Kersten messages a life out of me," he once said, "with every rub."

Hugh Trevor-Roper writes in his introduction: "Since historical accident drew me into this controversy, and human interest prevented me from dropping it till I had satisfied myself on every point, I may claim an intimate knowledge of the matter, and it gives me great pleasure to be able to publish the facts in the form of an introduction to this book. . . . As far as honesty of purpose and authenticity of documentation are concerned I am pleased to support with such authority as I possess the accuracy of these memoirs of Felix Kersten."

CONTENTS

PREFACE

With this book I put before the British public notes of my talks with leading men in National Socialist Germany, particularly with Heinrich Himmler, minister of the Reich and head of the SS. When I wrote down these impressions in the war years, coming straight from my meetings with these men, I had no idea of embarking on a piece of historical research. These observations came into being rather as a diary of my struggles with those in power on behalf of suffering humanity. I had to write from the heart of my impressions and experiences, and to describe what I saw and heard.

It was as a doctor that I met the men who held power in Germany at that time, and in an atmosphere such as usually prevails in the relation between doctor and patient. This meant that they were more free and unconstrained, often laying aside the mask with which men like to conceal their innermost feelings. My constant and passionate efforts to serve humanity and to rescue those whose lives had been despaired of were usually quite beyond their comprehension. Yet they sometimes showed themselves disposed to grant my wishes for the good of those who were oppressed and persecuted, simply because I was of service to them as a doctor and because our encounters were personal, beyond the limits of their grim and inflexible world.

Today much of what I describe may seem dull and not very striking. I lived through it all in that exciting time in which every talk and every meeting had a deeper significance, often concealed in the background. In its wider context every fact had its importance for me. My observations have since been revised only in so far as to group excerpts in chapters relating to a common theme. These pages of my diary may have some historical value. They were written under the direct impression of experience, in an incessant search for the truth.

My records are far more extensive than all that I have published in recent years in Dutch, Swedish, German—and now in English. For this reason the selections from my diaries in the present work ⸌

not correspond in every detail with these other works: *Samtal med Himmler*, *Klerk en Beul*, or *Totenkopf und Treue*.

A selection which should best give a true picture of my experiences has been undertaken in co-operation with my English translators and publishers.

FELIX KERSTEN.

Stockholm,
Sweden,
12th August, 1955.

INTRODUCTION

by

H. R. TREVOR-ROPER

FELIX KERSTEN, the author of this book, was Heinrich Himmler's personal doctor during the Second World War; he has also been decorated for outstanding services to humanity during the same period. This combination of activities might well seem a paradox; and since paradox naturally generates controversy, Kersten has been the centre, since the war, of a good deal of controversy—from which, however, he has at last emerged triumphant. Since historical accident drew me into this controversy, and human interest prevented me from dropping it till I had satisfied myself on every point, I may claim an intimate knowledge of the matter, and it gives me great pleasure to be able to publish the facts in the form of an introduction to this book. The contents of the book are certainly so extraordinary that readers may well wish for some assurance about the author's credentials.

First, how did Kersten achieve the strange position of Himmler's doctor—and indeed more than doctor, for he was, as he has himself admitted, almost a 'father-confessor' to that terrible ogre of the Third Reich? It is a cosmopolitan story, for Kersten is a cosmopolitan figure— at least a North European cosmopolitan. A Balt of Germanic origin, born in Estonia in 1898, and therefore originally a Russian subject, he fought in 1918 as a volunteer in the Finnish war of liberation against Russia. In 1920 he became a Finnish subject. Thereafter he studied manual therapy in Berlin under a famous Chinese specialist, Dr. Ko, and quickly became himself one of the most successful practitioners of this unorthodox but valuable art. His professional success began in Germany, where the aristocracy and the plutocracy of the 1920s alike resorted to him; but since both these classes are international, their patronage soon carried him abroad. Thus, among the aristocracy, Duke Adolf Friedrich of Mecklenburg passed him on to his brother, Prince Hendrik, the husband of Queen Wilhelmina of the Netherlands. This was one of the most important incidents in Kersten's career, for in time he became a member of the

9

Prince's household and made his home in Holland. But he practised in
Germany too, and there another recommendation led to even greater
consequences. This time it came from the plutocracy. In March 1939
his patient, Dr. August Diehn, President of the German Potassium Syn-
dicate, approached Kersten with a peculiarly urgent request. "Herr
Kersten," he said, "I have never asked a favour from you before; now
I have one to ask. Will you examine Heinrich Himmler? I think you
would find him an interesting patient. Besides, if you succeed with him,
you may do us a great service. Perhaps you can persuade him not to
nationalize private industry."

Kersten examined Himmler. He found that he suffered from intestinal
spasms, causing great pain, sometimes unconsciousness. Hitherto doctors
had treated him with narcotics and injections, but without effect. Kersten
treated him manually and the result was astonishing: in five minutes
the pain was relieved. Himmler was delighted: he begged Kersten to
remain in personal attendance upon him; but Kersten refused. The war
had not yet broken out; Himmler was not yet able to command; he was
therefore forced to remain as merely one of those German patients whom
Kersten would attend in the course of his regular professional visits to
Germany from his base in Holland.

Such at least was the intention: the issue was different. For by next
spring—the spring of 1940—when Kersten visited Germany, a state of
war existed, and it was while Kersten was actually in Berlin that the
German armies suddenly invaded Holland and cut off his retreat. The
Dutch royal family fled to England. It was therefore with all the advantages of power, and against a background of threats, that Himmler
now repeated his demands to Kersten. Faced with the alternative of the
court or the concentration camp, Kersten chose freedom: he became the
personal medical adviser to the Grand Inquisitor of the Third Reich:
the extraordinary part of history began.

To us, living and having always lived in a liberal society, the position
of court doctors in the Third Reich must always seem extraordinary.
What power was wielded, at Hitler's court, by his doctors, what ver-
tiginous politics surrounded them, what devouring intrigues divided them!
I have described elsewhere those strange events, which Bormann's letters,
written from the very center of the court, have since vividly illustrated.[1]
Himmler's court was hardly different; nor is the explanation really so
far to seek. All tyrants, isolated in dangerous eminence—especially if they
are, like Himmler, fundamentally weak men—require confidants whom
(perhaps wrongly) they suppose to be outside the vortex of political rivalry

[1] *The Last Days of Hitler*, 2nd ed., 1950, pp. 65–79; *The Bormann Letters* (1954) *passim*.

around them. Court fools, astrologers, priests, mistresses—all these have
filled a classic *rôle* in the past. The modern valetudinarian despots have
given the same *rôle* to their doctors. Hitler relied on Morell and (until
he was ruined by Morell) Brandt; Himmler upon Gebhard and Kersten.
To him Kersten, upon whom he became more and more dependent, was
always "my good Dr. Kersten", "the magic Buddha" (as he described
him to Count Ciano) "who cures everything by massage";[1] he addressed
him in almost tender terms, allowed him great liberties, listened calmly
to the most outrageous requests; and Kersten, holding as he did the keys
of physical salvation, became to Himmler the all-powerful confessor who
could manipulate at will the conscience as well as the stomach of that
terrible, impersonal, inhuman, but naive, mystical, credulous tyrant of the
New Order.

How did Kersten use these extraordinary opportunities? The facts
are now well attested. Thousands of Dutchmen, Germans, Jews and indeed others owe their survival to his intercession. All who sought respite
for doomed men and women learned gradually where it was most useful
to turn. The Finnish Legation in Germany used him to rescue Norwegian
and Danish prisoners;[2] the World Jewish Congress credits him with the
rescue of 60,000 Jews;[3] particularly he devoted himself to the interests of
Holland which, before the war, had become his real home. Thus in 1941
Hitler proposed to transport up to three million 'irreconcilable' Dutchmen
to Polish Galicia and the Ukraine and referred the execution of the proposal to Himmler. Fortunately Himmler happened at that time to be in
a low state of health and particularly dependent on Kersten. Kersten
persuaded him that the additional strain on his health of carrying out
so vast an operation might well be fatal. The operation was therefore
postponed till after the war. Himmler afterwards regretted his weakness
in this matter. The Führer's decision, he sadly admitted, had been right;
its postponement "was all the fault of my wretched health and the good
Dr. Kersten".[4]

Of course this loophole in the system of terror was noted at Himmler's
court. Some, the more liberal—for even at Himmler's court there were
some relatively liberal men, officials who obeyed orders without much

[1] Ciano, *Diary,* 7th October, 1942.
[2] Affidavits by Henrik Ramsay (Finnish Minister for Foreign Affairs, 1943–4), 13th
June, 1949, and by Professor T. M. Kivimäki (Finnish Minister to Berlin, 1940–4), 5th
December, 1948.
[3] Memorandum of World Jewish Congress (sd. A. Spivak & G. Storch), Stockholm,
18th June, 1947.
[4] Report of Dutch Parliamentary *Enquête-commissie,* 1950; since confirmed by depositions
of Ludwig Pemsel, 27th March, 1952, and General-Major Franz Müller-Dachs, 28th September, 1949. The plan to colonize the Ukraine with Dutchmen in 1941 is confirmed by Hitler's
Table-Talk (1953), p. 25.

conscience indeed but without any positive desire for blood—took advantage of it: Himmler's secretary, Rudolf Brandt for instance, and his chief of intelligence, Walter Schellenberg. These men continually referred the cases of condemned men to Kersten as the only man who could cause a sentence to be reversed or suspended. Others, of course, held the opposite view—particularly Ernst Kaltenbrunner, the Austrian thug who controlled, under Himmler, all security in the Reich. Kaltenbrunner would gladly have seen Kersten liquidated; but Kersten's position with Himmler was too strong. As Himmler once said to Kaltenbrunner, "if Kersten is bumped off, you will not survive him by twenty-four hours". So the loophole continued to leak; the gas-chambers and the firing-squads were quietly cheated; and Himmler himself saw perfectly well what was happening, but could do nothing: "Kersten massages a life out of me," he once said, "with every rub." [1]

By 1943 Kersten's empire over the mind of Himmler was so complete that he decided to emancipate himself from that too exclusive dependence upon him to which the war had condemned him. Since Holland no longer existed, he sought for another neutral state in Northern Europe and told Himmler that he now wished to move his home and family to Sweden. Himmler was dissatisfied: he did not wish to lose Kersten. But by now it was not Himmler who could threaten: the personal relationship between the two men had changed since 1940; and when Kersten gave Himmler the choice of never being visited by Kersten again or of being visited occasionally from Sweden, Himmler resigned himself reluctantly to the second alternative. In 1943 therefore Kersten, while keeping the German property, Gut Hartzwalde, which he had recently bought with his blocked German earnings, moved his base to Stockholm. This move marked another important stage in his career: it made him the agent of the Swedish Government in its humanitarian work at the close of the war, and, indirectly, it led to the attempts which have since been made to transfer to others the credit for his work.

Kersten's first important work for Sweden [2] consisted in his long and ultimately successful battle to save the lives of seven Swedish business men, representatives of the Swedish Match Company, who had been arrested by the Germans in Warsaw on a charge of espionage. It was the Berlin lawyer, Dr. Langbehn—afterwards executed as an anti-Nazi—who first suggested to the company's representatives in Berlin that Kersten 'would probably contrive to massage the men out'; and sure enough, in

[1] Interrogation of Frl. Schienke (Schellenberg's secretary) in England, 19th December, 1945.
[2] The first approach by Sweden to Kersten had already been made by the Swedish Ambassador in Berlin, Herr Richert, in the summer of 1942.

the end, Kersten secured the release of all of them, including four who had been condemned to death, and in December 1944 he was allowed to take the last three of them back to Sweden with him as a personal 'Christmas present' from Himmler.[1] In the early stages of these negotiations Kersten became personally acquainted with the then Swedish Minister for Foreign Affairs, Herr Christian Günther, and from that time he became an agent of Günther in Swedish humanitarian work in Germany. In the winter of 1944-5, when the defeat of Germany seemed at last imminent, this Swedish intervention became of international significance.

For what, in the last convulsions of Nazi Germany, would be the fate of occupied Scandinavia—of Denmark and Norway? Hitler had ordered the German armies to fight to the end everywhere. Could Sweden, the only neutral Scandinavian power, see her neighbours thus uselessly destroyed? And what would be the fate of the hundreds of thousands of prisoners—including Danes and Norwegians—in German concentration camps? Hitler had given orders that on the approach of the Allied armies all concentration camps were to be blown up and their inmates slaughtered. Policy and humanity alike required that Sweden intervene to prevent such useless destruction, such insensate murder. But where could such intervention be made? Where indeed but at the court of Himmler, the only alternative to the court of Hitler. Hitler ordered, but it was Himmler who executed—or stayed the execution; and to the ear of Himmler, Günther now had a direct private line in the person of Felix Kersten.

Thus the plan was made, in Stockholm, between Günther and Kersten and, after long preparation, Kersten duly presented himself to Himmler in Germany to see whether the tyrant, in the last days, would heed the voice of prudence and persuasion. Would he, asked Kersten, allow all Scandinavian prisoners to be sent to Sweden and be interned there? No, said Himmler, that was too difficult. Then would he, asked Kersten, allow all Scandinavian prisoners to be concentrated in one camp from which, if necessary, they could be transported to Sweden? To this Himmler agreed—provided that Sweden, not Germany, were responsible for supplying the transport for their removal. He agreed to allow into Germany—secretly of course—up to a hundred and fifty omnibuses to transport the prisoners to Sweden. Apart from the Danish and Norwegian

---

[1] The best, because reluctant, testimony to Kersten's work in this matter is contained in the record of the trial at Nuremberg of Walter Schellenberg. Schellenberg tried to claim that it was he who had saved the men, but as the witnesses were examined it became clear (as the Court observed) that their rescue was really the work of the then unknown Dr. Kersten.

prisoners, Himmler further promised, as a personal gift to Kersten, the lives of 1,000 Dutch women, 1,500 French women, 500 Polish women and 400 Belgians, provided he could obtain asylum for them in Sweden, and 2,700 Jews to be transported to Switzerland. The prisoners for Sweden would be concentrated in the camp at Neuengamme. This agreement between Himmler and Kersten was made on 8th December, 1944, and confirmed in writing on 21st December. On 22nd December Kersten arrived back in Sweden and reported to Günther the barely hoped for success of his mission.

All that remained to do was to send the omnibuses. By February 1945 this had been arranged. A column of a hundred omnibuses of the Swedish Red Cross was marshalled and set out for Germany. These were known as 'the white buses'; they were under the command of Colonel (now General) Gottfried Björk; and they were accompanied by the Vice-President of the Swedish Red Cross, an important social figure whom Kersten now, at Günther's request, announced by telephone to Himmler, Count Folke Bernadotte.

Folke Bernadotte played so large and, it will seem to some, so surprising a part in the rest of this story that it seems necessary to pause and forestall any possible misunderstanding. Since he is dead and cannot answer any charge, it is important that he should not be hastily accused or his motives rashly imputed. Nevertheless, the facts, amply documented, are clear. They show that he first sought to fill a larger *rôle* than had been assigned to him, and that afterwards, in a foolish attempt to monopolize the glory of the achievement, he allowed himself to claim a position which could only be defended by unfortunate exhibitionism and unfair persecution. How an essentially honourable man allowed himself to slide into such courses can only be surmised. Possibly to an energetic, if not very intelligent, man the position of a mere ambassador seemed inadequate. Possibly to a naive, rather vain man, unaccustomed to delicate and complex negotiations, his own part genuinely seemed more important than it was. Possibly there were many in Sweden who, uneasily conscious of an inglorious neutrality during the war, were only too eager to build up a Swedish prince as hero of the peace. And it should be remembered that many of Himmler's court, apprehending an early day of judgment, were only too eager to clutch at the visiting Folke Bernadotte, the kinsman of the neutral King of Sweden, as a future patron and protector whose vanity it was worth their while to flatter, and by flattery to delude. At all events, whatever the motives which led him afterwards to make his improper claims, Count Bernadotte paid dearly for them. But for the self-glorifying myth which he manufactured, it is unlikely that he would ever have been chosen as U.N. mediator in the Arab-Jewish war of 1948, or fallen in Palestine a premature victim of the assassin's bullet.

I have called Bernadotte a 'mere ambassador'. By this I mean that although he was empowered to discuss matters of detail with Himmler, he had no power to initiate or negotiate policy. Indeed, there was no policy left for him to initiate or to negotiate, for it had already been initiated by Günther and negotiated with Himmler by Kersten. Nevertheless, through Bernadotte's ignorance of policy, or perhaps through lack of clarity in explaining it to him, misunderstandings soon arose. For since his treaty with Himmler of 8th December, Kersten had been making, in concert with Günther, further arrangements. In particular, he had promised Hr. Hillel Storch, the head of the Swedish branch of the World Jewish Congress, to secure the release to Sweden, if possible, of a further 3,500 Jewish prisoners. To this Himmler had agreed, but suddenly Bernadotte (to the surprise of Himmler and dismay of Kersten) refused to handle non-Scandinavian prisoners. In the end, however, after a visit by Kersten to Günther in Stockholm, these difficulties were all overcome,[1] and on 21st April Kersten's work for the Jews culminated in one of the most ironical incidents in the whole war: the secret meeting, at Kersten's house Hartzwalde, between Himmler, the arch-persecutor of the Jews, and Norbert Masur, a member of the Board of the Stockholm branch of the World Jewish Congress, whom Kersten had personally brought from Sweden for that purpose.[2] That astonishing interview has been described elsewhere, by Masur himself;[3] in it the last details were arranged; and two hours later Himmler told Bernadotte that the Jews were free to go to Sweden—"I have promised my good Dr. Kersten and I must keep my promise; besides I have fixed all the details with Herr Masur"; and Bernadotte duly took them and was presented by a rabbi in Stockholm with a laudatory scroll.[4]

[1] At a meeting at the Swedish Foreign Office on 27th March, 1945, as confirmed by an official minute kindly quoted to me by Herr Åström, Counsellor of the Swedish Embassy in London.
[2] The original plan had been to send Hr. Storch himself to Berlin; but in the end, since Hr. Storch, a Balt, had no Swedish passport to guarantee his personal safety, this was judged too dangerous, and Hr. Masur, being a Swede, was sent in his stead.
[3] Norbert Masur, En Jude talar med Himmler (Stockholm, 1945). Some difference of opinion has since arisen between Dr. Kersten and Hr. Masur as to the relative importance, in connexion with the release of the Jews, of Himmler's promises to Kersten before 21st April and his agreement with Masur on that date. After a careful study of the contemporary Swedish, Jewish and Dutch evidence available to me, and an interesting discussion with Hr. Masur, I think it safe to conclude that Himmler undoubtedly made general promises to Kersten in March 1945, but that it needed Masur's bold personal visit to bring these promises into clear practical form.
[4] Bernadotte's initial refusal to take non-Scandinavian prisoners is confirmed by an affidavit by Gottlob Berger, Himmler's chief of staff, of 26th May, 1952. I have seen what

[Footnote continued at foot of next page

It is important to note that although Bernadotte seems to have been understood by Himmler as using the language of anti-Semitism—which may have been a tactical necessity—there is no reason to suppose that his motive in refusing to take the Jews was anti-Semitic. Indeed the evidence points in the other direction, for Bernadotte also refused to take French and Polish prisoners. It seems clear that his original instructions only allowed him to take Scandinavian prisoners; but on 27 March, thanks to the success of other negotiations, these instructions were widened to include all victims of Nazi oppression.

Meanwhile, on 12th March Kersten had completed Günther's programme by signing another treaty with Himmler. By this treaty [1] Himmler undertook not to carry out Hitler's order to blow up the concentration camps on the approach of the Allied armies, but to surrender them, under the white flag, with all their inmates, and to stop all further execution of Jews. Finally, on the night of 21st–22nd April, Himmler asked Kersten to forward an offer of surrender to the Allies. Kersten declined to meddle in politics and referred him to Bernadotte, who duly passed the message on to Stockholm.

Thus, in the last weeks of the Third Reich, the policy whereby so many lives were saved was the policy of the Swedish Government; behind it, indefatigable in his pressure and proposals, was the Norwegian Hr. Ditleff, who was head of the organization in Sweden for aiding prisoners of war, and who has rightly been called the driving force in these preliminary negotiations. The essential negotiator, but for whose influence that policy could not have been made effective, was Felix Kersten; the Jews owe a considerable debt to the intervention of Hr. Storch and Hr. Masur; Count Bernadotte could claim the honourable *rôle* of an instrument chosen to supply the technical but also essential means of execution. Unfortunately Bernadotte was not content with this *rôle*. No sooner was the war over than he was suddenly thrust before the public as the man who, on his own initiative, had both conceived and executed the whole plan. He alone, it was stated, by facing the hitherto implacable Himmler in his den, had managed the tyrant and, by managing him, rescued

Footnote continued from foot of previous page]
purports to be a copy, made by Rudolf Brandt, Himmler's secretary, of a very explicit private letter of 10th March, 1945, from Bernadotte to Himmler on this subject; but since its authenticity cannot be proved, I prefer to disregard it for the time being. According to Berger, Bernadotte sent several private letters (i.e. not on Red Cross notepaper and presumably not filed in the Red Cross files) to Himmler, and these letters were not among those which Himmler is known to have destroyed. If so the originals may turn up among Himmler's papers now in America.
[1] Of which a carbon copy survives and has been authenticated by the Dutch *Enquête-commissie*. The original was seen by Baron van Nagell, to whom Kersten showed it in Stockholm on 23rd March, 1943. Baron van Nagell has testified as to its form and contents.

Jews and Gentiles from death in the concentration camps. He was even credited with having ended the war. He was hailed as the Prince of Peace, the saviour and, after his death, the martyr of humanity. Much of this deplorable ballyhoo is not his responsibility. It would be unfair, for instance, to blame him for the inspired hagiography which, since his death, has only made him undeservedly ridiculous; but he cannot disclaim the three books which he himself wrote, the first of which, more than anything else, provided the nucleus of the legend.

This book was entitled, in Swedish, *Slutet*—in the English version, *The Fall of the Curtain*—and one of the most interesting facts about it is the speed with which it was produced. In spite of a disarming preface in which Bernadotte declared that it was only with great reluctance that he had yielded to the pressure of friends and consented to write this account of his actions, the book in fact appeared in the shops within six weeks of the events it described. Further, large parts of it had been ghost-written, at high speed, by Himmler's former chief of intelligence, Walter Schellenberg, who, at the end of the war, had taken refuge in Bernadotte's house in Stockholm and who (since he had a war crime on his conscience [1]) was eager to deserve Swedish protection. In fairness to Schellenberg it should be noted that in his draft (of which he still had a copy in his possession when he was finally surrendered to the Allies) some credit was given to Kersten and Masur for their work in the last days. Only from Bernadotte's final version were both these names altogether omitted. Even Günther, the Foreign Minister who had conceived the plan, received no recognition in Bernadotte's book. In that book the whole operation was presented as the conception and achievement of one great humanitarian, Folke Bernadotte.[2]

It seems that Count Bernadotte himself expected some opposition to his claims, for according to Kersten, one or two days before the appearance of the book he received a telephone call from Bernadotte advising him, somewhat bluntly, not to make any adverse comments on the forthcoming work if he did not wish to be sent back, as a Finnish subject, to Finland— then under communist *régime*. I would not mention this detail, since it comes from Kersten himself who may perhaps have misunderstood

[1] In 1939 Schellenberg, as a Gestapo officer, had been responsible for the kidnapping, on neutral Dutch territory, of two British intelligence officers, Captain Best and Major Stevens. This incident, which was of course contrary to all rules of war, and in the course of which a Dutchman had been killed, preyed heavily on Schellenberg's mind at the end of the war.

[2] Bernadotte was very energetic in spreading his own fame. On 17th April, 1947, he wrote to me suggesting that I had given insufficient attention to his achievements in my book *The Last Days of Hitler*, and he afterwards had his letter to me published in Sweden. Later, I discovered that he had sent copies of his letter to me to prominent Englishmen, for information.

Bernadotte's drift, were it not that it is partly confirmed by Schellenberg, to whom Bernadotte declared the same afternoon that he had given Kersten a 'knock-out blow' by telephone, and by an affidavit from the former Dutch ambassador in Stockholm, the Baron van Nagell, to whom Kersten promptly appealed for support. Baron van Nagell at once obtained an assurance from Günther that Kersten would never be molested. He also called personally on Bernadotte. "I was only allowed to see him for five minutes in the Swedish Red Cross Office," he writes, "but that was enough. I quickly reminded him that Dr. Kersten had done all the work and that he [Bernadotte] had only been charged by the Swedish Government to transport the released prisoners to Sweden. Finally Count Bernadotte had to admit that the rescue, ascribed to him alone, actually had two phases: first, the release of the prisoners from the camps in Germany, which was achieved by Dr. Kersten alone; and secondly, his [Bernadotte's] transport of the released prisoners." [1] Unfortunately a private verbal admission, however welcome, cannot effectively cancel a public and written claim contained in a best-selling book translated into a dozen languages. And unfortunately it must be added that this is not the only instance in which Bernadotte sought to prevent the publication of any version of these events except his own.

This public theft of the credit for his secret services was soon followed, for Kersten, by a more material blow. To protect himself against the possibility of extradition (which perhaps he over-rated) Kersten soon afterwards applied for Swedish citizenship, and his application was strongly supported by Hr. Günther, the one man who really knew about his secret work for Sweden. A correct understanding of Kersten's humanitarian work was important, Günther wrote, "since a number of earlier descriptions, especially of the relief work among concentration-camp prisoners, have given—unconsciously no doubt—incorrect proportions to the achievements of the various actors". Unfortunately for Kersten, in July 1945 the coalition government of which Günther was a minister fell from power in Sweden, and the new rulers of the Foreign Office adopted a different attitude towards the inconvenient foreign agent of their predecessors. According to later revelations by the Swedish Press [2] they refused even to reimburse Kersten his travelling expenses to and from Germany on behalf of the Swedish Government, and these had to be met by private subscription. And Kersten's application for Swedish citizenship, in spite of Günther's support, was suddenly, at the last minute, refused. [3] It had

[1] Affidavit by Baron van Nagell, 3rd October, 1949; letter to me from Baron van Nagell, 3rd March, 1953. Cf. also *Aftonbladet*, Stockholm, 23rd April, 1953.
[2] *Aftonbladet*, Stockholm, 23rd and 24th April, 1953.
[3] According to a letter from the Dutch Ambassador in Helsinki (Mr. van der Vlugt) to his Government, the refusal was made at the instance of Count Bernadotte.

become clear, the Dutch information officer in Sweden wrote to his head-quarters soon after the change of government, that "Kersten's presence will be tolerated by the Swedes only if he keeps himself in the background."[1]

Thus the name of the inconvenient Kersten was thrust back into obscurity and the genuine merits of Count Bernadotte were altogether buried behind the romantic myth of the national hero, which the irreversible machine of high-powered publicity was now thrusting before the world. It seemed that the truth would never emerge. For who knew the truth? A few Swedes—but how could they now resist the great name of Bernadotte in which so much national capital had been sunk? A few Germans, but why should they advertise the fact that they had been Himmler's councillors? A few Jews—but in September 1948 Bernadotte was brutally murdered by Jewish extremists and a sense of guilt inhibited that nation from seeming, by however light or relative a censure, retrospectively to justify the crime. Fortunately there was a fourth category of those who knew the facts. In Holland there are no such inhibitions; and so it was in Holland that the truth ultimately began to emerge.

In 1948 murmurs of the injustice done to Kersten reached the Dutch Government, and at the instance of Professor N. W. Posthumus, the distinguished economic historian who was then Director of the Dutch Institute of War Documentation, a special commission, consisting of one historian and two members of the Dutch Foreign Office,[2] was set up to enquire into the facts of Kersten's work during the war. Having collected, tested and examined numbers of witnesses and hundreds of documents, the commission made its report in 1949. This report, which has been invaluable to me in my researches into the same subject, proved all the charges made against Kersten—charges of having been a Nazi, or of having made financial profit out of his rescue work—to be malicious and untrue, and established the fact that Kersten had saved thousands of lives of all nationalities, on numerous occasions and at great personal risk and expense, besides saving Dutch people from transportation, Dutch art treasures from confiscation, and Dutch cities and installations (the City of The Hague and the Zuyder Zee dam) from destruction. In consequence of this report, which was at first secret but has since been released, Kersten was made a Grand Officer of the Order of Orange-Nassau, receiv-

[1] Report of Mr. Dijkmeister, the Dutch Information Officer at Stockholm, 22nd November, 1945.
[2] The members of the Commission were Mr. Snouck Hurgronje (Secretary-General of the Foreign Office), Mr. Van Schelle (Counsellor of the Embassy), and Professor A. J. Rüter of the University of Leiden.

ing the insignia from Prince Bernhard of the Netherlands in August 1950.

In Sweden, committed to a rival version of the facts, this foreign recognition made at first little impact. The Dutch report received there no publicity. A copy of it sent with a personal letter to the new Swedish Foreign Minister, Herr Östen Undén, was not acknowledged. In 1952 Kersten's application for citizenship was again rejected. In 1952 therefore, having myself by this time made extensive independent enquiries, I decided to publish the facts. This I did in an article in the American magazine *Atlantic Monthly* for January 1953. This article, which for the first time stated the facts about Bernadotte's attempt to monopolize the credit, created something of a sensation in Sweden, and the Swedish Foreign Office was moved to issue an official *communiqué* upon it. The *communiqué* denied some of my conclusions, but as it quoted no evidence of any kind, only darkly hinting at papers among the archives of the Foreign Office, I do not regard it as convincing.[1] Shortly afterwards, however, a document was published which, being a year old, may well have been the basis of its *communiqué*, as it also appears to have been the justification for the refusal of Kersten's citizenship in 1952. This was a *pro-memoria* on the case of Dr. Kersten written by Dr. Uno Willers, who, at the time of writing, had been head of the Swedish Foreign Office Archives: an extraordinary document which simply repeats, without evidence, all the old charges already disproved in detail by the Dutch Parliamentary Commission. Its intellectual character is sufficiently shown by its statement that Kersten's 'fascist tendencies' are proved by his participation in the Finnish war of liberation of 1918. Professor Posthumus, in a reply to Dr. Willers, had no difficulty in disposing of such rubbish.[2] Point by point he traced Dr. Willer's allegations to their sources and proved their falsity, and he even showed that the Swedish archivist, in his zeal to discredit certain documents, had been misled by an inability to distinguish between original documents and carbon copies. Even in Sweden this grotesque document only brought the Ministry into contempt. Five members of the Riksdag challenged the Government on its treatment of Kersten, roundly declaring that it had refused citizenship to a public benefactor on the basis of a worthless and malicious compilation. On 29th April, 1953, a stormy debate took place in the Riksdag in the course of which the Swedish Government's treatment of Kersten was roughly criticized as small-minded and ungrateful. Six months later the Government yielded. On 30th October, 1953,

---

[1] The *communiqué* was issued on 3rd February, 1953. I replied in detail in *Svenska Dagbladet*, 4th March, 1953, and, in English, in the *Atlantic Monthly*, April 1953.

[2] Letter from Professor Posthumus to the Nobel Committee of the Norwegian Storting, 10th June, 1953.

Felix Kersten was admitted to Swedish citizenship. Truth had triumphed over slander in Sweden.[1]

Such, in brief outline, is the story of Felix Kersten and the work for humanity which he contrived to perform as a foreigner, without any power except the power of physical and intellectual manipulation, at Himmler's headquarters. No man's story would seem at first sight less credible, and most of those who have first heard it—including Professor Posthumus himself, the inspirer of the Dutch commission—have greeted it with scepticism, but no man's story has undergone a more searching scrutiny. It has been examined by scholars, lawyers and hostile politicians. And it has emerged triumphant. Human memory and human judgment are always fallible, but as far as honesty of purpose and authenticity of documentation are concerned I am pleased to support with such authority as I possess the accuracy of these memoirs of Felix Kersten.

[1] Since this introduction was first published, in January 1956, the Swedish Foreign Office has published a White Book (*1945 Års Svenska Hjälpsexpedition till Tyskland*, 26 April 1956) in which some more details about the Relief Expedition are given from government records. This White Book is avowedly provoked by my writings, which it criticises with some heat. I have replied at length in *Dagens Nyheter*, 27 April 1956. Here it is enough to say that whereas the Swedish White Book corrects a few errors of detail, often very pedantic detail (which I have now myself corrected for the American edition), it at last admits that Kersten's services (which had previously been denied) were 'incontestable', 'clear and important', and that Bernadotte's account 'certainly fails to do justice' to his collaborators.

I

TALKS ON FREEMASONRY

1. VISIT TO THE MASONIC MUSEUM

Friedenau, Berlin
7th February, 1940

A FEW days ago Himmler asked me whether I would care to visit the Masonic Department at the Reich's Security head office. He believed that I had quite the wrong idea of what Freemasonry really meant and would like me to take a good look round. To this I agreed.

Today I had a look at the Department. First of all there is a huge card index which includes the name of every member on the lists confiscated from the dissolved lodges. On each card is the lodge and rank of the member in question, his political and economic standing; there are special documents for important personalities whether in Germany or abroad. I was allowed to take out a few cards and, in order to test their accuracy, I chose those whom I already knew to be Masons. The details were correct.

I was then taken to a complete Masonic temple, where the ritual of the Masons was explained and a lecture given on the alleged dangers of the movement, its international relations, its powers and influence. I was shown papers illustrating the work and methods of the Masons, seeking to prove that they used poison to remove traitors from their own ranks. There were skulls all over the place, a coffin marked with Masonic signs, aprons and insignia—really quite a gruesome display. I can witness that this, together with expositions of Masonry which were delivered with some skill, did not fail to make an impression on the visitor. There had been conducted tours of the Department every day until the outbreak of war. Thousands of Party leaders, Hitler Youth, Army officers and civil servants passed through. I was assured that officer courses in Berlin usually concluded with a visit to the

Masonic Museum. Altogether it was a very clever method of presenting the alleged menace of this 'super-national power'.

Finally I was shown an enormous library, which contains everything written about Masonic activities, whether by Masons themselves or their enemies. It has been assembled from the wealth of volumes in the Masonic temples which had been closed down, brought together to form one great Masonic library. To the bibliophile it is certainly a unique collection; it also includes material on occult healing methods, particularly those of the Chinese and the Indians, which to me were of very great interest. I talked with one of the specialists, an intelligent young scientist who had the idea that he was engaged in a bitter struggle with those who—after the Jews—were the world's most dangerous enemy; and he meant to play his part in achieving victory over this 'scourge of mankind'.

I learnt that the idea of arranging a Masonic Museum of this kind came from Heydrich, head of the Security police. At the same time he had set up an information centre for all governmental and Party offices. When it was decided that a man was a Mason, that also decided his fate as a Party member, Government employee or Army officer. A number of important people had already lost their posts for this reason. In particular Heydrich had led the campaign against Dr. Schacht, President of the Reichsbank, on the grounds that he was a 'high-ranking Mason'.

I took my departure with the firm resolve to get fuller and more comprehensive information from Himmler.

2. HIMMLER'S IDEAS ON MASONRY

Friedenau, Berlin
15th February, 1940

The chance came today when I told Himmler that I had made full use of his offer and had visited the Masonic Department.

"Now what's your impression of the Masons?" he asked.

I replied that I had come away with the idea that all outstanding men of the last two centuries had been Masons. I had never known that before: there must be some great intellectual force behind Masonry for it to possess such powers of attraction. Unfortunately nothing had been said about that in the lecture, which only depicted a terrible super-national secret society, spreading its net over the nations, while in the centre, like a spider, sat a small number of men who issued orders.

According to this exposition these were basically the same who stood at the head of the Jewish world organizations.

"So you have come as far as that," laughed Himmler. "Of course there is a definite idea behind it, the idea of the French Revolution with its demands for Liberty, Equality and Fraternity, its humanistic ideals and the rights of man. But this is only camouflage to catch the broad masses of the Masons, work on their minds, sway them or at least neutralize them. It's a diabolically clever trick by which the Masons bring thousands under their influence who are themselves worthy and respectable, whether they are in public offices or the professions, in management or industry. These poor misguided people believe they are serving a great humanitarian ideal, quite unaware of how they are being abused. This is especially true of our good Germans, who are always ready to be taken in by any ideological swindle."

How exactly similar was this, I thought, to the judgment passed on National Socialism by its enemies, particularly abroad. How many times had I not heard similar assertions. So I asked Himmler: "What would you say, Herr Reichsführer, if you heard such a judgment as this on National Socialist Germany?: 'A small group, consisting of Adolf Hitler, Himmler, Göring, Goebbels, Rosenberg, Ley and a few others, are making use of National Socialist ideas, especially the racial and pan-German doctrine, in order to catch, fool and sway the broad masses to their own plans for world domination. The ordinary good National Socialist credulously accepts this and thinks he is serving a great ideal, whereas being a German, and therefore ready to be taken in by any ideological swindle, he is blind to the realities behind it.' "

"You're a Jesuit, Herr Kersten," said Himmler, laughing, "but you can't seriously compare our work for our people with the ideological fantasies of the Masons and the French Revolution. Here we are concerned with entirely concrete matters which are quite obvious and which every man can easily grasp for himself."

"Supporters of the French Revolution asserted the same thing. Then there were entirely concrete matters of which I will only name a few: the freeing of the peasants from dependence on their landlords, the artisans and merchants from the oppressive chains of the corporations; freedom of the person from the notorious *lettres de cachet*, warrants for arrest which were bought for cash and enabled their possessor to imprison any unfortunate person named by him in them. Furthermore it was a question of freedom for scientific research and freedom of conscience from the compulsion exercised by the Church. All these were extremely real and concrete demands. They gave the French Revolution its driving power and its explosive quality, above all its terrific effect on the broad masses. You don't seriously think, Herr Reichsführer, that the ordinary man had any enthusiasm for the abstract ideas of Liberty, Equality and Fraternity, unless they had a concrete application to his daily life? For the peasants liberty meant an escape from armed strife, for the commercial towns free business efficiency, and for scholars the free exercise of scientific research, conscience and activity in every department of life.

"Moreover, Individualism, which you combat so strongly in the interests of the community, still has outspoken supporters today in wide circles of European culture. When these people talk of freedom of the person or freedom of conscience and opinion, they don't confine themselves to intellectual questions. I have no need to tell you whom they regard as their concrete enemies. No wonder they see Masonry as a defence of these ideals and feel drawn to it. Among the supporters of National Socialism there are similar traits of psychological interest."

Himmler answered: "And why do the masses support us? Perhaps you will tell me that, as you know so much about it?"

"Willingly, Herr Himmler, but don't take it in bad part if I give you my frank opinion. Do you seriously think that the masses follow you because they have a special respect for National Socialist ideology? That only comes about because they get something out of it. The worker who earns good money, the widows who compare the pensions they get with those granted in the previous war, come to the conclusion that National Socialism is a good thing. The industrialists make huge profits from armaments and find that they can get on very well with you. Parents have no more worries about clever children, for the State pays for their special education in the 'Napolas', is grateful if they want to become officers in the army or the Waffen SS and lets them continue their studies, which is all very pleasant for the parents. You promise land in the East to the younger sons of farmers, who before had to sweat out their lives as labourers. They take a deep breath and sing with enthusiasm: 'We'll ride to the East.' "

Himmler beamed at me and said: "Now, Herr Kersten, isn't that marvellous? Real practical National Socialism—and that again shows the influence of National Socialist ideology."

"You may call it that," I answered, "but I assure you that the greatest nonsense can be propounded ideologically. If you maintain and extend these measures, you will have the support of the masses not on account of but *in spite of* your ideas. You only need to change the focus a little and it's easy to argue that the National Socialists, as masters of the people's psychology, know precisely how to win over the masses—the inner circle has only to throw them a sop, lull them, fool them, sway them—and here we are back again at your version of the Masonic ideology.

"But what interests me most is something very different. Do you really believe, Herr Himmler, that there is a small group of high-grade Masons behind every political and economic event, regularly holding their secret meetings at which they make decisions involving peace and war, decisions affecting the history of peoples and governments? Your men in the Masonic Department said something like that to me and even seemed to believe it."

"I not only believe it, Herr Kersten," Himmler answered, "I know it. You forgot to add that these high-grade Masons are identical with the inner circle of the Elders of Sion. Thus the Jewish rulers of the world have used Masonry as a camouflage for their own international power. With Masonic help the Elders of Sion mean to break the resistance of the intellectual and spiritual ruling class of the Germanic world. For they only approach and convert the intellectuals, lawyers, doctors, evangelical parsons, industrialists and politicians, not artisans and tradesmen, especially not the workers. There's another super-national power to send the workers to sleep, the International Trades Union, which is directed by the Masons and their Jewish leaders."

"But, Herr Reichsführer, this is fantastic," I objected; "the Masons surround themselves with secrecy in order to exert a certain special influence on their supporters. It's natural that much is falsely urged against them on this account, but where are any real proofs of your assertions?"

"Herr Kersten, of course I can't put the criminal's confession on the table before you with his own signature to it. To get a clear picture you must examine the activities of the Masons in the last two centuries under the microscope. Then you can confirm this: leading Masons had a part in the overthrow of every government. They had a hand in every severe financial crisis which has brought the economy of a country to the edge of the abyss. Masons occupy the important positions in the economic and intellectual life of a country and draw other Masons after them. The decisive men who waged the First World War against us were Masons. The Second World War again finds World Masonry united against us. In some Anglo-Saxon countries it's quite impossible to achieve any position in industry or politics unless you're a Mason. Aren't these proofs enough, Herr Kersten?"

"Not for me, Herr Reichsführer," I replied. "Masonry attracts many owing to its humanitarian programme and the help and support which it gives to its members. They know that they will have opportunities for advancement, for making useful friends and bettering their position. Small wonder that men of initiative make use of this source of influence. The teacher becomes a Mason because his headmaster is one, the business man because he finds his director is one. It is human and easy to understand that men keep in touch with those they know. It's really a kind of natural selection which makes people become Masons. It's just as natural that the same men should turn up again in economic and political life. You take it as a proof of your theory and are triumphant when you can show that Masons had a part in any economic or political disaster. Then you draw the further conclusion that this is a plot of super-national powers which are responsible for almost everything. But you could just as easily prove that lawyers are behind every economic or political disaster. I'm only surprised that with your hatred for the legal profession you haven't done that before now."

"What do you mean?" Himmler asked me.

"It's very simple," I answered. "You only need to find out what is the profession of the leading men anywhere and you'll be able to confirm that thirty to forty per cent of them are lawyers. You, Herr Himmler, now have it in your power to draw your conclusions about this group of plotters and proceed against them as you have already done against the Masons. You won't be short of arguments. You could explain that all lawyers have the same training, speak their own jargon; their notions and methods are kept jealously to themselves; one brings another with him and rejoices when he finds someone on the other side with whom he can come to an understanding. They keep the game to themselves and in particular guard themselves against politicians who lack their special knowledge; they have international associations and understand one another by means of a language and training which is no less international. That's enough for you to draw the logical conclusion. I think, Herr Himmler, that you have become the victim of an ideology."

3. THE STRUGGLE AGAINST ALL ANONYMOUS POWERS

I was very curious to hear how Himmler would answer this. Unfortunately there was no more talk, as he was called away. But I was able to speak to a very frank and intelligent member of his staff and I remarked to him what a primitive thought-process it was, seriously to suppose that behind every political or economic event was a conspiracy of super-national powers.

"Only try to make that clear to the Reichsführer," was his reply, "he is firmly convinced. Extremely primitive is what he calls the opposite school of thought, which sees certain immanent laws behind political or economic events; he says this is only a camouflage of the real motives, evolved by the wire-pullers to deceive intellectuals who, having lost the use of their instincts, promptly fall for it. He hates every form of anonymity. He's like those peasants who never speak of the Government, but treat such and such an official, Meyer or Müller, as their personal friend or enemy. For instance if the Reichsführer is told, 'The Ministry of the Interior has arranged it,' he asks, 'Which Ministry of the Interior?' meaning who is the official behind it. You have to know that, if you're going to speak to him on such matters. He is always looking for the controlling power.

"For him there is no such thing as 'The Economy'. He begins to rave if anyone speaks to him of the immutable laws of economics. For him 'economics' is Herr Flick, Herr Stinnes, Herr Krupp or Herr Thyssen. His immediate answer is always, 'Very well, what does Herr Krupp or Herr Stinnes want?' He thinks that almost every important man is controlled by anonymous forces behind him and is the exponent of these forces. His mind and his conduct is wholly set on finding out who handles those controls. He puts his information service on to this, making them draw great charts to depict the various influences graphically. He can stand for hours on end before these charts with Heydrich, discussing and pondering. The sphere of industry, with all its ramifications and market agreements, offers great opportunities for this.

"Heydrich encourages this basic trait of the Reichsführer's. His Industrial Department has its own draughtsmen, who follow up these intricacies with the greatest exactitude. By this means he exercises great influence over the Reichsführer, who always listens to him when he expounds the system of controlling influences in his skilful manner. The Reichsführer nowadays only sees industry and the leading industrialists from this point of view. 'De-camouflaging' is Heydrich's name for this method and he considers it a masterpiece of his information service.

"Moreover the Reichsführer has adapted what he regards as his enemies' method and the basis of their power and has turned it to logical use as the basis of the dominant position occupied in the state by the SS. From this point of view the SS is nothing but an anti-Masonry—though the Reichsführer does not admit it—with whose help, and without attracting attention, he is trying to occupy the leading positions in the Government and the Party. The whole system of conferring uniforms and ranks on the so-called 'honorary leaders' can only be grasped from this standpoint."

"And how do these SS lodges work?" I interrupted.

"On the whole astonishingly well," came the answer. "This fact confirms the Reichsführer in his attitude. Recently he expressed it in this way: 'Since we have been so fortunate as to see this system transform the little dinghy which was the SS into the great armed cruiser that it is today, we have a glimpse of what our enemies could and did achieve while our people slept. At the same time this is a great stimulus for us to advance, with logic and method, along the path we have been following.'"

This struck me as a first-class explanation. Now I could understand much more clearly Himmler's blind and uncomprehending attitude to Masonry and to all associations which were at all like it. My visit to the Masonic Museum had shown me how he persecuted every association of this sort, even the so-called 'Teutonic Order' and the 'German League', generally regarded as harmless, but I had not before been able to fit this into the general problem.

4. NATIONAL MASONRY REJECTED

Friedenau, Berlin
20th February, 1940

Today I spoke to Himmler about this while I was treating him and asked the real reason why he even forbade national Masonic lodges. He answered at once: "Every lodge has secret masters to direct the leaders who appear openly. When some worthy doctor is chairman, how am I to know who's really behind him? One has to be logical in this and ruthlessly eliminate every weak spot where the enemy might break in. For this reason we have not let ourselves weaken by raising the ban on the three so-called national Grand Lodges of Prussia nor by offering alternative arrangements to their members, even though they could claim Prussian kings and princes of the blood royal among their members. This too is an outstanding example of the subtle methods employed by the leaders of the Masons. National lodges are founded, given far-reaching independence, suffered to have principles quite opposed to those generally demanded of Masons, with the result that kings and princes, who are not usually blessed with great vision, join them, hold high ranks and show themselves in Masonic aprons."

"And what do the Masons gain by that?" I asked.

"Are you still in the dark?" Himmler retorted. "First of all it's wonderful propaganda for the Masonic idea. If the royal house belongs to a lodge, then it is respectable in the eyes of the broad masses, the propertied and the educated classes. All doubts are at once silenced. The Masons no longer need to defend themselves, but only point to the king, their brother Mason. Is any individual going to be more clever than his king? Such membership automatically attracts all those whom the Masons particularly want, influential officials and politicians. Without any need for further action they have won over leading political and industrial figures to Masonry. The Masonic lodge now becomes the centre of social life with riotous banquets and celebrations for the king's or prince's birthday. It all seems like a great national and social club; cheap wining and dining offer no small attraction to the official unblessed with this world's goods.

"Meanwhile however the Masons are quietly and systematically extending their influence; lectures are given on themes dear to Masons; prominent scientists are won over; links are forged with other lodges and the desired result is achieved; at first neutrality, then union with World Masonry. It will perhaps surprise you to learn that the higher grades of this lodge are duplicated. Beside the Grand Master, needed as an advertisement, there is a man never seen who really occupies a far higher position in World Masonry, using and directing this 'shadow system' in a masterly way.

"Only *one* power has not allowed itself to be deceived, the Catholic Church. She is the inexorable enemy of all Masonry. It is certainly known to you that any Catholic is automatically excommunicated the moment he becomes a Mason. The Church knows very well why she is so inexorable. She herself works on Masonic principles; her religious Orders, in particular the Jesuits, are nothing more nor less than powerful lodges of the Catholic Church. She knows what she has herself achieved with this system and will suffer no opposition lodge, using every means to prevent her sheep from straying into it. One cannot be misled by the explanation that the Church is against the Masons because they pay homage to liberal ideas. By now these ideas have made such progress even inside the Catholic Church that warnings and prohibitions on that account are out of place. The inexorable stand of the Catholic Church against Masonry is the best proof of how accurately we have summed it up. Only the foolish Evangelical parsons have still not realized what is at stake. They join the Masons without realizing that they are digging their own graves."

"But aren't your SS really a sort of Masonic lodge, Herr Reichsführer?" I now asked Himmler.

"How can you say such a thing?" came the answer. "Have we unknown leaders or a system of Masonic grades? The SS is an Order with leaders who are known and objectives that are openly stated. It is the Germanic form of association for men who are pledging themselves to high aims. If you must make a comparison, then make it with the Germanic knights whose objective was defence against the East. But no real comparison is possible. The SS is a special creation of the National Socialist state, with aims proper to that alone, and can no more be transferred to other states than National Socialism itself."

"I don't quite understand that, Herr Himmler," I answered. "Then why are you setting up Germanic SS formations which are composed of Norwegians, Danes, Dutch and Flemish?"

"That's something very different. They are fighting units with a single task, to assure living room for Germanic peoples in the East. They have nothing to do with the other sphere in which the SS operates."

"If all that you and your people have told me about Masonry really represents your firm convictions," I went on, bringing the conversation to a close, "there's one thing I don't understand. Why have you at one and the same time made implacable enemies of the Jews and Masons on the one side, and their professed enemy, the Catholic Church, on the other, instead of at least treating with one side and playing it off against the other? Why have you been drawn into the Second World War with both enemies in your rear?"

"Unhappily, my dear Herr Kersten, I can give you no answer to that," said Himmler, tight-lipped, "that is a thing which the Führer alone had to decide. To talk about it, now that the die has been cast, is quite pointless."

"You honour Frederick the Great and regard him as a shining example?" I asked at the end of the treatment.

"Certainly," Himmler replied.

"But he was a Mason and allowed nobody to deceive him."

"That was a special case," said Himmler.

II

TALKS ON THE JEWS

Berlin
3rd March, 1940

IT HAPPENED that I had occasion to remark to Himmler that I had never understood Anti-Semitism; the Jews had at least been a great stimulus in almost all departments of life. Every people had a certain percentage of elements they had no reason to be proud of—one had to take care not to make sweeping generalizations. It would be equally easy to assert that 'all Germans are pedants, fanatics and imperialists', simply because a few could be so described.

Then Himmler started: "Wherever the Jew appears, he tries to do business. There's little to be said against the acquisitive instinct as such, but a great deal against the Jewish version of it. The frontiers of a nation and the industrial interests they enclose are a matter of indifference to the Jews, provided trade flourishes. They weave a network of connections with their fellow-Jews in every country."

Everyone wants business, I answered. Non-Jewish business people also worked for their own prosperity.

Himmler said: "Of course the Germans should trade with the whole world, but for the benefit of Germany as a whole, not only for their personal enrichment without considering the community." There were leaders of industry who acted in this sense. One need only think of such a man as Röchling. The so-called German Jew doesn't work for Germany, but only for the Jews. Scattered over the whole world, they were international in their outlook. Himmler emphasized: "The Jewish Empire (*das Judenreich*) comes before all others, draining them of their materials, their strength, their riches, their influence, in order to transfer everything to their own Jewish Empire."

My answer was: "These are fantastic ideas springing from anti-Semitic writings. There are many examples of Jews staking their lives, again and again, on behalf of the country in which they have made their home."

There were rare exceptions, Himmler said. There were also cases of treachery among non-Jews, when the overwhelming mass of the people remained decent. Those Jews who fought for the land in which they lived were, from the Jewish point of view, outsiders or traitors, cut off from Jewry. Agents of the Jewish Empire were often to be found among those Jews who were entrusted with war-work at home or behind the front.

I objected that I could not conceive such a Cloud Cuckoo Land as a Jewish Empire.

"This Cloud Cuckoo Land is based," Himmler retorted, "on the entire Jewish people. The Jew can stand any climate. In places where non-Jews can't live, the Jew manages, conducts a flourishing business and lives happily. This question of climate is also the reason why Jewish blood and Jewish traits always dominate in racial mixtures.

"The Protocols of the Elders of Sion and Masonry give the Jewish Empire an outstanding executive. It's a sort of intellectual Ghetto—but so transformed than even non-Jews can give their services to it without realizing. The Old Testament, the creed constructed centuries ago to suit the Jewish race, gives it a basis and a code. It's partly instructions in good behaviour, but only towards other Jews, partly inflated mysticism, partly cruelty and revenge, all with a good percentage of sexual obscenity. Thus the book offers something to everybody and has a continual appeal."

I replied that I knew a number of Jews who had become Christians. To him such a union between the two might seem impossible.

Himmler retorted that he knew a number of Germans who were either Catholics or Protestants or Mohammedans or nothing at all, but still remained good Germans. "If you want another proof, think of the Balkan peoples, who have lived for centuries under the Turks, often becoming Mohammedans, yet after all that time have not forfeited the least element of their national character. A Jew may become a Christian, but he remains a Jew and is spoken of by other Jews as one of themselves. He cannot escape from the circle which has left its mark on him. He will even become a particularly useful pawn in their game, because he is half-camouflaged and the people among whom he lives accept him as one of their own number."

"But Bismarck himself said that a dash of Jewish blood would be useful to the German people, or something to that effect," I interjected.

"Can you imagine Bismarck married to a Jewess?" was Himmler's answer. "I can't. That phrase of his was used figuratively. He meant that Germans should be greater realists in the sense of advancing Germany's position in the world. They have exactly the opposite disposition to the Jews; they make a footing for themselves abroad but at once abandon their nationality and their fatherland. You should read, moreover, what Luther said and wrote about the Jews. No judgment could be sharper."

After a pause he added: "And while we're on the subject of history, Pope Gregory VII was a friend of the Jews. His election was financed by them. His son also became Pope. The grandson of this Pope, Jewish again, was also a Pope. That was the state of affairs in the so-called Holy Church. This Gregory VII announced that nobody could give orders to the Pope, for he was sacred; he was able to depose princes and emperors; God had put all power into his hands; he could even release subjects from their allegiance. For that's what this Jewish fellow did and a German emperor had to stand for three days barefoot in the snow doing penance to him. What blasphemous arrogance and what confusion to the Germanic conception of loyalty this man brought into the world! That took place in the year 1077 and, in Bismarck's own words, it still sears the soul."

"But that happened a long time ago. Much has changed since then. You can draw no consequences from it for the present."

Himmler replied: "Nothing has altered. What the Jew-Pope achieved then is still having its effect centuries afterwards, and the Jews of today are pursuing exactly the same policy with their Elders of Sion. Then it was the papal throne, now it's an industrial throne, an even better camouflage. But often the curtain is drawn aside. Listen to this: when after the First World War the East European Jews came streaming into Germany, who received them? The so-called loyal Jews of Germany. Their feelings were with them, not with us. What did those East European Jews not achieve? They all became rich and prosperous. By the help of our own people? No, only by the help of the so-called loyal Jews. They assisted them while the figures of German suicide caused by hunger climbed to new heights. Why did these loyal Jews help them? Because they belonged to their community, not to ours. The drama, music, the cinema, art, journalism, all were turned topsy-turvy to serve Jewish ends. Their Old Testament spirit rotted everything."

I declared to Himmler that his proofs were invented. It was not possible to assert that all Germans were poets or thinkers, because at certain times there had been a few more poets or thinkers than at others.

Himmler still brought his proofs out of the dim and distant past: the Germanic people with their decisive force had always erected states; he called this "the heroism of the sword" and "the heroism of toil". They had not been able to do otherwise; it was simply the quality of their race, formed over the centuries by special circumstances and influences. The Jews on the other hand had been formed by quite other circumstances into a quite different race, which did not live by the sword nor by hard work, but by a particular type of business dealing. Even in what was called its respectable aspect, there was something of haggling and the oriental bazaar in its methods. This haggling never respected a nation's intellectual values or culture. Everything was bartered, cheapened and internationalized. "The Jewish Empire got its working capital and its material substance out of the bankruptcy of national character. That is its strength. Ours lies in our national, cultural and social structure. The Jew in himself is neither better nor worse than any other people. But each must be bounded by its own form of existence and culture. Otherwise there can only be a struggle of life and death. Do we germanize the Jews? No, but they turn us into Jews."

I answered: "You take your arguments from a time which lies seven centuries away. Science and world commerce have long ago transformed your field of ideas into something quite different. Living reality has already given the lie to all scientific dogmatism."

Himmler said: "I'll answer you very simply. In spite of world science and commerce it disgusts me when I see a Jew strolling on the Bavarian mountains in *Lederhosen* (leather shorts). I don't go about in a caftan and ringlets. There, in terms of racial feeling, are two different worlds."

"You're also annoyed," I replied, laughing, "if a so-called typical Prussian goes about in *Lederhosen*. That is Bavarian regionalism which cannot be abolished even in Greater Germany and now has even attached itself to the Jews. And how can you, as a man knowing history, make use of the Elders of Sion as arguments for your case against the Jews! You must surely know that they have been condemned as an indisputable forgery."

"They've only been condemned by the Jews or by Jewish bribery. You should know that."

My only answer was that with such methods one could reject all historical evidence and cut the ground from under one's feet. Discussion became quite impossible if you thought that all evidence was invented to state a case and that all documents were false. Such weapons were dangerous and could be turned against oneself. What would he say if all National Socialist history was regarded from that point of view?

Himmler was silent. But I felt that I had given him something to think about.

III

MEDICINE AND HEALING

BESIDES history, Himmler was extremely interested in the art of healing. This often happens with men in poor health who are unable to find the right medical treatment. They give themselves up to the search for help in their sufferings, entering an entirely new field, discovering widespread interests and sympathies. With Himmler it was not quite like that, although it played its part. He was pre-endowed, one might almost say, with an interest in medicine by his family. He enjoyed recalling that his great-grandfather had been much respected on account of the herbal mixtures and juices with which he used to help his neighbours; his grandmother also knew the secrets of herbs. He was proud of these ancestors and only regretted that they had taken their knowledge with them to the grave, without handing it on.

His own experiences in hospitals and with doctors, his outstanding gift of keen observation and a sure instinct, had convinced him of the need for reform in medical treatment. The schoolmaster side of his character, which was always urging him to teach and to reform, came into action here and early made him a sharp critic of doctors and their affairs. But here too he added positive proposals to his criticisms. Surgery alone received his unqualified respect.

His work as a farmer had made him keenly aware of the problem of nutrition and its importance. He considered its human application, saw how often a knowledge of proper food was lacking, how little planning there was, and busied himself with this question, the solving of which was of decisive importance to him. He was also concerned with the reform of therapy. He was violently opposed to 'injections' and 'patent medicines'; he stood for the return to simple remedies and those offered by nature herself. Herbs and their juices he regarded as an inexhaustible treasure. He called them 'the Lord's remedies' which God had placed immediately before our doors. That people neglected

38

these herbs, which grew on the mountains of his Bavarian homeland, was to him clear proof of how far the slow death of civilization had already gone.

Himmler knew the most important herbal works of the Middle Ages. He often talked to me about Hildegard of Bingen and the successful cures she achieved by immersion in straw, and about Albertus Magnus, the outstanding botanist of the Middle Ages. Himmler himself possessed the significant herbal work of the sixteenth-century Hieronymus Bock and was proud that Theophrastus of Hohenheim, the famous Paracelsus, was a South German. Kneipp he saw as a reincarnation of Paracelsus. "Isn't it extraordinary," I often heard him say, "that this area has produced two such important men, one of whom"—meaning Kneipp—"has renewed the work of the other, which had already been forgotten?"

Himmler was very well read on medical subjects. Naturally he was interested in 'preventive medicine' as it is called today. But he had a good general knowledge which he got through the reports of his offices, particularly the Security Service and later the Ministry of the Interior, which he read in great detail. When I once asked him why he went so deeply into these questions, he explained: "In all the departments of life which concern me the doctor has his share and I have to see that he is pulling his weight." On another occasion: "Doctors are entrusted with many departments of life which particularly lend themselves to a guidance which would be followed readily enough. Quite apart from restoring people to health, the doctor should guide them towards an ever increasing mastery of life. But, with a few exceptions, he only tries to patch people up and repair their injuries. Why? Because he has only learnt how to patch people up, not how to guide them. So we have to undertake that ourselves." Here too he wanted first to try out his methods within the framework of the SS before they were applied more generally.

I had numberless talks with Himmler on medical questions. I quote a few which seem specially important to me and characteristic of him.

1. SURGERY AND NATURE-CURES ACKNOWLEDGED

Friedenau, Berlin
15th August, 1940

Today Professor Gebhard from Hohenlychen was with Himmler. He values Gebhard, whom he knew from his school-days, as much for his human qualities as for his great ability as a surgeon. During my treatment Himmler was still wholly under the influence of this visit; his strong interest in all medical questions had received a fresh impetus.

"A surgeon's work is important," he began. "It's exact work, and if he also has a little imagination, and is not only after money, he is usually a complete man. Men such as Gebhard or Sauerbruch stand for something; you have to take off your hat to them. All praise too for the doctor who does scientific work in a laboratory, often experimenting on himself at the risk of his life. They are real heroes in white coats. One day they will get the highest honours of Greater Germany. On that I am in full agreement with the Führer. But I haven't a great opinion of the rest of so-called medical science. They make one mistake after another and know how to camouflage their mistakes as science."

I remarked that it was human to err and that the representatives of other sciences did the same; he had only to consider Keppler's astronomy or the chief changes in physics and chemistry in the past hundred years.

"Quite, quite," answered Himmler, "that may be, but no one is so arrogant as the doctors, who somehow claim an infallibility that is hardly to be endured. That begins with the University Professor and goes right down to the little country doctor in Lower Pomerania. Were you ever at Wörishofen, Herr Kersten?" When I said I had been, Himmler continued: "Then you've never before seen so many nature doctors in one place. Do you know why? Simply because it's good business. How they laughed at Kneipp, treated him as a wretched quack and persecuted him to the point that his name was never mentioned in scientific circles, although he was the man who was curing all Europe. His treatment only made use of water and natural remedies, not expensive chemical mixtures and preparations. But it was soon taken up once people saw how much money there was in it and how patients hurried to put themselves into the hands of such doctors. But before that Kneipp's teaching had to be given a scientific basis—which meant expressing it all in secret medical terms and making it much harder to understand what Kneipp had said with sublime simplicity. Then the time was ripe for the medical schools to take it up.

"Here and there natural methods of healing are studied in the academies, but what a miserable rôle is assigned to them! You know yourself with what scorn a correct practitioner looks down on the man who cures with water and herbs, and how he despises nature doctors.

Yet every doctor should be a nature doctor and bend all his energies
to helping men by the simple means of nature."

"Then the Catholic Church has at least done some good in bringing
forward such a man as Kneipp," I responded.

"You are mistaken, Herr Kersten, Kneipp was not fundamentally a
parson. Anyone who has listened so profoundly to nature, and known
how to speak so nobly of the healing powers of herbs and water, must
be remote from the unnatural, which is embodied in the Church. But
naturally the Church has taken him over and you'll see in a few decades
he'll be first beatified, then canonized; and if men go to Wörishofen
and get cured, that'll be not because water and herbs have cured them,
but because St. Sebastian, which was his name, has helped. All the
immersions of knee and thigh, all the partial and total immersions
ordained by Father Kneipp, will become pious rites. You laugh, Herr
Kersten, but perhaps you will live to see it. For the simple man who
lives under the laws of the Church, the knee immersions of 'Saint'
Kneipp have more effect than those of ordinary Sebastian Kneipp. The
Church has already made the first step in raising Kneipp to the prelacy.
There you are!"

I asked Himmler why, if he had such a high opinion of Kneipp, he
had not tried his cures for removing his stomach pains.

"I have tried," Himmler assured me, "but they don't help me. I
can't stand cold water. I've often reflected on this. There must be
something wrong with Kneipp's system, that he orders the same thing
for everyone. That's always so with prophets; each man has to look for
what's right for himself. Alternate warm and cold baths do me more
good, warm better still, and hot best of all. But that's against the
dogma and I'm sinning against our saint. In other ways, however, I
follow him entirely. I eat simply, as you know; and the glass of red
wine which I take would also be allowed me by Father Kneipp and he
would regard my diet as quite suitable."

We had to break off the treatment and also the talk, because
Heydrich came. He was being sent from Himmler to Göring and had
to receive a few instructions. Apparently Heydrich had told him something agreeable, for Himmler came back to me in the best of humours
and said: "What I wanted to ask you was, do you know Priessnitz?"

"Only from the Priessnitz papers, Herr Himmler."

"Priessnitz was a very respectable man, racially more sympathetic
to me than my Bavarian fellow-countryman, Kneipp, who looked just
like a brewer. You should have seen the man's finely marked peasant
features. I have read the book on Priessnitz as well as Kneipp's writing,
although it's hardly known at all. Highly original thoughts! What

impressed me most was how he arrived at the water-cure. When he was still a shepherd's boy he had observed how a roebuck, which had been shot in a hunt, cured its lame leg by going daily to a spring and putting it under cold water. Priessnitz was able to confirm how from week to week the leg healed and after a time the animal was completely cured. Priessnitz copied this. That's a true nature-cure. It's a great joy to me to know that the place where this man made his first cures in the most primitive surroundings, what is now the Priessnitz Sanatorium on the Gräfenberg near Freiwaldau, once again belongs to the German Reich. Few people know about Priessnitz because he had nobody like the Catholic Church to advertise him. She regarded him as a competitor. For the Catholic Church there's only one water-saint, and that's Kneipp. She can't tolerate an Evangelical and keeps quiet about him; some even declare, as I have often heard seriously maintained, that Priessnitz took it all from Kneipp, although he lived before Kneipp."

Himmler took his departure, still smirking as he went and saying: "You should read that book about Priessnitz. Remind me to give it to you. I would be interested to have your opinion on it, and a few cold immersions wouldn't do your corpulence any harm."

I also talked about this subject with Brandt and asked him whether Himmler had really read these books in detail. "Certainly," Brandt answered, "he often takes himself for something of a Kneipp and gives advice to this man or that. For instance he ordered a wet, cold stocking as the only possible remedy against my headaches. I tried it once, in order not to have to keep on lying to him. A horrible business, very much against the grain, but it really helped. Yet in spite of that I prefer headache tablets; it's simpler and it helps too."

"Now, my dear Brandt," I said to him, "I have you in my power, for I'll tell Himmler."

"Don't do that or I'll have to sign an undertaking every day that I've used the cold poultices. He can't bear them himself; that's his great worry. If it wasn't for that, the whole of the SS would be 'Kneipped' and 'Priessnitzed' and a successful cure at Wörishofen would be the first step towards promotion. You laugh, but Heydrich has already started in his department; he's opened a campaign against fat men. They are forbidden in the SS. It's lucky that you're not in it, Herr Kersten, you wouldn't have much of a time. Under the charge of a Berlin doctor each man's capabilities were tested in detail, then it was prescribed what he might and what he might not eat, then there was weighing and more tests. At the head of it were Heydrich and Himmler benevolently watching over the whole thing. Certainly this would have become a general practice in the SS if the war had not intervened and food rationing started. A little while ago I jokingly asked the diet doctor what his attitude to rationing was. He very seriously informed me that it had fulfilled his life's work: the rations made necessary by war contained exactly those quantities which he considered correct and suitable to a healthy man. You see, even war is good for something."

2. IGNORANCE IN DOCTORS. STRUGGLE OVER FOOD INDUSTRIES

Friedenau, Berlin
20th August, 1940

"What do you really think, Herr Kersten," so Himmler briefly greeted me, "is real honey better than artificial? You and any sensible man will naturally decide in favour of real honey. But read this: the exact chemical constituents of real honey are known, so that it can be produced synthetically, with a proportionate admixture which makes it much better than anything the foolish bees can contrive. You need only to go to such and such a factory which has brought about this miracle. The certified food chemist Müller confirms it and the chief doctors in certain hospitals describe the favourable results they have obtained with the use of artificial honey. Now it is only necessary for the Press to spread the news, and the public which has lost its instincts will feel that it is doing something special for its health when it eats artificial honey instead of real which has the further advantage of being cheaper. You see, that's how money is made, and my own SS doctors, whom at least I thought had more sense, fall for it. One of them seriously proposed to me that, on the basis of these discoveries, I should order large quantities of artificial honey for the Waffen SS. The artificial is everywhere, everywhere food is adulterated, provided with ingredients which are said to make it last longer or look better or enrich it or anything else that the advertisers of the food industries care to say."

"The reason for that," I put in, "is that the cake which has to be shared out won't go round, so people try to enlarge it."

"That may be true in war-time, but not in peace. The root of the matter is that we are in the hands of the food industries, which by means of their large capital and the advertising it makes possible prescribe for us what we may and what we may not eat. Men in cities, who in winter live largely on tinned food, are already at their mercy, but now they are attacking the countryside by refined flour and sugar and white bread. The war has made a break in these proceedings; after the war we shall take very energetic measures to prevent the ruin of our people simply for the benefit of the food industries."

"And how will you do that? You can't prescribe for men what they shall eat and drink, nor forbid them the enjoyment of white bread, special flour or tinned foods. That would please nobody."

"There's no need to act so impetuously. First of all much can be achieved by skilful direction from the Government. For instance we have only to declare that bread must contain a fixed percentage of wholemeal. That is already of basic importance to the diet of the German people, especially for growing children. We're giving them bread which is not robbed of its most valuable constituents, as results from the refining processes of milling."

"And what if men prefer white bread, as is the case in England and France?"

"Then we must influence them by propaganda to show the damage caused by refined foods. There's no lack of examples. The wrong diet always plays a decisive part in all the troubles of civilization, from the general loss of teeth to chronic constipation and digestive ailments, or difficulties in assimilating food, bad nerves, and defective circulation."

I asked Himmler where he had obtained this detailed knowledge, to which he replied that diet was part of a farmer's work. If everything was in order in the stables and the cattle still did not thrive, then the farmer knew that something was wrong with their fodder. He paid attention to it because it directly affected his earnings; but as for men, they stuck to the beaten track, indifferent to the best modern science on diet, such as a Bircher-Benner, a Ragnar Berg or a Hindede had provided in the most exemplary way. He had read the wealth of material in Bircher-Benner and Ragnar Berg's writings among others most carefully and learnt much from them. They had confirmed truths which had come to him by intuition. Parts, especially in Bircher-Benner, were exaggerated, but the fundamentals were certainly correct and had to be admitted, even if one was oneself neither a vegetarian nor a believer in raw foods. After the war he would see to it that knowledge of this kind was widely spread. The first approach must be to housewives and mothers. In their hands lay a gigantic responsibility, which only needed to be shown them with all its consequences. He was certain that extraordinary success could thus be achieved. Folly and ignorance always caused the greatest damage to public health. He intended to have films produced on the wrong and the right diet, in which their results would be vividly portrayed. He would see whether this battle could not be won. "I will have experiments made in the ranks of the Waffen SS with different forms of diet, and test the capabilities of my men under them. The results will be shown in films before the general public."

"And what do your doctors say to such undertakings?" I asked Himmler, as I knew that in that quarter there was scepticism about his efforts for reform.

"That is a real difficulty," Himmler answered with complete frankness. "They grew up in the old school and are still under its influence; they are more or less against my ideas and resist in their hearts. I don't take that in bad part, but I demand of them that they should concern themselves with the question, test it seriously and not simply avoid it because what is suggested to them is something they didn't learn at their universities. They must be patient, as I am, and advance step by step. I will make a start with the rising generation of doctors. Isn't it madness that the majority of country doctors haven't the least idea of diet? For them albumen is just albumen, fat is just fat; they only consider calories and don't know that vegetable albumen has quite a different effect on men from what it has on animals. They also ignore the fact that fever cases do best on fruit and that miracles can be achieved by fasting for bad cases of rheumatism and gout.

"They let patients keep to their old habits of life, instead of first asking, 'What is your diet?' and going on from there. 'Our medicines should be our diet and our diet should be our medicines,' said a great doctor of antiquity. You will know the saying. Today our medicines are injections and our diet tinned food, and the majority of our doctors accept that without thinking. I will begin on this by giving the right directions for my Waffen SS and appoint no doctor whose basic knowledge of this subject has not been established by special lectures, however good his general medical knowledge may be. This business is far too important."

Without waiting for an answer, Himmler went on: "From this standpoint the next to tackle are the hospitals. It's a scandal that while a hospital may have a kitchen for special diets, the general feeding of patients is never carried out from the standpoint that our diet should be our medicine. They calmly give pork and pickled cabbage to rheumatic cases; heart cases get liver sausage with bread and butter, pickled gherkins and black tea. Men with serious nervous disturbances, for whom a diet based on raw food and fruit often works wonders, receive the same diet as an otherwise healthy man who is lying in plaster of Paris on account of a broken leg. There is only one system and that is based on financial economy. These poor patients are so mistreated; if their bowels are not working, they're given an aperient which completely ruins their health; others are similarly treated. How much the hospitals could save, if their sick bays were really turned into health centres! I know what I'm talking about, I've been in hospitals. And today it's just the same. This is where we will begin, by building model hospitals, whose importance will lie not in the amount of their equipment, but in the high standard of their diet."

"But you can't do without equipment in modern hospitals," I intervened.

"Naturally there must be a certain amount of equipment, but do you really think that with all this equipment we treat more patients and cure them better than the doctors of the past, a Paracelsus or a Hippocrates, a Kneipp or a Priessnitz? I only know that the number of sick is increasing, the hospitals make still greater claims, specialists grow like mushrooms and results decline. Something must be wrong. We must think it over and go back to nature-cures, which are based on the right diet.

3. MEDICINE AND THE MANUFACTURING CHEMIST

3rd February, 1941

For a few days Himmler had been suffering from headaches and lack of blood in the brain; his eyesight was impaired and his work interrupted. I was able to bring him relief. At the beginning of today's treatment he fetched a box from his safe and handed it to me. "Look, these are all the headache cures which I used to take before you came. As the headaches got worse in spite of them, I had stronger doses prescribed. When they no longer had any effect, the doctors shook their heads and declared that there was nothing more they could do. Nobody had the idea of taking me in hand and treating me with manual theraphy as you do, Herr Kersten. And here's another collection of headache remedies."

Himmler showed me a second much larger box, in which there were some thirty different sorts of remedy, which he had received as samples for the health centres of the Waffen SS. "See what a good thing headaches are for the manufacturing chemist. It's the same with remedies for digestive troubles, rheumatism or gout. You would have to laugh, if the matter wasn't so serious. With our diet we're in the hands of the food industries, and our medicines are decided by the pharmaceutical manufacturers. The doctor is pressed into service as salesman for these industries, the chemist as their clerk. It was a point of honour with chemists in times past to prepare the doctor's individual prescription for each patient. That was really an important social task. But today only a few doctors write out individual prescriptions. The chemists have taken over all this; a manufactured remedy is the answer.

"Can you blame the busy general practitioner that he takes the easier way, instead of writing out individual prescriptions? Examining the patient has become a farce. In how many cases is there a proper examination? The doctor has five minutes, three for filling up forms, two for hearing the patient and ordering a remedy. In most cases there's no need for the doctor to see the patient. He need only sit by the telephone, wait for a call, write out a prescription and send it to the chemist, where the patient can fetch it himself. At least that saves much time which it would be senseless to waste in useless talk."

I laughed and said that was going a little too far; a trained doctor could recognize even in the brief time at his disposal whether an illness was assumed or serious, in which case he could hand the patient on to a specialist. It was the general practitioner's job to sift out cases.

"Sifting is the right word for it," answered Himmler. "The general practitioner sifts to such effect that many of the people he treats turn their backs on official medicine. These doctors don't realize how much trust they have squandered and how widely they have discredited their profession. I see it only with deep regret. The doctor fulfils a very important *rôle* in public health; we can't afford to have the medical profession continually losing ground through a chain of highly various circumstances."

"But how will you alter it?" I asked Himmler. "Will you, as I have already heard from Herr Ley, nationalize medicine after the war?"

"What are you thinking of, Herr Kersten? That's really the most foolish thing we could do. I can understand that Ley should have something like that in mind; it's in accord with his inclination to collectivism, which we're wholly against. Besides that wouldn't improve the least thing. It would only add to our present troubles by making the doctor a civil servant. That would be the complete eclipse of the medical profession, the destruction of all initiative and all those positive, creative elements which we so badly need for the reconstruction of medicine as a whole. If Herr Ley talks to you again about this, you can quietly tell him that; this is no joking matter for me."

"I'm very glad to hear it, Herr Reichsführer," I replied, "I will tell

Ley with pleasure, but I still don't know what your plans for reform are."

We were interrupted and Himmler invited me to dinner for one evening that week. I was curious to hear what proposals he would have to make.

4. HIMMLER'S PLANS FOR REFORM

7th February, 1941

It was a most interesting evening. We had hardly finished the meal before Himmler returned to the subject of our previous talks. "It's no use producing new schemes for university training, Herr Kersten—they're already being mass-produced. One generation of doctors after another have amused themselves with such schemes but nothing has been done, because men of the old school are entrenched everywhere and they're cunning enough to sabotage even the best of plans. It would be a labour of Sisyphus to do battle with them. But if we appoint a few men to take our side in this controversy—men who share our ideas—then the forces of reform can gather around them.

"Here as elsewhere it's much better to begin from the bottom. Because numbers of ignorant men credulously accept whatever he prescribes, the doctor never thinks twice about ordering manufactured remedies. We must shake this credulity of theirs. Once we make it clear to people, especially to mothers, that these medicines can at best allay symptoms, but not cure the sick person, that the simple remedies which Nature offers, the Lord's remedies, are the best and most helpful, then they will ask their doctor for them. I would like to see the mother who doesn't want what's best for her children. Now the poor woman believes that the most expensive chemicals are the best; in another twenty years she'll think differently. The doctor will swing over of his own accord, once he sees that otherwise he'll lose his livelihood.

"Why are there already such numbers of homeopathic doctors? Because there exists a nature-cure movement which demands such treatment. Why do you find, over and above Wörishofen and the Kneipp baths, so-called Kneipp doctors? Because the Kneipp Association stands behind them. I once got the figures for membership of the Biochemical Association from the health department of the Security Service. It's astonishing how many belong and demand biochemical treatment, quite apart from whether one believes in it or not.

The law of supply and demand does not only apply to economics. We'll do our best to awaken the demand for treatment by natural methods; and then the doctors themselves will also find means of satisfying it."

Smirking, Himmler went on: "We'll do something else to help, you may be sure. We'll incorporate the most open-minded young doctors in the SS and thus we'll institute a genuine, general reform; as soon as they've got their degree we'll give them special training in nature-cures and then we'll teach them how to turn this to practical account. It's almost incredible how little knowledge of therapy a young doctor has. If I was a doctor it would upset me to set out and practise on human beings in such circumstances as that. The doctor of today is stuffed with theoretical knowledge and the niceties of clinical diagnosis, but he is unable to use simple remedies for curing a sore leg, eczema or rheumatism. Any old woman in the country can do better with her herbs. Paracelsus made the point clearly enough when he said: 'The man who understands disease is a philosopher of medicine, but the man who cures it is a doctor.'

"We'll supply this need and—once they come to practise—I believe these doctors will be grateful to us for having given them a solid training in those simple remedies which often produce the best results. They'll also learn how the old doctors treated and cured their patients. They'll share in all those valuable therapeutical arts that modern medicine, in its arrogance and defective sense of history, has thrust heedlessly aside. They'll learn how to remove kidney and gall-stones without an operation, how to deal with goitre, how to cure rheumatism and gout properly, how to handle arterio-sclerosis—matters in which modern medicine is more or less helpless—but the old doctors understood them. Besides the teaching of Kneipp and Priessnitz, we'll get first-class specialists to teach them about the Finnish 'Saunas' and the magnificent results they bring. We'll have these baths in every small town after the war; and as our soldiers will already have experienced their marvellous effects, people will take to them all the more easily.

"I'll gladly pay for this special training out of SS funds. Then we'll cleverly group these men in strategic positions throughout the Reich and at the same time make it a part of their duty to set up local nature-cure associations and recommend special baths. You'll see what a movement we shall inspire! I have gone into all this with Gebhard, who is very understanding about the plan. Once the war is over, we'll make a start. Very soon the chemical industry will swing over and adapt itself to the changed demand. This will all happen quietly without any fuss; nobody will be able to stand in our way. We'll leave them no point at which to attack us. One day success will come and our labours will have brought about the type of reform which is never achieved by discussion. The legislation which follows will simply confirm our achievements. That's what is known as organic growth, Herr Kersten, and it's just the same in every walk of life. Law must be the expression of life and only enforce what life has already established. That's what I did with my SS; first I laid the foundations of power, and then power dropped into my hand.

"Meanwhile," Himmler continued, "we're already doing something in that direction. You'll perhaps have heard that I'm proposing that people should plant herb-gardens everywhere, in the country and even in towns, wherever possible. I know that I'm laughed at on that account, but that doesn't matter, I know what I'm doing. By these means we're retaining and renewing old knowledge. We're getting people into the way of helping themselves with natural remedies in their little day-to-day indispositions; thus they acquire the habit of this sort of treatment. Once it has helped them, they'll demand similar treatment from their doctor in more serious matters."

"In other words," I objected, "you're leaving people to cure themselves."

"Don't be misled by such a typical doctor's argument. Every normal man first tries to help himself. Either he does nothing and trusts in his sound constitution to throw off disease, or he does what his neighbour tells him or—as in the old days—he has recourse to some trusted remedy whose effect he knows. Look at the peasants in Bavaria. Do you think they run to a doctor the moment there's something wrong with their cattle? Of course not—still less so on their own account. They'll treat a cut, for instance, with plantain and wait to see what good that does. They poultice their own sick horses. They drink an infusion of wormwood and gentian to cure their own aches and pains. They grow elderberry bushes beside their cottages, knowing its properties—and they treat it as a crime if a man should dare to cut one down. If they get splinters in hand or foot they poultice them with resin according to an old recipe, instead of cutting them out. They know about all those noble herbs, shave-grass and arnica, gentian and dandelion, plantain and pewter-grass. They gather them themselves—and at the right moment when healing powers are at their zenith. Kneipp too was a Bavarian peasant's son, who built on what he learnt in his youth. But ask in the towns about such herbs; nobody will have the least idea of them or of their healing properties. Unhappily this awful ignorance is now afflicting the younger generation even in the country. The more this happens the more we're in the

hands of the industrial chemist. Now you'll understand why I'm so set
on restoring this lost knowledge to be the support of our people. It is
a great undertaking."

Himmler fetched from a shelf the famous herbiary of Hieronymus
Bock. It was the German translation of 1554 by Melchior Sebizius
bound in the finest pigskin. He opened it and showed me the beautiful
wood-cuts. He had been through the book in detail, underlining and
making notes. It was clear that he knew his subject. He concluded by
giving me a lecture on the power of certain herbs, especially the
centaury and the popular balm, an infusion of which he drank himself.
He spoke of the wonderful curative properties of the ivy and of the
high esteem which the juniper enjoyed in Bavaria.

Much of what Himmler said was certainly exaggerated. All the
same, for a layman, he has an astonishing knowledge in this field.

IV

CIVIL SERVANTS AND HONOURS

Friedenau, Berlin
23rd August, 1940

As I was going to treat Himmler this morning, Heydrich came to the door with a document which he gave Himmler to read. "Now what else could you expect from such a fellow?" said Himmler. "Don't worry about that. I don't take it in bad part—after all, he's a civil servant and can't change his nature. I'll talk to Frick about the whole affair." With that he gave the paper back to the disconcerted Heydrich.

But he had not got the matter off his mind. He walked up and down, then, standing before me, he started one of his instructive monologues. They are always most informative and it is only necessary for me to put in a word from time to time in order to learn his innermost thoughts.

"This is a fine mess," he said. "Heydrich had got hold of an official in the Ministry of the Interior who seemed a good racial type—and trustworthy. He talked to him for hours, introduced him to our way of thinking and wanted him to be a reliable informant, as we must know what's happening in the offices over there. The official agreed, Heydrich arranged for me to receive him—and what happens? The official reports the whole business in an elegant memo to his minister and now I must suffer the consequences. With Frick there's nothing much to fear—he hardly ever gets to the Führer, but just imagine if it had been Goebbels!

"These things arise through not taking the mentality of civil servants into account. How could a civil servant understand the ideals of the SS? He only considers what is going to help his career or bring him promotion and honours. The civil servant is always servile; he humbly accepts everything that is passed down to him from above—

why not?—he simply passes it on to the fellow below. Meanwhile he'll do everything in his power to show the boss on whose goodwill he depends how loyal, honourable and decent he is, how industrious and conscientious. He behaves in this fashion not because he approves of it but for the sake of his career. Now if Heydrich had realized this, he'd have been a bit more subtle: he'd have tried to win the fellow's heart and could have done so by persuading him that what he was being asked to do would be a simple and comfortable means of forwarding his career. But see what will happen now. You'll find this honest fellow on the next list for the Führer's Birthday Honours. If Heydrich had only told him that he would get him into the Reich's Chancery or arrange for his promotion to the presidency of some committee, he would have become a willing tool."

"But then have you no high opinion of the civil servant's code? The Prussian civil service has a great reputation all over the world," I put in.

"Certainly—so long as there was a monarchy, which gave its civil servants direct orders, satisfying their desire for a career while keeping them on the rails. The Kings of Prussia, such a man as Frederick William I, knew the mentality of their civil servants and treated them as they must be treated. Read their history and you'll learn a lot. These so-called civil servants were simply servants of their prince, who referred to them with scant respect. He cleverly made use of their human weakness too for his own plans. What an advantage to the state when it doesn't need to pay its civil servants a large salary and instead hangs a ribbon round their necks which costs practically nothing, what a saving! How clever to confer a third-class honour on a civil servant which will stimulate him to work day and night so that in another five years he can achieve the second or perhaps even the first class! What a contest between competitors when one has the order with, the other without, the clasp. A man will accept a lifetime of underpayment simply because at the end of it he will be fully entitled to call himself privy councillor.

"I once found the greatest pleasure in contemplating the seniority lists of civil servants in the old states of Prussia and of my own Bavaria. What a wealth of statecraft lay hidden there! During our struggle for power, when the civil servants oppressed us as only they knew how, I used to swear to make an end of the whole system the moment we came to power. Now, knowing the history of the Prussian state, I think quite differently. The civil servants are a necessity. But you need to understand their mentality exactly before you can make use of it.

"The means of doing this is by honours, titles, promotions and documents giving recognition to five, fifteen or twenty years of faithful service, which the lower ranks of civil servants can hang in their rooms—as indeed the higher ones too would like to do in their heart of hearts. It was very foolish of the Weimar Government to abolish honours and thus rob itself of a cheap and very important weapon.

"On the other hand just consider the industrialist's scorn for such honours. He sees what's really behind them. After the war we'll have an entirely new system of honours and titles; we'll do our best to cope with the vanity and inferiority complexes of civil servants, until we've trained a new type of man who'll no longer need such concessions to human vanity. He'll embody the motto of the SS: 'Being is more than seeming.' But that will take time."

"Then you condemn all honours as worthless?"

"By no means," Himmler answered. "There's a real value for instance in the life-saving medal or the Iron Cross—though these also inspire a lot of scoundrels. The Mothers' Cross is the best of all; one day it'll be the greatest honour in Greater Germany. Sentries will have to present arms to a woman with the Mothers' Cross in gold; she will have a right to an audience with the Führer and she'll enjoy boundless honour throughout the land. You smile, Herr Kersten, and perhaps think that I have a romantic imagination. But you'll find that a delegation of women with the Mothers' Cross will have precedence on parade over the Führer's bodyguard—and just consider the effect of that!"

"And what if mothers bring ten children into the world simply in order to win the Mothers' Cross in gold?"

Himmler laughed. "You're not going to compare mothers with civil servants, Kersten. I would welcome such ambition, for the women would undertake it at the risk of their lives. God grant us plenty of such mothers."

I've thought a great deal about this talk today. What sort of a man is Himmler? A crass rationalist coldly taking account of human instincts and using them for his own ends? Yet at the same time a romantic? He spoke with deep emotion when he told me about the Germanic woman with the Mothers' Cross in gold taking precedence over the household troops; and he plans to make the SS salute every woman who has the Mothers' Cross, even the ordinary one. But all his utterances fluctuate between these two poles and cloud his vision of reality.

When I have a chance I'll ask Himmler what his criterion is for

CIVIL SERVANTS AND HONOURS

promotion in the SS. As far as I can see he plays on human nature no less here than in the case of those civil servants he so much despises. He has openly admitted to me that men like a smart and flattering uniform and that it makes them comply with his wishes; this view is expressed in the uniforms he confers on his so-called honorary leaders, who are granted a rank suited to their administrative post.

V

HOMOSEXUALS

AT THE end of the treatment today Himmler related to me the following case, which was greatly troubling him: about a year ago he had
learnt that one of his SS leaders, a man with a good record, was homo-
sexually inclined, at times actively. He had had the case examined and
the facts were confirmed. The man was reduced to the rank of private
in the SS and gave his word of honour that he would renounce this
inclination; he was offered the opportunity of rehabilitating his good
name on active service at the front.

I couldn't help laughing, so grotesque did the situation appear to
me. Himmler noticed and angrily demanded: "Why are you laughing?
For me the matter is deadly serious. It concerns the existence of one of
my leaders."

"What amused me," I replied, "was that you and your men believe
that homosexuals can be cured by giving their word of honour. What
a truly simple method that would be! Just try to change the sexual life
of a man of thirty by means of his word of honour: you will discover
that nature is far stronger than any word of honour."

"That is quite different, Herr Kersten," replied Himmler, "that is
normal sex. This case is an abnormal one."

"From your point of view, Herr Himmler, but not from the homosexual's. According to his psychology he is normal and we are
abnormal. I can imagine what happened in this case of yours. The man
naturally broke his word of honour and now you're casting that at
him as a further reproach. But it's you who are to blame, Herr Himmler,
for you had no right to exact a promise from such a man."

Himmler admitted the facts and told me that the man had distinguished himself highly in the meantime and had been advanced to an

even higher rank, but now there was fresh proof of his abnormal sexual behaviour. There was only one answer: further degradation, expulsion from the SS, a prison sentence and finally the concentration camp. It was terrible for him to have to do this, but it was no good; he had to be logical. He asked me whether a doctor could not do something, so that he could make one more attempt.

I replied that I could only give an answer to that when I had seen and examined the man himself. Pathologists and psychotherapists had gone into the whole problem with a skill to which I could make no claim. But I was generally acquainted with their researches; there was a comprehensive literature on the question. Homosexuality was sometimes related to abnormal glandular development; but if the person in question was simply a case of arrested development, still there was always a disturbance of the whole personality. The problem of homosexuality was overwhelmingly medical, not moral in nature. It was very questionable whether the state should punish it. That he should not want to have homosexuals in the SS was understandable; but it was less easy to understand, in the light of the researches I had mentioned, why the man in question should have to repent of his disposition in a concentration camp.

"I can tell you why, Herr Kersten," Himmler responded; "it's because we mean to get rid of homosexuals root and branch. They're a danger to the national health. Just think how many children will never be born because of this, and how a people can be broken in nerve and spirit when such a plague gets hold of it. If a man has an affair with his pretty secretary, at most she will exert some influence over him, but she won't affect his ability to work. In certain circumstances there will be a child. But when a man in the Security Service, in the SS or in the Government has homosexual tendencies, then he abandons the normal order of things for the perverted world of the homosexuals. Such a man always drags ten others after him, otherwise he can't survive. We can't permit such a danger to the country; the homosexuals must be entirely eliminated.

"Our forefathers knew what they were doing when they had their own homosexuals drowned in a bog, but let those belonging to conquered peoples, the Romans for instance, go unpunished and even encouraged them. Politically speaking, these were wise measures which we should do well to copy. The homosexual is a traitor to his own people and must be rooted out."

"And if he has children?" I objected. "There are a number of men who have both sexual tendencies, live a normal married life and have quantities of children."

"So much the worse," was Himmler's answer, "for then the homosexual tendency will be inherited. I have long been considering whether it would not be to the point to castrate every homosexual at once. That would help him and us."

"That would only involve you in fresh trouble," I retorted, "and fundamentally wreck the man's whole character. It would also prevent his ever finding his way back to a normal life. Yet there are a number of cases in which this can happen, by renewing the development which has been arrested. A clever psychiatrist can treat the root causes which have disturbed the personality."

Apparently this was news to Himmler. He only answered: "You're not going to tell me that psychiatrists can cure homosexuality. They're a trade union for pulling people's souls to pieces, headed by Freud, their Jewish honorary president—though they may quietly disown or supersede him for their own ends."

Here too, as so often, Himmler stuck to his own prejudices without seeing and reflecting on the problem from all sides. The way his Germanic forefathers treated homosexuals played a great part in his own psychological attitude. I pointed out to him that the problem of homosexuality in a modern state had to be looked at, judged and treated in a very different manner from that of Germanic barbarians 2,000 years ago. There were often outstanding intellects, too, among homosexuals. It would mean considerable bloodshed to imprison and liquidate the lot. If he wanted to get the matter into a proper perspective he would have to consider homosexuality from a medical standpoint.

"I am convinced," I emphasized, "that a homosexual's homosexuality appeals as little to the doctor investigating it as it does to me. But you can't reproach a sow's ear for not being a silk purse. You must consider the basic causes and circumstances. Only then can you find a solution or at least form a right judgment. You simply see the symptoms and want to take action against them, without knowing or weighing the causes."

"That's quite enough, Herr Kersten," retorted Himmler, irritated, "I don't want to know anything about these men and their alleged virtues. They're repugnant to me with their womanish attitudes and behaviour; you had better be on your guard too! Just talk with women about them. They keep a very sharp eye on these rivals of theirs and hate them so much that they would gladly burn the lot."

Himmler was no doubt right about the attitude of women towards homosexuality in men.

HOMOSEXUALS

59

11th November, 1940

Today Himmler asked me: "Now what do you propose? These researches you mentioned must have some bearing on the matter."

"That's a tall order," I answered; "I will only put forward a few points as they occur to me. First of all let parents and teachers and those who bring up the young be well informed on homosexual matters. Keep them on the alert for these tendencies and give them the chance of using their influence and understanding while they supervise. Don't limit boys to the companionship of their own sex in the period of adolescence. Encourage mixed schools; it's important that boys should mix with girls of their own age. These produce youthful friendships, 'crushes', increase of individuality and the development of man's underlying need for woman. At the same time you can see how boys are getting along and which of them are in danger of homosexuality. These require special treatment."

"That's splendid, Herr Kersten," Himmler broke in, "I will nominate you as my adviser on homosexual matters. The Hitler Youth has already taken up something like that, but nothing has yet been done for a fundamental solution to the problem."

"For heaven's sake, Herr Himmler, don't do that to me," I answered, frightened by the effect of my proposals. "I would avoid such a thing in any circumstances. Do you think I would set myself up against Herr Heydrich and always champion the homosexuals against him? That would suit Heydrich! No, Herr Himmler, please don't ever say that such an idea had even been considered."

"But why do you hesitate, Herr Kersten?" Himmler asked me.

"I can soon tell you that," I answered. "You know yourself that, ever since it was known how severely you were dealing with homosexuals, it has become a source of the most malicious denunciations. In earlier days if you wanted to get rid of anyone you said they were a witch or in league with the devil. Today you accuse them of homosexuality and proceedings are set in motion. I will have nothing to do with it, not even as a doctor."

"But at least you'll still see the SS leader of whom we spoke?"

"That I'll gladly do and give you a report, but certainly nothing more."

Gut Hartzwalde
17th November, 1940

Today I carried out Himmler's wishes. The man had a good appearance, the blond blue-eyed type: I could not help thinking how upset Himmler must be to have anything of this kind happen with such an outstanding representative of the Nordic race. He would have suspected an inferior dark-haired type in advance and drowned him in a bog without thinking twice about it.

When he was eighteen this man still knew nothing of the opposite sex; his first sexual experience was masturbation. Then he read some hackneyed phrases about dirty habits which made him pause. He recognized himself as a terrible sinner. He experienced all the consequences of which he had read, from weak-mindedness to pains in the back, which he put down as the beginning of spinal disease. But how should he escape from this condition? He could not find his way to a woman; his behaviour seemed to him so disgraceful that he did not dare approach one. But as this was advocated as the only way of overcoming the masturbation habit, he went to a prostitute, which ended in a fiasco and gave him such a shock that it caused an unconquerable repugnance to women.

Next he was seduced by a very clever intellectual, who first of all induced him to consider homosexuality from the intellectual angle, read Plato's *Symposium* with him and showed him that many important men were homosexuals. He had soon convinced him that, while the embraces of women were good enough for the mass of men who were primitive in their outlook, homosexuality was better suited to their intellectual superiors; it was to be viewed as a higher form of development. So he found an ideological background for his own resistance to women. He became an enthusiastic supporter of the idea of men's clubs to form a community pledged in 'body and soul'. He devoured contemporary writings on the significance of men's clubs in political reconstruction. But if these clubs were to fulfil the functions of an exclusive governing class they had to avoid any interference from women. He dedicated himself to this idea. It seemed a logical step for him to pass from the Homoerotic to the Homosexual. In all seriousness he informed me that if the SS were to fulfil its task and become 'an order dedicated to sacrifice', it had to follow the same path; this was not for the majority, but only for a chosen inner circle.

When I remarked that the Reichsführer of the SS had set himself against that and made it his principal aim to increase the number of children, even to the point of advocating bigamy and bastards, he only gave a superior smile and observed that the Reichsführer could do nothing against the movement's immanent laws. When I wanted to know why he had given his word of honour to renounce his homosexual inclinations, he was at first evasive. Then he admitted that there was an element of cowardice in this; he had known beforehand that he would not be able to keep his word of honour; he despised women and any man who associated with them. I asked him whether he would give his word of honour again, should Himmler demand it. He said he would refuse and was quite ready to suffer as a martyr for his creed.

It was clear to me that no doctor could do anything for him. A fundamental disturbance in his development when still young, a refusal to accept normal sexual experience, had resulted in his over-compensating himself in two ways. One was the idea that homo-sexuality was a superior way of life; the other was that, in the form of men's clubs, it was necessary to a governing class. So it came about that the champion of these ideas was by no means the ordinary instinct-dulled type of homosexual; his was more an accentuated tendency towards homosexuality, only occasionally and decreasingly active. Even in his errors he was not wholehearted.

In other ways he had shown himself to be an extraordinarily brave and daring soldier and officer, as had been expressly recognized by his superiors. He wore with pride the honours they had bestowed on him.

The problem of how to help the man remained, how to keep him from the automatic sequence of events: arrest, being reduced to the ranks again, a sentence and the concentration camp, as Himmler had described to me. It would be best if he was to go abroad, so that he might be automatically removed from a circle where he was always under observation. With this in mind I asked him whether he would care for work in a mission abroad, as I might be able to help him to get it. He beamed with joy as he said 'yes'. I got him to promise that, in the event of a trial, he would give no far-reaching explanations as he had to me, but simply make light of the matter and leave the facts to the prosecution.

Gut Hartzwalde
20th November, 1940

During today's treatment I had a chance to speak to Himmler about the case. It would have been quite useless to tell him how things really lay; it would only have meant the certain downfall of a man who was by no means fundamentally bad. Therefore I had to be very cautious and adroit.

Himmler at once asked me: "Now then, what did you find out? Is he curable? Can I give him another chance? I already had it in mind to put him in charge of a particularly difficult unit where he can prove himself afresh. What do you think of him on the whole?"

"He has already proved himself quite enough, Herr Himmler," I replied. "You should get the man out of it, so that he can breathe a different air and no longer live in a circle where he is always being watched, where his every word and act is regarded from a certain angle. Anyhow you won't get at the facts in this case and that's certain. Your own police inspectors with their psychologically ignorant methods surely won't succeed in producing any better suggestions than mine. I would advise you, as the final court of appeal in the SS, to make the arrangements I suggest. I am quite ready to provide minutes of my interrogation on which you can base your decision."

I saw that Himmler was visibly relieved. He immediately asked for the minutes, rang and dictated his decision. I had certainly had no idea that I would achieve my aim so rapidly.

Hartzwalde
21st November, 1940

I made use of his favourable mood and proposed to Himmler that he should send this man who was loyally devoted to him abroad on some mission or other. "Under no circumstances, Herr Kersten," Himmler answered. "Don't you know that the enemy Intelligence make great use of homosexuals and go systematically to work when they think they have found a good subject? I would only expose the man to new dangers, and the Reich to measureless damage, if he should fail."

I laughed out loud and asked Himmler who had told him that: in future he should only employ eunuchs in the foreign services, for it was certainly proved that every intelligence service made particular use of women and how successful they had been was not unknown to history.

Himmler informed me in all seriousness that Heydrich had considerable evidence of the political consequences of homosexuality. Since then officials of the foreign service and all those whose work took them abroad were specially watched and tested with this in view.

I couldn't help laughing, for it was really such a convenient way of exercising control over Ribbentrop's department and demanding the removal of anybody undesirable on the grounds that he was a homosexual. I saw that I could not do much here and wanted to leave the matter, but Himmler—who was really glad that a way had been found to save him an unpleasant decision—returned to it and told me that he would give the man a position on his Norwegian staff; if that proved successful, there would still be time to think of sending him further afield.

So the case had a practical solution. But I could not prevent myself saying to Himmler: "Would it interest you, Herr Himmler, to know that our *protégé* has modelled himself on Frederick II?"

"What are you implying by that?" Himmler retorted. "You're not trying to suggest that the great king had abnormal tendencies? I know those dirty Jews who assert things of the kind in order to take our heroes from us and drag them in the mud. Any great man who has done wonders for his people must somehow or other be abnormal, or at best demented. But with the best will in the world it's quite impossible to assert that Frederick the Great should be even suspected of homosexuality. Only mediocrity is normal and conventional because it produces no greatness and is therefore politically and economically 'safe'. To portray Frederick the Great as abnormal is the obvious malice of a sick mind. I know that his coldness towards his wife is brought forward as evidence. But just consider that poor-spirited creature; it's no wonder that he viewed her as a holy terror and refused to live with her. Why can't it be looked at in this way: as he could not live with his lawful wife, he gave himself up to an ascetic life as king, which fitted him for his great achievements. Instead of that, mud was slung and homosexual tendencies attributed to him—for which there was, moreover, no foundation in fact. If you looked you could only find indications, no clear and indisputable proof."

"It might be difficult, Herr Himmler, to prove such a thing," I objected.

"Then people should keep quiet," Himmler answered, "and bow in silence before his greatness. I would only say one thing to them: if a dozen so-called proofs were put before me, I would brush them aside and assert that they had been made up after the event, because my feelings tell me that a man who won for Prussia her place in the sun could not have had any of the tendencies of these homosexual weaklings."

This talk stayed in my mind for some time. Himmler only recognizes gods and devils. His heroes are like the gods. That they can be men with all too human traits—and for that very reason have a much greater effect when not conventionally portrayed—is a thought quite foreign to him which would seem like an insult to his heroes. To Himmler it was an obvious patriotic duty to support all propaganda assertions about his heroes. At first he did not understand me when I remarked that this was the way to abolish free scientific research, to which he attached great importance; it was also the way to create a science more or less controlled by the police, as every scientist knew what he might and might not write and proceeded accordingly. Anything taken from his picture of his heroes was either the work of small minds, too inferior to grasp such greatness, or came from the malice of enemies—Jews, Masons or priests. In the end he admitted that it was possible for even a National Socialist scholar, unexceptionable to his view, to reach the wrong conclusions. Then he must sacrifice them, Himmler said. The Church, too, asked that of her adherents, for the need of the people to keep their heroes and their respect for them came before all truth.

VI

RENEWAL OF THE RULING CLASS

1. THE BASIC BIOLOGICAL LAW

Hartzwalde
18th December, 1940

HIMMLER had seldom been out in the last few days. I expressed my surprise at this and asked the reason.

"Look here, Herr Kersten," he said, "it's like this: in these weeks of winter when Nature draws right back into herself, man has to do the same. He has to unburden himself and relax, share in the rhythm of Nature, so that he can experience in his own person the great event of the winter solstice, after which the rise of sap and strength begins again. I always pause at this time and breathe in its benediction. Countrymen understand that perfectly; they lie behind the stove and 'laze', as the townsman calls it. For people in towns know nothing about all that—to them one day is the same as another and they carry on their pursuits, indifferent whether Nature is in blossom or fruit or has surrendered to her winter sleep. Yet this countryman's rest is no laziness; it is rather a summons to new strength. This is the only reason why he is able to work so astonishingly in the summer, already in the fields at dawn and not lying down again until late in the evening. The same laws apply to other lives. The preliminary to all great achievements is to work and relax in the rhythm of biological laws."

These words made me think of Himmler's piles of documents which he went through every day, of his industriousness, and of the burden of work under which his secretary Brandt laboured, in which there was little question of relaxing and the rhythm of life. So I replied: "A fine theory, Herr Himmler, but neither you nor those around you, nor the ruling class in Germany as a whole, follow it, nor ever have. That's why Germans seem so uncomfortable to foreigners. You should make what you have just told me a rule of your own life and take a long week-end off every week, or—as the Swedes do—go into the country on Friday evening and not return until Monday. You would see what an effect that had on your decisions and on your thoughts."

"Obviously such things can't be done in war-time," Himmler replied, "even the Führer can enjoy no rest. But afterwards we will come to serious decisions in this matter. A long week-end is relatively easy to fix, as everyone is ready to fall in with it. Another scheme will also command general agreement: the Führer has it in view to set up conference places in the most attractive spots in the four quarters of the Reich. Here the leaders of the Reich will meet for important decisions, so that they can come to properly balanced conclusions, in peace and quiet, far from the daily grind. Every ministry will have a place of this sort within easy reach. The success of the undertaking will more than defray its costs. Leaders too are used to keeping things going when they're not there; they arrange for deputies to take their place.

"But we have a much greater problem to solve. The same laws as affect Nature and the individual are also true for the nation as a whole and for its ruling class. Look at the leading families: they come to power, keep going for a few generations and die out because they are completely used up. That can't have been in the plan of the Creator."

"On the contrary, that seems to me a law of life, Herr Reichsführer," I answered. "The man who attains leadership engages in a struggle in which there is no looking back. This consumes his life-substance. Moreover it is the same with peoples as with forests, as you are so fond of remarking. The old trees are still standing, but new ones are always springing up out of the measureless wealth and resurgence of the woods. A nation must have the chance to infuse fresh blood into its leaders."

"You're right there, but that's only one side of the problem," Himmler answered. "I admire too the way the English have solved it. They have arranged matters so that their upper class is always recruited from a rising class. Specially deserving and outstanding men are raised to the peerage, so that the old aristocracy of birth is reinforced and transformed by a new aristocracy of action."

I spoilt this pretty picture by remarking that deserving Jews were honoured in this way in England, so that a Benjamin Disraeli became a Lord Beaconsfield, a Rufus Isaacs a Lord Reading, an Alfred Mond a Lord Melchett; and they were a boon to England. Himmler naturally did not like this and said that it could only be understood in the light of England's mistaken indifference to racial laws. "The English don't know the Jews, they only get them at secondhand, whereas we have them straight from the East."

2. THE ENGLISH UPPER CLASS AS A MODEL

21st December, 1940

Today Himmler returned to the topic of the English upper class and said: "We should have made discreet use of the English system of reinforcing their nobility; then we would certainly have had less degenerate a nobility today."

The example of England was responsible for the Führer's decree whereby only a proportion of the sons of SS leaders might in their turn become leaders in it; the remaining positions in the upper ranks were left open to the proven best of the nation; this would systematically produce a new aristocracy of action. Another English measure had made a very strong impression on him. In England only the eldest son inherited the title and possessions; the remaining sons and daughters were reabsorbed into the national life and transmitted their good blood into it. You could call that conscious racial breeding. In Germany on the other hand every fifth or sixth person you met was a count or a baron, which meant nothing, so that counts and barons and princes swarmed; they usually had no money and so little self-respect that they tried to coin money out of their titles and made use of them as cheap advertisements for insurance companies, banks or court dressmakers. The public was foolish enough to fall for such frauds and preferred to have at their disposal a Count von Tannenfels than a plain Mr. Fritz Tannenfels.

After the war energetic measures would be taken. Only the actual owner of an estate would in future have a title. The former upper class would be judged by its reliability and the proofs it had given of itself during the war. Moreover the eldest son would inherit under the same conditions as were already in force for the inheritance of property. Members of the aristocracy who administered their estates inefficiently would be dispossessed in the same way as incompetent farmers and the next in succession would become the ground landlord. Farms would be shared out to other descendants. In future there would only be *one* Count von Tannenfels, to keep up the tradition of the family name. Other branches of the family would be plain and simple, Tannenfels; but they might take the name of their estate as was the custom with farmers in Eastern Germany. A former Count von Tannenfels who happened to occupy an estate in Blumenau would become Fritz Tannenfels zu Blumenau. "That's something; it sounds well and above all people know what it means."

"Then you want to set up a new upper class in the East, Herr Reichsführer?" I put in.

"Exactly, my dear Herr Kersten, a real farming aristocracy in which the old nobility will take its place beside our farmers there. They can prove themselves there, get new blood and take things quietly for a few generations, before they're called upon to serve again. Until now the nobility has decayed as soon as it lost touch with the soil from which it sprang. For the same rhythm of achievement and relaxation holds good for families as for individuals and the seasons of the year. We must regulate ourselves by the laws of Nature."

3. *STATE FARMS*

23rd December, 1940

We continued the talk. Himmler said: "This principle also holds good for the ruling class of a people. Our scholars and industrialists usually come from the country, from families of small farmers or artisans. They get on, flourish for two or three generations, then become exhausted and die out. If a family lasts longer, you'll usually find when you investigate that specially favourable circumstances have intervened. For instance, Evangelical parsonages are, biologically speaking, fountains of youth. Although I don't want to have anything to do with the narrow-minded clergy, I must confess that they have achieved marvels in this field: they have leisure, usually they choose the wives they need for their round of duties and they reside in their country rectories like the lesser gentry.

"We can't afford the dying out of valuable blood after a relatively short period of activity. Imagine," said Himmler, "what would happen if all the leading men in politics and industry died in their thirties. What an outcry there would be! The whole medical profession would be mobilized to find the reason and remedy the state of affairs; but no heed is paid when almost the same thing is happening, simply because it is spread over two or three generations and doesn't leap to the eye in the same way."

"Then do you want to put the ruling class back on the land every second or third generation?" I asked Himmler. "That seems a purely mechanical process."

"Not like that, of course," was Himmler's answer, "but it's obvious to me that they must somehow be brought into contact with the soil again, to renew themselves from that permanent source of strength. It's only a question of the means. The first step will be to endow the intellectual, industrial and political ruling class with farms which they will not be allowed to sell, of an area proportionate to their services, so as to restore their contact with the land. If a politician or a scholar has a farm, he will naturally make it his home and his wife and children will pass their holidays there. The children will go to the country as a horse to pasture; this wonderful experience of the soil will last throughout their lives.

"But we'll do more than that. We will see to it that, when farms cannot be handed over as private property, smaller farms will be lent as 'state farms' to members of the ruling class. Certain posts will automatically carry with them the right to such a farm, for which there will be a special 'state tenure'. The farm must not be too far from the place where the man works, so that he can reach it by car conveniently. If his work takes him to a different part of Germany, he will surrender this farm and receive another. The farm mustn't stand in the way of his employment. By these means we'll get another considerable group of men back into direct contact with the soil."

23rd December, 1940
in the evening

In order to make clear to Himmler the psychological fallacy behind his thought-process I started off: "Have you considered that these men are no farmers? In a short time your 'state farms' will have been so mismanaged that you will no longer be able to recognize them. Each man will indulge his hobbies and make experiments which will arouse the contempt and laughter of real farmers. After the first fine enthusiasm has worn off and he sees what he has let himself in for, the townsman will be so sick of his farm that he will curse the hour that he ever set eyes on it."

"Naturally we've considered that," was Himmler's answer. "The urbanized civil servant obviously knows nothing about the management of a farm. These farms will be looked after and administered as state property by a manager appointed by the Government, who will see to a number of farms, something like a local bailiff."

"Then you're simply providing your ruling class with a country house on the cheap, Herr Himmler. The bailiff, not receiving orders from the so-called owner, will not think much of him; and the owner, having nothing to say, will feel that he is generally superfluous. There will be sources of friction: his urban wife will find these constant stays in the country boring and will prefer to accompany her husband into the city on Sundays, rather than while away her time in Lower Pomerania. On the other hand he will have to insist on staying in the country as often as possible, in order to keep up appearances with his superiors; the time spent in the country will become a burden. So you will have achieved exactly the opposite of what you wanted. It is certain that in a short time you will have quite destroyed that instinctive desire and longing for the country which is common to most people living in towns."

"These dangers are naturally in our minds, Herr Kersten, and we will need all our skill to find a way round them. But what else should we do? We can't give full responsibility for his farm to a man who is not a farmer. He has first to get into the way of it; responsibility and possession are naturally our aims. The first steps are chiefly to see who can be trusted with a farm and who has to be rejected."

4. OVERCOMING THE EVILS OF CIVILIZATION

28th December, 1940

A few days later the talk on state farms was resumed. Himmler, who always obstinately pursued a subject until he had reached the conclusion he wanted, declared: "The objections you made have not convinced me. They are specious, but they won't hold water. You must remember what an important part the bailiff has to play. He will have to be very carefully chosen. He will not only have to superintend the work properly, but take the tenant of the farm in hand and introduce him, and especially his children, to farm management and to country ways and habits. Our first choice for bailiffs will be wounded SS leaders, coming from the same social class as the tenants of the farms; we'll prepare them specially for their task and give them courses in farm management. It's no mystery; where there's a feeling for it, it can always be learnt. Soon the tenant will be in a position to talk knowledgeably with his bailiff about appropriate measures. The bailiff will gradually become no more than an adviser and the tenant will assume his proper function.

"All that naturally takes time, much patience and goodwill, but it's worth while. If we only succeed in really bringing one son or daughter in every civil servant's family back to the land, for the simple reason that he or she has been bred on it, we have already achieved an immense amount. Then we'll give them a complete training in our agricultural colleges and assign them farms in the East. So we will have enabled our leading families to escape from the 'evils of civilization' in the city; healthily bred in contact with mother earth, they will present new families to the nation.

"Favourable living conditions for the ruling class, links with the country, the return of some sons and daughters to the land, that is the way to renewal. What do the initial difficulties count against that! One day it will be assumed that every leading man is at the same time a farmer. Then men will no longer waste their time in idle gossip, but like farmers they'll discuss the care of their estates, and solid country thinking will dominate all our political and economic decisions."

Enthusiastically Himmler continued: "Then the Germanic race will begin to flourish anew and its existence will be assured for a thousand years. We must lay the foundations for that and not allow ourselves to be put off by the difficulties which are to be encountered at the commencement of every great undertaking. Above all we must, in this as in other matters, make a start first and then see how things are going, advance step by step, do what we must, correct our mistakes and not move on to new objectives until we are quite convinced that we have found the right way."

5th January, 1941

Today the talk continued. I remarked: "But, Herr Himmler, you can't ask the industrialist to think like a countryman and to overlook the fact that Germany is first and foremost an industrial power and that her strength lies precisely there."

"You're forgetting that our captains of industry—I need only mention Robert Bosch—often have more of a country outlook than our urbanized upper class. These industrialists usually have their own estates and know the worries that go with them. I'm only too glad of it. From a political point of view it's of the first importance. Country ways of thought go far beyond what is usually expressed by the phrase. They mean that your thoughts and decisions draw their strength from the roots of the earth and the inner reserves of the nation. Unhappily our ruling class has lost these ways of thought."

"But what's going to happen to the great majority of your civil servants and officials? Will you abandon them to the 'evils of civilization'? What about the workers?" I asked Himmler.

"That is a problem of quite a different sort," was his answer. "In the country as in small and medium-sized towns it is correspondingly easy to solve. Here we only need to strengthen the movement towards allotments and ownership of property. They'll bring about revolutions in health which will extend in ever-widening circles. We have a model for this too in Württemberg. It's the healthiest region of the Reich and entirely free from economic troubles owing to its special mixture of industry with small farming properties."

"In the city," Himmler went on, "it's a matter of far-reaching changes and new accommodation, which the Führer will tackle with all his energy after the war. Plans have already been worked out. Instead of huge workers' tenements there will be houses able to accommodate at least four children, so constructed that the housewife will be relieved of many of her burdens. They will of course have bathrooms and lavatories. Each of these houses will possess an extensive garden.

"Wherever possible official posts will entail the possession of land on a scale commensurate with the official's salary, as used to be the case with teachers. This will have a special importance in the choice of a wife, as the civil servant who knows that he has to manage a farm will not select a girl or woman so urbanized that she is unable to cope with it. Children will no longer be a burden but a necessity. You can't explain to a civil servant that he must have plenty of children, when the basic facts of his life, the smallness of his salary, poor accommodation and confined circumstances are all against it. We must create conditions to suit human needs, otherwise we're only moving in the realm of utopias. And you're always trying to charge me with being utopian in my plans," concluded Himmler with an ironical smile.

5th January, 1941
in the evening

This evening I was with a small group of Himmler's colleagues and, to complete my picture, I raised the same topics which I had recently had the opportunity to discuss with Himmler on several days. I explained what I had heard from him. On all sides there was agreement and confirmation, given joyfully and devoutly. Hard-headed men spoke with enthusiasm on this subject, their eyes shining, using almost the same expressions.

I asked myself what was this extraordinary manifestation that I had encountered. Apparently I had touched on their holy of holies. Certain words had the effect of magical formulae upon them: 'Back To The Land', 'The New Farmer', 'Own Your Land as a Free Man', 'Really Getting Down To It', 'A New Ruling Class', 'A Better Future', 'Racial

Breeding'—and above all the thought of 'The SS which Arranges Everything'.

"Yes, Doctor," said one of these gentlemen with great seriousness, "we know what we're fighting for without rest day or night. In a single generation Germany will already look very different and in two it will no longer be possible to recognize the Germany of today. It will be the paradise of the Germanic race."

I wondered whether it was because I had become so urbanized that I took all this so quietly. One can call it romanticism when one sees the strong impulses which move those men, but where does that get one? It is much more important to be clear about the cause of this crusade against city life and the 'evils of civilization', to discover the roots from which their convictions draw their strength.

Perhaps it's simply due to a number of different circumstances: the terrible sense of confinement in which Germans live, to which this antagonism to city life bears witness, coupled with German romanticism which regards the country as the fulfilment of all its dreams, a paradise in opposition to the city, a spring of youth in contrast to age and death. Himmler appeals to these basic feelings and shows his people the power of the SS which can realize their longings. They only need to do their duty, use all the strength they have, and each day will bring them a little nearer to what they long for. Each of those to whom I spoke already saw himself as a gentleman farmer in the East with a Germanic family of at least seven children.

They regarded their 'King Henry' as at once the guarantor of this paradise and the man who would lead them to it. Was Himmler here trying to copy Mohammed, whom he so liked to praise? Was he promising his valiant men a paradise—with land tenure to take the place of houris?

VII

THE CHOSEN WOMEN

Friedenau, Berlin
15th–17th January, 1941

TODAY I had to wait an hour before I could give Himmler his treatment. Heydrich was making his report to Himmler and the red light was on all the time; nobody might interrupt. Finally at noon I was able to begin. Himmler was in the best of humours and very talkative. He told me that entirely new marriage laws were being prepared; he had just been talking over the details with Heydrich. As the war would soon be over, they wanted everything to be ready for it.

Among other things these new marriage laws included new conditions for divorce. This would be legal if the marriage had gone for five years without children. Such a marriage could and must be broken up, for the state required as many children as possible and could not have the slightest interest in a childless marriage.

I objected that it was not only a matter for the state but for the feelings of the married couple themselves. I knew a number of childless marriages which were extremely happy. Such people would regard it as a tragedy if the state compelled them to separate.

Himmler would not listen to such objections. The good of the Reich came before the happiness of the individual. It was of small importance whether Herr and Frau Müller were happy; what counted was whether they had children. If they had none they must be given the chance of another marriage which might produce children. A proper family, in Himmler's opinion, only really started with three children; the state could not be expected to countenance a childless marriage. Existing marriage laws were controlled by the Church and needed reform. They must be replaced by a marriage law which breathed the Germanic spirit and opened the way to a new intellectual and spiritual rebirth for the German people.

Himmler was at the moment concerned with a very important aspect of this marriage law—the question of the '*Hohen Frauen*', or 'Chosen Women'.

"What are they?" I enquired, when he used these words. "Are you trying to provide something on the lines of the old German 'wise women' to be advisers to the Reich?"

"That's an idea that's worth thinking about," Himmler considered, "but the Chosen Women are quite another matter. You know, Herr Kersten, what we lack is that strong, purposeful type of woman that the Romans had in their vestals or the old Germans in their wise women, whom you have just mentioned. This type of woman has disappeared, yet she filled a definite place in the life of the state. Of course there's no lack of fine racial types among women, but they are immersed in their daily tasks or have to slave miserably at jobs which are quite unsuited to them. There are no longer any obvious positions in the state for them; there is nothing to attract them and stimulate them to great deeds."

I was still not very clear what Himmler had in mind and said: "Do you want to give women more rights and a proper position in the state, as the women's emancipation movement has demanded? Women would certainly regard that as a great step forward. It would also be a clever political move to win the women over to your side."

"We're certainly not going as far as that," Himmler replied. "We want to start in a small way from below and thus solve one of the problems which lies very close to our hearts. We're going to set up 'Women's Academies for Wisdom and Culture', in which a number of specially selected German women will be educated. Besides complete reliability in politics and wholehearted acceptance of National Socialist ideas conditions for admission will be: high intellectual gifts, grace of mind and body, and an entirely Germanic appearance."

"You mean that only blonde-haired and blue-eyed women will be admitted to these schools?" I put in.

"Naturally," said Himmler. "Of course I know that some brunettes have outstanding intellectual qualities and great charm, but we have to make a logical start and we will do so here. These Chosen Women will receive the best possible education. They will have a good grounding in history; they will learn languages and have the same basic training as officials in the foreign service; they must be quick-witted and know how to think and act swiftly in delicate situations. Daily games of chess will be part of the curriculum to develop their minds; and all kinds of sports, especially fencing, which is also an intellectual exercise, as it demands an instant reaction to every move of your opponent; there will be riding, driving, swimming and pistol practice. Naturally there will also be special courses in cookery and house-keeping. After passing a thorough examination these women will receive the title of 'Chosen Women'. This will be the highest distinction which a woman can reach in the Greater German Reich. The Chosen Women will stand beside those who have won the Mothers' Cross in silver and gold."

"By the time a woman has learnt all this," I objected to Himmler, "she will have aged a little. And what will you do with these elderly women when they have finally achieved the title of Chosen Women?"

"Elderly women!" replied Himmler, laughing. "What are you thinking about, Herr Kersten? These women must have finished their education by the time they are twenty-six or twenty-eight."

I imagined that these Chosen Women would go as advisers in the foreign service or to embassies and represent the Reich in a particularly impressive fashion. Their training on lines similar to diplomats and members of the intelligence service indicated this. I asked Himmler about it.

"It's true," Himmler replied, "that that is also work for which they are being considered. I'm convinced that they could be excep-tionally useful there. It's a great mistake that women are so seldom employed in the foreign service; their gifts of intuition and sympathy would make them more effective than men, who only rely on their reason.

"The same holds good for their efficiency in intelligence work, where their training, brains and charm will make it easy for them to score outstanding success. But such duties are reserved for later generations. They must first be used in quite different ways; we need them urgently to put right what is happening in our own ranks. Just look, Herr Kersten, at many of our National Socialist leaders' wives! They are good and worthy housewives, adequate during the struggle for power, but being unable to rise in the world, they're no longer suited to their husbands. They quarrel all the time. The husbands find other women; the wives feel that they and their husbands are drifting apart. On public occasions they make a poor showing. We must do something about the malicious gossip which persists in maligning our leaders' private lives, for these men are not private citizens and they're always in the public eye. The Führer has faced this and wants the situation altered fundamentally.

"We must find a way then to separate men from their wives honourably, when the men are so much needed by their country. The wives will receive a pension on which they can live quite respectably.

But their husbands must look for a wife among the Chosen Women who will be fitted to his future position. Such a marriage must be a model for all National Socialist marriages. In the event of scandal, the Führer is determined to be ruthless; the guilty man will be declared unworthy of marriage with a Chosen Woman and expelled from the Party. I will myself direct proceedings in the SS."

Here are other remarks of Himmler's on this subject: "As things are at present, women differ chiefly in that some can spend more money than others on such things as dress and appreciation of the arts. But the truly capable woman has no means of developing her great qualities except within her family. Such exceptions as there are can be counted on the fingers of two hands. Just consider the women of the past: Elizabeth of England, the Pompadour in France, Maria Theresa in Austria, only to name a few. They united charm and womanly feelings with diplomatic skill and a great capacity for action; and in this pleasing combination they showed a superiority comparable to that of the most outstanding men. We want to give the Chosen Women who don't inherit a royal status a chance to use gifts essential to the country. The way will be open to every woman who is suitable, while still at her most attractive age. Athletic grace and cultured intelligence, delicacy of feeling and subtlety of expression—these women will have all that. They will fill a gap in our leadership; their qualities will counterbalance the dullness of men."

Before I could comment, Himmler went straight on: "Now you'll see why I attach so much importance to having only blonde, blue-eyed types as Chosen Women. They will be a permanent ideal for the whole nation; others will watch them and follow their example. So they must also embody the ideal physical traits: no compromise is possible here."

Berlin
18th–19th January, 1941

Yesterday we were interrupted in our interesting discussion of the Chosen Women. During today's treatment Himmler at once picked up the threads. I had had time to reflect on the whole problem and had prepared a few questions.

My first was: "Then are the Chosen Women obliged to take the man who asks for them?"

"In principle, yes. You must realize that this is the fulfilment of the great vocation for which they have been trained. Personal preferences have to take a back place, as was customary with royal marriages. Yet the women have a certain right to refuse. This is permissible if the Chosen Woman has herself selected a suitable husband from the circle in question; she will have the chance to make her own choice there. But there will be a time limit to her choice, after which the right of selection returns to the men. The Führer has decided that the final decision will rest with the Reichsführer of the SS, who must not delegate it but exercise it himself.

"At first it will only be a narrow circle among whom the Chosen Women may marry, but in time this will be enlarged. It will depend on how many of these women can be trained. The ultimate aim is that it should become a matter of course for the leaders of the Party and the SS to marry this type of woman, so that we'll never again suffer from conflicts of the sort that are troubling us now. At the same time— without making any fuss—we will be creating a new upper class to replace the present one, which is often thoroughly degenerate. This will come about simply through guiding the choice of wives instead of leaving it to chance. It's a unique opportunity and can lead to a complete rebirth of the Germanic race.

"In the SS these measures will take effect in one simple decree making marriage to a Chosen Woman a condition for promotion to the higher ranks. Imagine what that will be like, when in future our leading men will only marry women who are both gifted and charming, noble in soul and body! A generation will arise which will be a spring of youth and renewal both for the German people and the Germanic race as a whole! I regard it as a great honour that the Führer has entrusted this task to the Reichsführer of the SS—a special recognition of the policy I have followed within the SS."

Himmler was highly enthusiastic, as always happened when he spoke about his Nordic ideas. Here indeed they had found expression in a complete system and could be seriously put into practice. It was always a cause of grief to him that his SS leaders still continued to marry brunettes, in spite of all the propaganda for the blonde, blue-eyed type. But he himself had to countenance such marriages, if he was to avoid making his Settlement and Racial Head Office a storm centre; every SS man had to seek permission there before he married. Only in the case of a Jewish or coloured woman was permission refused. With the realization of his plan for the Chosen Women, Himmler had his first chance of rejecting a certain type of woman and going in for racial breeding, which was one of his pet ideas.

He always maintained the theory that men could be bred just as ssfully as animals and that a race of men could be created possess-
highest spiritual, intellectual and physical qualities. It was only

necessary to face the problem seriously, above all to make a start without being put off by the violent prejudices which men had ingrained in them from their upbringing and in particular from the teaching of the Church. The Church had a great interest in preventing the formation of a fine Germanic type, for she had need of the inferior racial type, the only one ready to accept her teaching. The real hundred-per-cent German on the other hand was the born enemy of clerical doctrine.

Himmler never tired of talking about this theory. He had specialized knowledge at his disposal and made use of the most recent experiments in the rearing of animals and plants. On the one hand he gave the effect of a preacher, presenting his ideas with the faith of a fanatic; on the other hand a scholar who developed the Mendelian laws in detail and considered their application to the breeding of men. Through breeding he meant to produce Nietzsche's Superman. He was firmly convinced that definite intellectual and spiritual traits were inherited no less than physical ones; and he regarded anyone who denied this as an enemy of the Germanic race, a personal enemy whom he would have liked to throw into jail, before such fallacies could do further damage.

When he saw blond children, boys or girls, he became pale with emotion. It has often happened, when I was out driving with him, that he would stop the car, take children in his arms, talk to them, write down the name and address of their parents, give them a present, and say to me: "Look, Herr Kersten, what a marvellous child—that's what all our people should look like. One day I'll have him for my SS."

Sometimes this got Himmler into trouble. Brandt told me that one day when he was visiting a seaport he came upon a large, good-looking blond docker, went up to him and said: "You're going to join my Waffen SS. Have you seen service?" The man said he had and Himmler next asked: "What rank? Private, of course. It's always the same. People like this are never promoted in the army. Make a note of this, Brandt: from now on this man is a corporal in the SS." To the man he said: "You will report at once as personally promoted by me to be SS Unterscharführer in Adolf Hitler's bodyguard. The details will be arranged."

The man duly reported; his papers were looked over and he had his medical. Meanwhile the first anonymous letters came in denouncing him. Who was the man Himmler had picked? A man engaged in the bawdy trade, who had often been to prison! When the Reichsführer heard it, he was overwhelmed; he would never have believed such a thing of a blond man. It upset him very much to give the man up, cancel his promotion and send him home again.

I thought of such moments when I listened to Himmler talking about the Chosen Women. He looked at me and realized how sceptical I was. "I see," he said, "once more you are full of doubts. But just question me—it's always healthy and informative. The Socratic method is based on questioning."

I answered, laughing: "So you regard me as a disciple of Socrates? But don't forget that Socrates' aim was to use his questions to convince his listeners how wrong they were. Well, first of all, Herr Reichsführer, I don't believe that you will find enough suitable women for your scheme. What woman is going to be willing to surrender her own freedom of choice and accept a man who's forced on her? Particularly not after an education the whole point of which is to develop her personality."

"There you're making a great mistake, my dear Herr Kersten," was the answer. "The greater the task, the greater is its attraction. We have been able to confirm that again and again when forming our picked units. The hardest tasks attract a definite type of man, who can and must live dangerously. We'll find the same thing here. Some women will be only too glad to have at their side a man highly placed in the Party and the Government, glad to help and advise him— women who like this sort of life and don't want to be bothered with housekeeping and small daily chores. It's generally hard to find them and to put their abilities to the best use in the state; but it's of the first importance and the tasks assigned them will attract the right ones and repel the others. You may be sure of that."

"I doubt whether this sort of political Amazon will give you much satisfaction," I answered, "and to create a happy family life for your leaders will also require a lot of doing. Do you really think a man enjoys having constantly at his side a woman who knows everything about his affairs, trained to criticize his decisions and who will be ready to do so? Just consider the type of women men really prefer. Not those trained to a man's own image and quite capable of doing his job in politics or industry—but the opposite type, the woman who understands nothing of these things, yet has her own peculiarly feminine qualities and acts accordingly."

"There are sure to be certain difficulties," Himmler responded, "but they will settle themselves. The great thing is to get it all going on the right lines and make an end of the present system, where hardly anybody bothers about who the chief leaders of the Greater German Reich marry. Once that is done improvements are always possible. If marriage with a Chosen Woman doesn't work out, there can always be another separation. However the Führer has expressly desired that this should not come before the ordinary courts, but only before one specially appointed. The Führer has reserved to himself the confirming of any decisions reached. We'll see to it that everything goes properly. Naturally, here as elsewhere we shall have to buy our experience."

Friedenau, Berlin
21st January, 1941

"What exactly will happen to the Chosen Women's children?" I asked Himmler today, to complete the picture. "Will they also receive special treatment?"

"I'm glad you asked that," Himmler answered, "I had almost forgotten an essential part of the scheme. Their children will be educated at the state's expense; they are to be the future leaders in the Party and in the Government. In particular I will draw on them for my leaders in the Waffen SS. But here too the Führer has looked ahead and made regulations to provide against the forming of a narrow class out of touch with the healthy elements of the nation. Only a proportion of the leaders are to come from that source. That's in accord with the Führer's general instructions on recruiting from the rising generation. Only recently he stipulated that in future no more than a fixed percentage of my SS leaders' children were to succeed them as leaders. The remainder are to be brought in from other professions, particularly from among farmers, where possible from the East. The healthy interplay of forces must be preserved—men must come from the country to the highest positions in the Party and in the Government, then there must be a return to the country to recruit strength and maintain the healthy balance of family life. The Führer has clearly recognized the great significance of this rule and gave me proper instructions on the subject long ago."

"I had understood," I replied, "that the SS leaders were to receive country estates as part of the system by which the Party leaders were to be tied to the soil."

"That's true," Himmler answered, "but that belongs to quite a different problem. The reason for endowing Party and Government leaders is to assure them a certain independence of mind and take away the feeling that they must keep their post at all costs, otherwise their families would be in difficulties, their sons' studies interrupted and the upbringing of their daughters jeopardized. Put yourself in the position of such a man. He can't help becoming a civil servant, clinging to his post and the pension which goes with it. That must be avoided at all costs. Against that, if he has a farm to which he can retire and lead an independent existence, then we acquire leaders much stronger in character, who can say 'No' and even throw up their posts without worrying unduly."

So ended our talks on the Chosen Women, which had filled me with a mixture of distaste, doubt and amazement. I had long to ponder on this curious blend of cold political rationalism, Germanic romanticism and racial fanaticism—and on Himmler's firm resolve to transform this effort of the imagination into reality. For there was no doubt of the sheer will-power which proposed to shape and develop the scheme. Himmler would have been best pleased if he could start at once on this task which lay so close to his heart; he only bewailed that the war was not yet over and that his plan was thus delayed.

VIII

FOREIGN POLICY WITHOUT DIPLOMATS

Friedenau, Berlin
24th–25th January, 1941

WHEN I went to Himmler yesterday morning, he was sitting over a heap of reports which he had been working through with a green pencil. He picked out one of them and said: "Read this, Herr Kersten —the marked passages are enough. They are reports from our diplomatic gentry on the military strength of France and Belgium, written before the campaign in France. Most illuminating—according to them, we would be permanently held up and bled to death in front of the Maginot Line. Meanwhile a powerful Franco-Belgian and English army would encircle our flanks and achieve our certain downfall. The reports are very well written in a fine style—quite classics of their kind —based on unimpeachable sources."

Himmler handed over the papers. I read the report of a German diplomat on the comparative strengths of Germany and the Western powers and on the dangers threatening any German attack on France. Apparently the man knew his subject; he had been many years in the foreign service abroad, lost his post as a result of the war, and, out of a deep concern for the welfare of his country, had pointed out the perils which would beset it, militarily and politically, in any break with the West. From the military point of view the report had been refuted by the German victory in the West.

Himmler informed me that the Führer had had some of these reports produced again and been much amused by them; he had read out the significant parts and handed them over for further study. They fitted perfectly into the general picture which the Führer had formed of diplomacy. They showed up not only the incompetence but the menace of diplomats in such a way that the Führer had decided to reorganize the diplomatic system entirely with the ultimate intention of abolishing it altogether.

"But how are you going to manage relations between two countries," I enquired, "if there are going to be no diplomats in future?"

Himmler said: "It's very simple; you only need an efficient consul, who will control commercial affairs, passports and visas; that will be his total field of activity. He will be absolutely forbidden to concern himself with what has hitherto been the realm of diplomacy. If nations have matters to adjust with one another, in the sphere of foreign relations, then they will send a special mission provided with the most detailed instructions. In future anyhow there will no longer be career diplomats, who believe that it's for them alone to give an opinion on all matters which affect other countries and who treat everybody else who dares to express an opinion as a complete fool. It wasn't so in earlier times; then nations sent missions to each other. The missions drew up treaties and then went home again.

"That is a far healthier way of doing things than setting up permanent diplomatic missions, which I resent all the more because they are the licensed agents of the enemy intelligence. They take your breath away; you can't tolerate them, once you have really understood them. I agree with the Russians, who make short work of these gentlemen and so restrict the field of their activities that they can hardly stir. With us too it's only the other side which profits from this licensed spying, because our own diplomats are so foolish that they are children at the game."

I countered by saying that I had got to know, both in Germany and abroad, very many highly able diplomats, who knew their subject thoroughly and had rendered great services to their country. Everyone made mistakes at times, but you could not condemn the profession as a whole simply because here and there a diplomat made a mistake. Göring's anti-aircraft guns were not judged by the planes they missed.

"No, Herr Kersten," said Himmler, "that's not the way to look at it. You must view it quite differently. The diplomat is first of all a civil servant with all the weaknesses of a civil servant. We have already discussed that subject. As a civil servant he is chiefly concerned with his career, his ambition for promotion and honours. The attaché wants to become secretary, then first counsellor of an embassy; later he dreams of being an envoy, then a full ambassador on an equal footing with a minister. But that can only be brought about by making himself agreeable to his superiors. While the ordinary civil servant tries to earn success by really hard work, these gentlemen give proof of their abilities by the reports they write on the country to which they are accredited. If these reports are to be useful to the writer's career, they must correspond with the views of his superiors.

"I have myself some people working with me who simply can't bear it if I heard nothing of them for a few days; their whole object is to put some exciting event before me at least every other day, or to cable me for a decision on some matter or other. I began by taking it all seriously, but gradually I realized that they were always the same people, who simply wanted to make themselves important. When they get up in the morning they're already thinking of what special information they can send their boss. They seize on every item of news for that purpose—they make it seem reliable, whether it is or not. Do you think it's any different with these gentry of the foreign service? They live on news and trade on it just like professional news agencies. A character who is absolutely selfless and excels in summing up a situation can respect himself and his employers and rise above human weaknesses. But where will you find such a man? I even catch myself at it, when I'm making a report for the Führer, underlining more heavily than I need things which I know he will be glad to hear, taking into account his cast of mind, which is perfectly known to me. Yet such things should never be done, for they destroy the objective value of any report.

"I've noticed the same methods in the reports which are put before Göring or Goebbels. They're suited to the bosses' cast of mind, but the bosses never know how rotten they are, nor how dangerous are their results."

29th January, 1941

"You were saying the other day, Herr Himmler, that diplomats were civil servants and took their colour from their superiors. Then it must be quite easy to change them round at any time as the need arises."

"You're confusing two separate human traits," Himmler corrected me. "There is the impulse to rise and make a career, and also the impulse to defend what you've won, even though by so doing you bring harm to yourself. Wounded vanity has its place here. A man wants what he has said and advised to be considered true and irrefutable. I have yet to meet a diplomat who won't use his special knowledge to show that any policy adopted against his advice must be wrong, and that the real situation is quite different from what the Government thinks. The ambassador has a way of feeling that he is a great man in his own right and that everyone, even his own Government, has to bow before his knowledge and experience.

"In Germany it's particularly bad because so few Germans get abroad—the Führer and most of the leading men have never travelled —and on the basis of their so-called foreign experience the diplomats think that they can treat the rest of us with the superiority of specialists; it's a thing you always come across when the so-called specialist talks with a layman on his subject. Anyhow their position has been shaken as never before owing to their being so utterly wrong about the consequences of marching into the demilitarized zones in Austria, the Sudetenland and Czechoslovakia and about the war in Poland and France. Yet in spite of this the same people who have been proved so flagrantly wrong, and had their lack of judgment so clearly exposed, still have the impertinence to send memoranda to the Führer and lay down what our foreign policy should be.

"In no other walk of life would you find anything comparable. A defeated general is quite content to keep quiet; but the strategists in foreign affairs, the defeated ambassadors, still go on talking. Instead of keeping their false assumptions to themselves and thinking them over, they go further and assure us that the next step will certainly lead to catastrophe, as they have long prophesied; and secretly they hope for disaster, so that they will be proved right in the end. In Russia they make short work of such people: they accuse them of sabotage and have them liquidated. Life is more dangerous for these gentry over there." After a short pause, Himmler added: "I am thoroughly convinced that the Führer's plan to do away with career diplomats is the correct one; I've really come to the conclusion that he's right.

"We would have got further in this matter if Ribbentrop had not persistently intervened and influenced the Führer to postpone the whole matter until after the war, privately thinking that he would have reorganized his own department in the meantime. The old school of diplomacy is quite repugnant to him because they don't take him seriously—a fact of which he is well aware and which he repays with outbursts of hatred—yet he has a terrible fear that the ground will be cut from under his feet. It's simply for this reason that he tries to keep the old system going—in particular the diplomatic intelligence—and attempts to infuse fresh blood into it. Since basically he does not understand a thing about diplomacy, he has to let the old school have its way, with the result that everything goes wrong. On the other hand *we* have both the personnel and the experience in intelligence matters; what couldn't we do, if only Ribbentrop had a little more sense! As it is I have to limit my activities and only intervene at decisive moments with my reports. Valuable material is wasted because I can't let it come to an open conflict with Ribbentrop, or else I have to bring it to the Führer's notice by other means. But just give me a chance; my hour will come yet!"

Himmler realized that he had exposed his cards too openly and broke off with the words: "But on the real point, the battle against the old school of diplomacy, I'm completely at one with Ribbentrop."

IX

HESS

I'VE been here for more than a week with Rudolf Hess in the Hotel Dresen. Hess is very busy and excited about recent events—the French armistice—and suffering in consequence from severe stomach pains. Meanwhile he was in the Forest of Compiègne and came back yesterday.

During the treatment, still charged with tension, he sketched to me the course of recent events, and spoke of the future, which he envisaged as an era of fruitful Franco-German co-operation.

"You forget England," I told him. "Her whole history, the laws of her political life, her very nature will never suffer her to leave things as you imagine. She will be going against her own existence if she does not take appropriate counter-measures. You're also forgotting the toughness of England. The English haven't such a Utopian cast of mind as the Germans."

Hess replied: "We'll make peace with England in the same way as with France. Only a few weeks back the Führer again spoke of the great value of the British Empire in the world order. Germany and France must stand together with England against the enemy of Europe, Bolshevism. That was the reason why the Führer allowed the English Army to escape at Dunkirk. He did not want to upset the possibility of an understanding. The English must see that and seize their chance. I can't imagine that cool, calculating England will run her neck into the Soviet noose, instead of saving it by coming to an understanding with us."

15th May, 1941

Yesterday I was arrested for five hours and was personally interrogated by Heydrich. He asked me in the form of a direct question

88

whether I had encouraged Hess in his friendly feelings towards England. I replied that I had not spoken with him on political, only on medical, matters. Heydrich laughed and said: "I don't believe a word you say, for I know that you're not on our side. But the day is coming when you will tell us the truth for once."

After an interrogation lasting five hours, Heydrich had to let me go. I've just heard that all doctors who had treated Hess in recent years have been arrested. I also learnt from a trustworthy source that during Heydrich's interrogation Himmler rang up and ordered my immediate release. That must be right, for towards the end of it Heydrich was called from the room and I was left alone for ten minutes. Then he returned and said that the Reichsführer had guaranteed me but that I should hold myself at their disposal.

It was a year ago that Himmler asked me to examine Hess; since then I have treated him too. I established that he was suffering from trouble in the gall-bladder and stomach pains. In Hess I encountered a man who was quiet, friendly and grateful. He frequently spoke of his home in Egypt, for which he longed. He often said too that he would be happiest if he could retire to the loneliness of the Bavarian mountains. But he emphasized even more that he had only one wish: to meet a hero's death while flying. But the Führer had forbidden him to fly, so that he was condemned to sit at his desk.

Hess was a good and helpful person, very modest in his way of life. He was a vegetarian, surrounded himself with clairvoyants and astrologers and despised official medical views. He was constantly saying that he could not go on with this existence. He was firmly resolved to stake his life on a great deed in the service of Germany. Once, when headquarters were in Belgium and Hess had to go to an interview with Hitler, he asked me to accompany him. We drove through towns and villages which had been shelled during the recent heavy fighting. Later Hess said to me with tears in his eyes that it was horrible to see these once flourishing areas so laid waste. The war should not last any longer. The world must come to see that Germany was unconquerable. And he, Hess, had to stretch out his hand, to bring about a reconciliation between Germany and the other nations.

Another time he told me that he had to concentrate all his powers and harden himself—he needed all his strength for the deed which would secure the salvation of Germany. When I asked what he meant by this 'salvation', Hess replied that he could not tell me, but he was preparing for an act of historic importance.

X

ENCOUNTERS WITH HEYDRICH

1. HEYDRICH THE MAN

Gut Hartzwalde
10th February, 1941

ONE of the most interesting men in Himmler's circle is the Head of
the Security Police, the SS Obergruppenführer Reinhard Heydrich. I
often had occasion to observe him at first hand. He had the right of
admission to Himmler at any time and sometimes put in an appearance
in the middle of a treatment, to give him some urgent papers. He is a
very striking person, tall, slim, blond, an extremely Nordic type, a
brilliant speaker in the concise military style. In contrast to Himmler,
who is often rather stiff, he expresses himself incisively and with
polish.

I have often been able to listen to the arguments with which
Heydrich supported various proposals of his own. They were at times
masterpieces of exposition: a short sketch of the person or subject,
then his arguments, effectively built up to the decisive trump card
which he played last of all, then his conclusion, which Himmler could
hardly resist. Sometimes I had the impression that after one of these
expositions Himmler was quite overwhelmed. For he often went to the
telephone a little later and had Heydrich told that the measures they
had discussed could not be put into effect at once—he would have to
talk the matter over with the Führer first. Then later he would send
him his countermand in the form of what purported to be an order
from the Führer.

On the other hand Heydrich behaves towards Himmler, who
always treats him with the most open friendliness, with quite inexplicable servility. He addresses Himmler as 'Herr Reichsführer'—a
thing absolutely forbidden throughout the whole SS—instead of simply

'Reichsführer'. Heydrich's side of the conversation between them goes like this: "Certainly, Herr Reichsführer, if that is the Herr Reichsführer's wish I will have the necessary arrangements made at once and report back to the Herr Reichsführer. Yes, certainly; yes, yes, indeed!" Doubtless as a political personality Heydrich is far more dynamic than Himmler. He knows that and shows his superiority in mustering his arguments; Himmler just isn't in the same class. On the other hand Heydrich draws back at once the moment Himmler manifests any opposition or puts forward a different point of view. Himmler seems to possess some sort of secret power over Heydrich, before which Heydrich submits unconditionally.

Himmler's people haven't a great opinion of Heydrich. In such a narrow circle, where Heydrich's and Himmler's adjutants are constantly meeting and the staffs have known each other for years, everybody learns everything about the bosses' characters. Nothing escapes them, so that all are in a position to form a reasonably true picture of the bosses.

In general the adjutants play a very curious part in the National Socialist state. If they were to get together they could almost rule the Third Reich. Outwardly Heydrich is on friendly terms with the head of Himmler's personal staff, Gruppenführer Wolff; but from Brandt I learnt how intense is the antagonism between them. Heydrich sees in Wolff his rival as the Reichsführer's eventual successor. As he can't get rid of him, he tries to be friendly.

Yesterday Brandt was again talking of Heydrich's great political gifts, thus expressing his master's opinion, but he added a very harsh judgment on Heydrich the man to which I attached great weight, as it had been formed in a varied experience over the years. Heydrich, it seems, has no friends of his own; his friendships all have a political motive and he gives them up once they have served their purpose. Friends from his naval days turn their backs on him.

Himmler's staff is not ill-disposed towards women; Himmler himself regards them with respect. He is even markedly chivalrous. If he can help a woman in trouble, he will. It may be that the decisive influence in this is that he has really modelled himself on his Germanic ancestors—how often have I heard the phrase on his lips: 'To the Germanic peoples women were sacred, and sacred was the hearth.' But the fact remains. Never have I heard an obscene word on his lips, nor would anyone dare to use any such expression in his company. Heydrich however is outspokenly cynical and brutal in his attitude towards women; they feel this and avoid him. Thus it comes about that this very fine-looking man hasn't much success with though you'd think they would flock to him. If he has occasion to go out in civilian clothes with his adjutants, it's they who make the running, which often leads to great complications—and Heydrich reacts strongly against the poor wretch who has bested him and walked off with the woman. Heydrich can never come second. Wherever he is invited the question of rank is always a problem; he can never be a good loser.

His fencing master is always in terror when he has to act as referee. He has of course been taken into the ranks of the SS, so that he is under Heydrich's orders. He has nothing to laugh about if Heydrich loses. This is regarded as disloyalty at the very least, if not a crime against the service. Heydrich much enjoys shooting, less from any love of the open air or the excitement of the chase than because he *must* make a kill. If he doesn't succeed, the day is wasted for him. If he doesn't get a shot in, he takes it as personal malice on the part of the keeper—who can do nothing about this.

Heydrich used to practise daily with a pistol; he wanted to be the best shot in the SS. He gave up simply because he can't bear failure. He admitted himself that he was constantly at his desk, while the others competed outside. Again, he wanted to face issues of life and death, so that he could look death in the eye and give proof of his courage. He succeeded in being nominated an officer in the Luftwaffe by Göring and after sixty operational flights in a fighter he received the Iron Cross, first class. Then his military ambition was at last appeased.

Brandt laughingly told me that what Heydrich would like best would be to send his whole staff into the field and have them killed so that he could report to the Führer: "The entire staff of the Security Police has fallen on the field of honour"—and be able to say, as against the Wehrmacht: "The Wehrmacht should just try to emulate us."

It was Heydrich who encouraged Himmler in the idea of letting the Waffen SS take part in an exercise using live cartridges against each other; a couple of dead or wounded were of no consequence. Himmler had occasion to mention this to Göring, who replied with a deadly serious face: "My dear Himmler, I already do that with my Luftwaffe. The 'Courage Test' is a part of their training." Very interested, Himmler asked him what it comprised. Göring replied: "It's quite simple, just a little parachute jumping test. Twice with the parachute, the third time without." Since then there has been no more talk of a Courage Test for the SS.

Himmler's people are really afraid of Heydrich. Brandt told me that they never knew what means he would employ, what traps he would lay. Recently he has aroused much mistrust because he has found

a way to Hitler. This is how it happened. In Himmler's absence
Heydrich made an urgent report to Hitler with exact details of an
attempt on his life. He produced evidence which overcame Hitler's
distrust: at a conference a man with a rifle equipped with telescopic
sights was going to shoot him from a building across the street. This
and Heydrich's summary of the affair must have made a great impression on Hitler. Heydrich was summoned to him at times when
Himmler was not there. One day he might have got the better of
Himmler. But there was no satisfaction in this for Heydrich, since
Himmler always knew of it and was able to take the necessary counter-
measures.

2. HEYDRICH'S OFFER

Gut Hartzwalde
25th February, 1941

A few days ago Brandt told me that Heydrich had a very poor
opinion of me; he had told his people that he suspected me of being
an enemy agent, or at least an active sympathizer with foreign powers,
and that I was using my position with Himmler to prejudice the Party;
one day he would produce his evidence. The cause of his hostility was
the fact that there should be anyone close to Himmler who was not
under his control, whose influence he could not watch. I had to
reckon with Heydrich's making a move some time or other.

I was not surprised, therefore, when after I had treated Himmler
today Heydrich expressed a desire to talk with me. I replied that I was
ready at any time, today if he liked. Heydrich agreed and we made an
appointment for the evening in his official quarters. As the conversation
began, he pressed a button—a casual visitor would not have noticed it
—and his microphone became live. Brandt had already put me on my
guard about this. Quietly I said to him: "My dear Herr Heydrich, if
you want us to talk undisturbed, I would rather invite you to
Hartzwalde."

"Why? We can chat just as well here," was his answer.

"But it's *I* who would press the button there," I answered, laughing.

Heydrich did not take it in bad part; he turned the thing off and
said with a smirk to emphasize the allusion: "You seem to be very well
acquainted with listening devices and well versed in political matters."

"Anyone who has business in this building," I said, "must be
prepared—and incidentally I've no political knowledge whatever."

"So much the worse," Heydrich retorted, "apart from the fact that I don't believe it. But you are treating the Reichsführer, and it happens with great men, when a doctor relieves them from pain, that they regard him as their deliverer and are ready to lend an ear to his insinuations. So it would be better if you were really well informed and in a position to decide on the opinions which you pass on to him."

I took that as a very unfriendly remark and reacted accordingly. Yet I was better pleased when he was frank than when he was as slippery as an eel; and I was very curious to see how he would go on.

At first Heydrich felt his way with some care. I would certainly be interested, he thought, to have a look at source material on the spirit and achievements of the SS. I turned at once and replied that I had read all that had been written on the subject, heard much about it from Himmler, and had already formed my own picture of it.

"Then we are already a little further than I had supposed," Heydrich replied, without noticing that he had lost the first round, "but you will surely be interested to read reports on the situation in Holland and Finland and see how we assess things there."

Now I knew that he was aware of the information I got from my Dutch and Finnish friends; and that he imagined that certain alterations made by Himmler to his plans were to be traced back to my intervention. I at once took up his offer and told him that the reports would indeed be of interest to me; Holland and Finland were the two countries which were specially close to me and I had a share in their fate.

For a moment Heydrich reflected whether he should take the next step, then he let the cat out of the bag: "Do you know, Herr Kersten, we could really be very helpful to you. When people come to you and ask you to intervene with the Reichsführer, then it must be your task to form a really objective picture of the condition and character of the person in question, before you go to the Reichsführer. It's always painful to have to change your attitude afterwards. Until now you must have had a lot of trouble in getting the necessary facts; we'll gladly do that for you. What you decide, and whether you regard the information as correct or not, is your affair. In return I only ask you, when you do make use of this material, to tell the Reichsführer that *I* have supported you, so that he has the feeling that I am loyally cooperating with a man he values so highly."

That sounded very well and was very illuminating. I at once realized that Heydrich had only suggested this in order to learn the names of those who applied to me for help, so that he could take the necessary counter-measures, prepare Himmler beforehand, and thus prevent me from being of any use. I replied that I was extremely grateful. An open refusal would have made an open enemy of Heydrich. Then I would have lost any chance of helping my *protégés;* furthermore I could only suppose that—as it was known that all measures were being intensified—appeals for my help would also increase. I was firmly resolved to allow Heydrich no glimpse of such matters, but I hoped that my answer—that I was extremely grateful— would be answer enough for a man who was used to immediate compliance. He seemed to take my remark as being to the point, showed pleasure, and offered me any other help of which I might stand in need. Then he asked me to supper.

At the meal he was very open, told me of his shooting experiences and the number of his trophies, showed himself an accomplished talker and host. In the middle of the conversation Heydrich asked me with an innocent expression whether it would amuse me to pay a visit to his newly established 'House of Gallantry' in Giesebrechtstrasse. It had been opened in agreement with Ribbentrop specially to offer something to foreigners in Berlin. For the moment, it was true, it had still to be subsidized, but he hoped that it would soon be self-supporting. I laughed out loud. He smirked and told me that since the house had been opened Ciano was a more frequent visitor to Berlin; it also had a certain attraction for prominent Germans. It had been necessary to establish this house, as otherwise foreigners in Berlin fell into the hands of the worst type of prostitute.

"How attentive you are," I said, laughing, "to care so much for the health of your guests."

For the rest I had already been told how interested Heydrich was in this house simply from its value as an intelligence service and also on personal grounds; and that he had already had successes with its 'ladies'. Beyond that it gave him particular pleasure to have records made of the intimate talks of these important gentlemen, and on suitable occasions, when they crossed his own plans, to make use of such material. He was without scruple in these matters.

"I have been advised to open a similar house for homosexuals. What do you think about it, Doctor?" Heydrich suddenly asked towards the end of our conversation, clearly in the hope that I would supply medical arguments for it.

"What attentiveness!" I answered with irony. "That would be the finest monument to your warm heart."

He grasped the point at once. "And so you know nothing about diplomacy and politics? You're more than the simple medical man you pretend to be." His whole face beamed; it seemed to amuse him to find someone using his own weapons.

I began to make ready to leave. "Well, Herr Kersten," he returned with a sarcastic smile to this subject we had discussed, "if you would like to take a look at the Giesebrechtstrasse—of course simply from a medical point of view—it's at your disposal at any time. You need only call on me. Then perhaps I will take you myself. You could come in your white coat too; that would be fine. I'll put one on as well and act as your assistant."

"Splendid, Herr Heydrich, that's your best idea yet, to become a masseur in the Giesebrechtstrasse."

That was almost too much. I felt that he was beginning to lose his benevolence, so I took my departure, thanking him for a pleasant evening. He took me to the door himself, the sentry saluted and he gave a superior nod. I drove home, still amused as I sat in the car.

3. *HEYDRICH A NON-ARYAN*

Gut Hartzwalde
20th August, 1942

Today I treated Himmler, who was suffering from exceptional pain. When he was at last relieved he lay back and relaxed and what I had so often experienced happened once more. His thoughts, dammed up, poured out like a waterfall and he relieved himself by confiding them to me. Talk turned to Heydrich's death. Hitler had been deeply disturbed by it. Heydrich's death meant 'more to him than a lost battle'. Heydrich was one of the few men who knew the right way to treat a foreign nation. If he had trampled on the Czechs with hob-nailed boots, the English Secret Service would have kept a careful watch to make sure that nothing happened to him. But because he had made a statesmanlike and intelligent approach to win over the Czechs, he had become a dangerous enemy for the English and their plans, and had to be removed. Shortly before he was murdered he had called together his officials and junior SS Leaders and given them orders to go gently in Bohemia and Moravia; in the long view that was more successful than severity, as the Protectorate was a civilized country. A really tragic fate. It would be very difficult to find a substitute for this highly gifted man. Hitler had had other great tasks in view for him. He, Himmler, would have great difficulty in nominating a successor to control the police.

"There's a rumour that Heydrich was not entirely Aryan. That can hardly be true, can it?" I asked.

"Yes, it's true enough."

"Did you know that before, or have you only learnt it since his death? Does Herr Hitler know it?" I replied, astounded.

"I already knew it when I was still head of the Bavarian political police. I discussed the matter with the Führer at the time; he had Heydrich brought before him, talked to him for a long time and received a very favourable impression. Later the Führer informed me that Heydrich was a highly gifted but also very dangerous man, whose gifts the movement had to retain. Such people could still be used so long as they were kept well in hand and for that purpose his non-Aryan origins were extremely useful; for he would be eternally grateful to us that we had kept him and not expelled him and would obey blindly. That was in fact the case."

While Himmler talked, I remembered the servile way in which Heydrich had always approached him and my eyes were opened.

Himmler went on: "The Führer could confidently impose anything on Heydrich—even action against the Jews—which no one else would care to do and rest assured that it would be carried out perfectly."

I could not keep myself from saying: "Then you have made use of one of their own people, whom you had under your thumb, to exterminate the Jews. That's a really devilish trick!"

"What do you mean?" Himmler replied. "Just you read Machiavelli and his teaching on *raison d'état*; you'll find something very different there. Do you think that times have changed? Methods have only become more refined. Machiavelli wouldn't have behaved a jot differently if it was a question of saving the state and employing force which he could keep permanently under control."

I was silent at that. Himmler ended the conversation by asking me specifically to keep quiet about what he had just told me.

4. HIMMLER ON HEYDRICH

Gut Hartzwalde
25th August, 1942

Today I brought the talk round to Heydrich again and told Himmler the opinions about him that I used to hear in the rank of the SS. Himmler agreed that there was much truth in them. Heydrich had at bottom been an unhappy man, completely divided against himself, as often happened with those of mixed race. Such people suffered from persistent inferiority complexes and tried to react in one way or another. Then such phenomena appeared as had become increasingly noticeable in Heydrich.

"You know, my dear Herr Kersten, Heydrich constantly suffered from the fact that he was not racially pure. He wanted to prove that the Germanic elements in his blood were dominant, by distinguishing himself, particularly in the field of sport, in which Jews do not play any part. He had a childish pleasure in winning the Silver Sport Badge and the Riding Badge, in being the victor in fencing bouts, in shooting well or in bringing home fine hunting trophies, or in getting the Iron Cross First Class. But in all that he was only pursuing a purpose, he found no real pleasure in it, even though he pretended to himself that he did so.

"I've been able to watch him closely over the years and I know what I'm talking about. How sorry I was for him, when he proposed men for the SS drawing particular attention to their excellent racial origins. I knew then what was going on inside him. He never really found peace; something was always upsetting him. Often I've talked to him and tried to help him, even against my own convictions, pointing out the possibility of overcoming Jewish elements by the admixture of better Germanic blood, citing himself as a case in point. How pleased he was when this attitude to those who were a quarter Jewish found expression in the racial laws; though this sprang only from political reasons, in order finally to regulate the Jewish question. For the time being, it is true, he was very grateful to me for such help and seemed as if liberated, but nothing was any use in the long run."

Himmler stopped talking, carefully lighted a cigar and, gazing at the blue rings of smoke, went on as if talking to himself: "In one respect he was irreplaceable. He possessed an infallible nose for men. That again was based on his own inner conflict. Because he was himself divided, he was sure to sense such divisions in others. He saw the ways which friend or foe would take with a clarity which was absolutely amazing. His colleagues hardly dared to lie to him; he could always tell. He could read their motives like an open book. He was certainly not an easy boss to have; they were right to fear him. He imparted his own restlessness to them and drove them as he himself was ceaselessly driven. Altogether he was the embodiment of distrust —the 'hypersuspicious', as people called him—nobody could endure it for long.

"If, disdainfully curling his lip, he declared, 'Herr Reichsführer, the man is a scoundrel,' then there was something in it and in a relatively short time he had triumphantly produced the proofs. On many of the reports brought before me which I handed over to him for his opinion there would appear the inscription—'Don't believe it—simply a rumour—a wild invention.' When I asked him whether he had investigated the report in question, he told me not yet, that this was simply his feeling. He was usually right. He never forgot names once they had cropped up; his gift for correlation surpassed everything, he was a living card-index, a brain which held all the threads and wove them all together. Taken all in all, he was a born intelligence officer and the ideal head of the Security Police."

Himmler went on: "He was extremely useful in another way, in the struggle against the Jews. He had overcome the Jew in himself by purely intellectual means and had swung over to the other side. He was convinced that the Jewish elements in his blood were damnable; he hated the blood which had played him so false. The Führer could really have picked no better man than Heydrich for the campaign against the Jews. For them he was without mercy or pity.

"Yet he also had positive traits. He despised every flatterer and regarded those who denounced others as morally defective, even when he himself made use of them. Anyone who attempted to organize intrigue inside the SS aroused his hatred. He demanded the strictest scientific impartiality for SS enquiries in all the fields under his supervision. Then of course he made Machiavellian use of the information he got for his own purposes. And when he tackled a task, he spared neither himself nor others.

"For the rest it will interest you to know that Heydrich was a very good violinist. He once played a serenade in my honour; it was really excellent—a pity that he did not do more in this field."

"Is it true," I put in, "that he was in fact no hero?"

"I have never been quite clear about that. Yet when mortally wounded he grasped his pistol and shot at his assassin. In the matter of courage too he had the same infallible nose for the weak side of a character, and he had no hesitation in putting to the test any of his colleagues who did not seem to him free from cowardice."

XI

HIMMLER'S HATRED OF LAWYERS

TODAY at lunch Himmler told me with great amusement that Hitler had again been making fun of lawyers and had poured scorn on their being rebaptized 'Defenders of Justice' by Reichsleiter Hans Frank, leader of the National Socialist League for Defence of the Law. Was Frank really so foolish as to imagine that he could do away with lawyers by renaming them? But there was one good thing about it, for now he—Hitler—could go on about lawyers even in Frank's presence without those gentlemen, the Defenders of Justice, feeling in any way offended.

Himmler took this opportunity to put before me his own conception of lawyers. It was solicitors who affected him most. For them he nourished a really fanatical hatred. He described them as 'the thieves of the legal profession, cheats and exploiters', going in the outward guise of honest men, calling themselves the friends and helpers of the oppressed, but really setting their whole mind and conduct on getting the victim into their net so that they could fleece him properly.

This is how Himmler described their activities: "In his need a poor man comes to a solicitor, either because he has got into trouble with the law or because he needs help against an oppressor. The first thing that happens is that he must pay an advance—these friends and helpers of the oppressed naturally can't do anything without an advance. In order to gull him, his case is presented to him as extremely difficult and complicated, so that he's at his wits' end from fear, swallows the bitter pill and pays up. The next thing is to draw out proceedings in order to collect the largest possible profits. The official fixing of fees helps here, prescribing the rates which the solicitor may charge, so that appearances are completely preserved. Whatever happens the advance must be spent. When that's done a new one is demanded; it's extortion without end.

"However, I've closed one door on their doings in the war. None of these Lord's Day bandits will be exempt from service; I've given strict orders to take in all those who are at all fit for service. I've made the same arrangement for tax-consultants, who do nothing but make the state lose the taxes due to it, working out day and night how this can best be done and getting fat fees for it. That is another anti-social profession which will disappear once we have won the war. Can you understand how a state can recognize a calling whose sole aim is to do that same state out of its well-earned money? Imagine a man sitting in a private firm, doing nothing but advise its debtors how best they can escape paying. What would happen to him? He would be flung out of the window, and that's what we're going to do with these tax-consultants. I'm taking care to do my bit towards it now by seeing that all tax-consultants shall be called up regardless; that's already a step nearer the final goal."

"But, Herr Himmler," I responded, "you can't simply get rid of all lawyers. You at least need some to become judges in a civilized modern state."

"You're very wide of the mark, my dear man," was his answer. "These legal gentry have already made it beautifully clear to us that we couldn't live without them and that everything would go topsy-turvy. We will produce evidence to the contrary. We only need to alter the laws. After the war they will be entirely remade and become clear, straightforward and generally comprehensible to everybody, so that the legal arts of exposition will no longer be needed to find out what the law means. For don't you realize that the laws have only been turned into a sort of arcane wisdom—incomprehensible and stuffed with clauses—so that the lawyer can make a living and the training of ever new generations of lawyers appear justified?

"Just take the trouble to consult one of these famous commentaries—as they call them—to their law-books. You will shudder to find pages of explanations in the commentary over a single phrase used by the lawgiver; and there are considerations set down about what he meant or might have meant by it, what he certainly did not or perhaps might not have intended. Lawyers are a lodge just like the Masons; the same men who make the laws give expositions of them and gaze with immense arrogance at any man so intellectually limited in their eyes as to dare to offer his opinion on any of these so-called 'legal questions'. These questions are the private preserve of this caste and of its priests! Woe to him who pokes his nose into it all!"

Himmler had talked himself into such a passion that, entirely against his habit, he poured himself out a second glass of red wine and hastily drank it down.

"Even if you get rid of the lawyers," I answered, "and institute the finest and most easily understood law-books in the world, you have still not abolished the quarrels, whose causes have to be argued out and decided. Who is going to do that, if there are no longer any lawyers?"

Himmler replied: "Do you really think that the Führer has not considered that? Once we have new laws, then we can take the best and most honest men from other callings and professions. Where the law has left the question still open, they will pronounce just judgments based on the Germanic feeling for law. You know how much I have concerned myself with Germanic law, the laws of the West and the East Goths, the laws of the Saxons, the Suabians and other Germanic tribes. Where it is at all possible, I will promote the publication of the texts of their law-books. What sublime legal terms you find there, what wonderfully clear language, which anyone can understand, bound up with a profound knowledge of the basic laws of life, the preservation of the breed and the Germanic race!

"Just read one of these law-books and then one of the famous legal works of today and you'll see what I mean." Himmler had one of these texts fetched and read me outstanding passages which he had marked. I saw that he had worked through the text and underlined the points which seemed most essential to him. He got more and more enthusiastic, as I had always noticed with him when it was a matter of things which had to do with the Germanic idea. Nor did he limit himself to the Germanic idea alone, as it found expression in German lands, but even thought, as he expressed it, in a 'Greater Germanic' manner. Wherever Germanic customs, habits and codes of law had found expression, whether in Italy, France, Sweden, Norway, England or Spain, they always had in Himmler a profound admirer.

However superficial in judgment of a particular institution, Himmler seemed here to dispose of an astounding knowledge which he tried to deepen whenever he could, getting hold of the best experts and talking with them for hours on end. Then the most important matters had to wait, to the despair of his adjutants; the number of visitors with appointments went on piling up. But Himmler quietly continued to talk, like a scholar far from the cares of the world, about runes, Germanic customs and habits, putting forward what lesson could be learnt from them for the present day, what knowledge he had already drawn from them for the SS, and how these thoughts could be made to live again in the nation. His only worry is that this can't be done at once, but is stopped by the war, which at bottom he hates as it also prevents his dearest wish, the internal construction of a Germanic state.

With a sigh he turned to the adjutant who, having waited impatiently, at last came in: "My God, Herr Kersten, it's already an hour over the time; we are always being disturbed, but I must go. Today of all days the representative of the Minister of Justice is waiting for me upstairs. If only he had heard our talk about lawyers! But come to supper this evening, and I will show you some exceptionally fine things which I have at home."

17th July, 1941

Yesterday evening I went to supper with Himmler as arranged. He at once received me with the words: "Now, have you thought over what I said to you yesterday morning about these legal gentry? I know what your objections will be, that in a modern state it's no longer possible to give a new lease of life to Germanic ideas on law. But look at Switzerland where the 'Thing' still meets; just get someone to tell you how the English have managed to protect themselves against Roman law; then you will see that neither the modern state nor its economy need stand in our way. If there is only the will, some courageous steps in this direction can be taken.

"Think of it, Herr Kersten: Roman law and the lawyers it brought with it who suppressed the old Germanic people's law are like a mortal cancer menacing the German people and the Germanic race as a whole. If we want to build a new Germanic Reich, our task is to cut this cancer out of the body politic. We'll not suffer any outcry from the lawyers, and it will be a matter of indifference to us whether other states—swayed by their legal caste—describe us as having no culture. Before another century has passed there will be a new Germanic people's law, in which the general Germanic feeling for law, based on the ideas of our forefathers, will triumph anew. Then the ages dominated by Roman law and the lawyers formed by it will be seen as an evil dream, a monstrous mistake; and all will admire the clarity and the inexorable nature of the measures taken by the Führer."

Himmler seized one of the books lying beside him in which he had himself made notes and after a few pages read me the following phrases:

" 'I, the judge, enquire about the law; I ask the free men, who tell me, the judge, what the law is.'

"See, Herr Kersten, that's how our forefathers thought. They asked the free men about the law and the free men told them. Where then were our learned legal gentry? We did wonders without them; the Germanic race flourished and prospered."

He glanced at me in triumph and went on: "We must once again make it clear to Germanic man where his real strength and greatness lie; we must appeal to the presiding genius of the race and we must methodically eliminate every superfluous element. There will be a response. I see it daily in my SS. External circumstances must be suitable and men must be led away from the narrow limits of great cities to surroundings in keeping with their nature; and they will develop a new life in body, mind and spirit. The Roman lawyer is closely bound up with the town where everything is atomized. The countryside has offered the longest and most obstinate resistance to the compulsion of Roman law, and tried to defend its old common law and habits. Just read your history! We must renew links with the past."

"But you yourself make use of lawyers in your organizations! You have a supreme judge in the SS and another in the Party and everywhere I look I'm coming up against lawyers," I retorted.

"Supreme judges—whether in the Party or the SS—are no lawyers and never will be. And SS and Party justice must be quite differently constituted," Himmler answered. "Here there is already a tendency towards a new justice, which rests on the Germanic feeling for law and has freed itself from Roman legal notions. Just read the chief paragraphs of the code I've instituted for the SS. In the past we needed lawyers on our staff to protect us against bureaucratic measures, whose strength—which seemed invulnerable—rested on a network of paragraphs. We fought lawyers with lawyers. This was a matter of necessity.

"We try to train our lawyers by putting them in the SS and infusing them with our own spirit. But I must say it's a hard task and one which is constantly making me rack my brains. You're always catching them at it, breaking out and falling back into their old ways. Yet training has a strong influence, I can see that now. At the start it was particularly bad. Before I got it right it was the lawyers, not I, who controlled my staff. I had first to consult my legal gentry about all my measures to find out whether they were correct and corresponded with accepted legal ideas, the same ideas which we were bitterly fighting, which had put every possible obstacle in our way to power.

"I really can't tell you how grotesque the beginning was. Everywhere I was knocking up against people in SS uniform, in themselves dear, nice, decent people, who saw their task as that of supplying all my orders with a kind of legal respectability and pointing out to me at what points my measures contradicted existing enactments and were therefore not binding in law. They did that from the best motives, in order to save me, as they expressed it, from damages and recourse to claims, never seeing that they themselves were the prisoners of a system. I had to undertake a vast training programme. I got rid of the unteachable; I tried to infuse the others with my ways of thought and set them up against the legal line, tried to goad them into drawing up such laws as they could accept with a good legal conscience, to help forward the realization of our ideas.

"It always particularly amused me to see what a sigh of relief came from some poor pudding-head when a law was substituted which he could grasp, and how he would puff himself out and juggle with the legal paragraphs to make our measures legally unobjectionable. But you have to come to terms with the devil as they say; all lawyers are intellectually deformed in some way or other—it's in the nature of things—they're a kind of lay clergyman. Some set themselves up to guarantee security on this side, others to protect it on that—and how fine life is once you've grasped that you can get along splendidly without the lot of them."

18th July, 1941

"And how about lawyers in the administration? Do you also want to get rid of them?" I asked Himmler today, and was eager for his answer, because I myself possessed a number of friends, acquaintances and patients who occupied important positions in the administration.

"Proceedings are already well on their way," came the surprising answer. "First of all we have broken the lawyers' monopoly in principle and demolished the superstition that leading places in the administration can only be occupied by lawyers. But our notion has been skilfully attacked by the lawyers; unfortunately many educated men hold them to be in the right and take it as a mortal offence when such places go to engineers, outstanding organizers from other professions, building experts, economists and others. Then they think they can pronounce judgment that a post is not occupied by a professional man."

"But there must be a reason, Herr Reichsführer, why one always falls back on lawyers and regards them as specially suited for such posts," I objected.

"Certainly, I can tell you the exact reason," Himmler replied. "It consists in the fact that people take for granted that the whole nature of administration lies in the application of laws and that the lawyer who has been trained to apply and interpret the law should understand this best. But that is a fundamental error. The nature of administration lies in mastery of vast planning tasks, especially an administration such as the National Socialist state, urged forward by its great work of settlement in the east. To apply and interpret law embraces only a very trifling part of the matter. The lawyer is entirely out of place in the work of planning, which a good administrator or the president of a board should carry out, a man who from the nature of the tasks assigned him must have plenty of imagination. The lawyer has learnt to think in an extremely one-sided fashion and in his daily work the application of law plays only a very small part.

"Really able administrators, who have long outgrown their legal training, with whom I have talked and gone into this question, have always confirmed this. A well-trained engineer or economist is much better placed here and does work of far more value to the state. Certainly he can take a lawyer on to his staff, if he thinks it proper—I've no objection to that; but we must make an end with the idea that the lawyer is the born administrator on account of his training. We have had excellent results too in choosing our administrative heads with the needs of present-day administration in mind."

"Why then does industry attach so much importance to lawyers, whom you regard as quite unnecessary to administration, and why do I find them everywhere holding important positions, ranking second or third, on your staff and in the government?" I retorted. "Simply because the administrative heads whom you had taken from other professions were quite prepared for the tasks they had to fulfil, and had to call on experienced lawyers, whose minds are trained to grasp the essential facts, to help them bring order into chaos."

"You must have a lot of lawyer friends, that you bring such stuff forward on their behalf?" Himmler enquired. "I see too that you have come well briefed. You bring me all the objections against which I have to contend daily; they're constantly being brought against me by lawyers in the administration, by state secretaries in the Ministry of the Interior or the Ministry of Justice. Such objections can't move me, but I'll gladly give you my opinion of them.

"What you assert about industry is entirely false. You don't really think that lawyers get the important posts there? Just look at the leaders of industry: are any of them lawyers? Not one. Experienced big business men and engineers occupy these posts. But they have their lawyers for the permanent struggle against competition and the government, to bring in the largest profits. Their lawyers are certainly trained for that. They don't head any big undertakings, they don't busy themselves in vast enterprises—but advise how to get round regulations most conveniently, how to insert conditions with double meanings into contracts which are particularly useful to their employers; or in other difficulties advise them how to do best for themselves in their struggle against competition and against the government.

"The lawyer here, it is very true, takes the second or third place; he is not valued on account of his position as a 'Defender of Justice', to use Frank's term, but because he is quite prepared to be a defender of what is illegal. In undertaking this the lawyer is nothing but an employee working for his employer. Woe to him if he doesn't arrange things in a manner pleasing to his master. He will be sacked without a thought.

"Recently Frank wanted to explain to me the significance of his 'Defenders of Justice' as an independent legal profession and asked for my co-operation with the Führer, of whose anti-legal attitude he complained bitterly. I laughed at him and told him that he should just explain to me the position of lawyers as independent Defenders of Justice in industry. He still holds this remark against me.

"The lawyer whom we find in industry is the prototype of the Roman lawyer, obviously needed for that sort of job. Yet I prefer this type of industrial lawyer to the others. They are at least capable of something, have some notion of the industrial set-up. For them this only means one thing: they admit that they are the representatives of vested interests. Their aim is a good salary—they want to do what they can for themselves and their families. That I can understand, but not the megalomania of the ordinary lawyers who boast that, just because they have studied law, they can and must have a share in everything."

So ended the conversation which had lasted over an hour. Brandt came in with urgent papers and Himmler returned to work. After a time I had a chance to talk to Brandt, told him of my conversation with Himmler about lawyers and expressed my astonishment that he was so well acquainted with all these matters and had all his arguments immediately to hand.

"You've touched on one of the fields where the Reichsführer is continually being compelled to fight—in his own organization, in the administration, against the Ministry of Justice—the lawyers are dug in everywhere, often holding the highest ranks in the Party and the SS, marshalling their arguments and forming a quietly united front against him. So he has to be very much on his guard, if he is to make any headway. There's no limit to his distrust of lawyers. How often it happens that he reads some paper which goes against all his ideas or upsets him in some way or other. Then he calls me and says: 'Brandt, just make certain what this fellow's profession is.' Then I know that the Reichsführer had smelled out another lawyer and wanted to know whether his nose was right. If it is, then he declares in triumph: 'Now then, didn't I smell it out again?' If it's something else, then the phrase is: 'But he could have been one and certainly is one at heart.' "

I pointed out to Brandt that Himmler had not answered my question why lawyers everywhere occupied the second and third most important places on the staff and in the administration.

"Yes," Brandt observed, "that is a very ticklish question which the Reichsführer prefers to avoid. He doesn't really believe it's a fact and remarks that it only comes from the exaggerated statements of lawyers themselves, with a position in the world, who exalt themselves without having to adduce any evidence for it. He has therefore ordered statistics to be compiled; finally to shed some light on the matter. But he is uneasy about the whole business."

XII

RIBBENTROP

A FEW days ago Himmler asked me to examine the Reich's Foreign Minister, von Ribbentrop. At first I was against this, not wanting to draw upon myself the hostility of the doctors who treated him. I also wished to preserve my incognito. But Himmler had already spoken to Ribbentrop about me and said that I had treated him for his rheumatism. I was not to tell the Foreign Minister anything about Himmler's stomach pains, which were to be kept a close secret. Ribbentrop had to think that Himmler was perfectly strong. Once he knew that Himmler was ill and unfit, he would intrigue and snipe at him even more than at present.

Ribbentrop then sent for me. He is suffering from severe headaches, giddiness, partial loss of vision and stomach pains. I have taken on the case.

10th March, 1943

Today I treated Ribbentrop again. On this occasion he asked me whether I was a member of the Party. When I said 'no', he was astounded that this should be possible when I had already been in Germany for three years. I told him that I was a doctor and that I only considered a man's sufferings, quite regardless of whether he was a monarchist or a democrat. I was only interested in helping him. Ribbentrop found my attitude devastating. Had I attended no political training course? And what did Himmler say to all this?

12th March, 1943

Ribbentrop has complained to Himmler about me. As I was treating Himmler today the latter said: "I'm aware that you're no National Socialist. But I had thought you were more discreet. For with men like Ribbentrop you must keep your mouth shut and not give your real opinion. You know yourself that you have to be doubly cautious with such people. Apart from that, you have no idea how often you are denounced to me in the course of each month."

Today Ribbentrop said that he had talked to Himmler about me and told him what an excellent doctor I was. But he had not been able to ignore my recent remarks on politics. Himmler had given him a firm assurance that after the war I would be one of the first to attend a political training course. With that he, Ribbentrop, had been satisfied.

Then we came to talk about England and I asked Ribbentrop whether it was true that he had greeted the King of England with 'Heil Hitler'. Ribbentrop declared that this was absolutely true. He had wanted to make clear to the King that a new period in the history of mankind had commenced. But the King had not grasped this. If England had then taken Hitler's outstretched hand, she could have gone peacefully about her business and survived under the powerful protection of the Greater German Reich. Hitler had assigned 'a definite living space' to England. But now she would lose everything, Ribbentrop concluded.

21st September, 1943

Today I asked Himmler to free me from the obligation of treating Ribbentrop. I could do no more for him. Himmler was very shocked and begged me to make another attempt, whatever the circumstances. Ribbentrop was irreplaceable. He, Himmler, had long reflected on the question of a substitute, but there was no real successor for Ribbentrop in Germany. For Hitler trusted no one so much as him. No one could explain foreign politics to him so well as the Foreign Minister. Ribbentrop's art of exposition was unique and it was entirely suited to Hitler's ways of thought. From my knowledge of Ribbentrop's attitude I remarked that what he could explain to Hitler could only be figments of his own imagination. Himmler said that didn't matter so much, as this war was not being won by diplomats, but by the Waffen SS, the Party and the Army. Diplomacy was quite beside the point. Basically it was quite unimportant what Ribbentrop said to the Führer. The great thing was that Ribbentrop's expositions pleased Hitler and kept him in the good humour he needed for the great military decisions of the war. After the war the diplomats, the most stupid people in any state, could start on the peace treaties; that would be a job for them.

I still wanted to finish with Ribbentrop and in the end Himmler agreed, since I was no longer able to help him.

XIII

SHOOTING PARTY AT SCHÖNHOF

26th October, 1941

YESTERDAY evening we arrived at Schönhof, at the hunting lodge of the Foreign Minister, von Ribbentrop. Today the whole day was given up to shooting pheasants. The bag comprised 2,400 pheasants, 260 hares, 20 crows and one roebuck. Count Ciano alone shot 620 pheasants; he's the champion. Ribbentrop shot 410 pheasants, Himmler only 95 and Karl Wolff (Obergruppenführer of the Waffen SS) 16. Other members of the party shot the rest, among them the Reich's Finance Minister Count Schwerin-Krosigk. Altogether there were eight shoots; each man used three guns. Ribbentrop asked whether I would shoot too; I refused, but went with them. The beaters consisted of 300 mountain troops from Vienna. The soldiers are glad to do this, for they get a couple of days' leave and are well looked after. They seemed gay and healthy.

I took up my position with the different shoots in turn, mostly being with Ciano or Ribbentrop. Ciano had fantastic luck; pheasants fell to him like gifts from heaven. He beamed and was in a radiant mood. When I stood for a moment behind Himmler, he uttered a kind of snarl and said to me: "Look what luck that Ciano has. I wish the Italians in Africa had been such good shots. In Albania they've scattered like sheep before a wolf. But here Ciano does fine! Where there's no danger, the Italians are heroes."

I answered, laughing: "Don't be so bitter. Don't begrudge him the pheasants!"

"Of course I don't begrudge him the pheasants," said Himmler. "For all I care he could shoot the lot by himself. Personally I find no pleasure in blowing the poor creatures to bits. Defenceless birds. I would never have come to this shooting party if the Führer had not expressly wished me to do so."

Suddenly a new drive of pheasants went up, most of them flying over Ciano's stand. Only two flew over Himmler's. He fired, but missed. He forgot that he didn't want to shoot any pheasants and said angrily: "It's just as if they were bewitched, they all fly to Ciano!" I couldn't help laughing to myself.

At the next drive I was with Ribbentrop. He was very pleased and said: "Isn't this shoot symbolic? As we combine to shoot down the pheasants, so we'll also combine to down the enemies of Germany! As the host I'm delighted that Ciano has such luck. He ought to have regular shooting practice; perhaps he may yet need it in Italy."

I enquired: "Do you mean that in a political sense?"

"Yes, of course," Ribbentrop answered, "I always think politics —even here, out shooting." While we had to wait a few minutes for the beaters, Ribbentrop added: "The Royal Family in Italy is preparing a stab in the back against Mussolini and us. There must be a drive there too—to sweep them all away. Then we'll be appreciably nearer to victory. The sooner the monarchy disappears in Italy, the better for the Axis powers." At this moment we heard the beaters and had to keep quiet. Ribbentrop shot two pheasants, then said to me: "It's not that I'm a bad shot either. But what's the matter with Himmler? He keeps on missing them. He ought to show what he can do. But probably his humanitarian feelings stand in his way."

At the next drive I stood behind Ciano. He was beaming. "Wonderful this shoot. Long time since I took part in such a good shoot. Fantastic beaters. Lots of pheasants. Why, Herr Kersten, not shooting? Everything well organized here. But women not pretty in Germany. Comic hens but no golden pheasants. No grace."

I said that he would soon be back in Rome with his Italian golden pheasants.

Ciano smiled. "Wonderful." Then his lip curled. "But these *Tedeschi* always look so angry. Why not laugh a bit? Even here out shooting. Otherwise all right. But no joy."

Ciano considered that when Germans hold important posts, then they look angry, and when they have minor jobs their faces are pursed up and expressionless. "Strange people!"

At three in the afternoon the shoot was over. There'll be more tomorrow. At five there was a large meal. Afterwards we all sat round the fireplace in the drawing-room. Strange to relate the conversation was not political. Probably Ribbentrop thinks of politics while out shooting and of shooting while at politics. He talked about horse-racing in England and Ciano about bull-fighting in Mexico. Ribbentrop said that after the war he would see to it that Germany led the world in horse-racing. I suppose German race-horses will be bred in a Party brown or an SS black. Himmler played little part in the conversation. At eleven he took his leave and went to his room giving as a reason that he had some papers to work on. He asked me to come with him and give him more treatment. In his room he said that he couldn't listen any longer to the silly chatter of those two fools and preferred to go to bed.

When I returned to the drawing-room, Ribbentrop said that he had a headache and asked me for treatment. He took his leave from his guests and we went to his bedroom. He said that it had been a magnificent day. He had proved to Ciano that in Germany they could arrange splendid shoots even in war-time. "Did you notice what an impression it made on Ciano? It's no longer possible in England, I believe."

After the treatment Ribbentrop felt better. I again returned to the drawing-room. Ciano received me with a beaming face and said: "Now all patients ill from a little bit of shooting?" I replied that the gentlemen were only somewhat fatigued. Ciano said: "I'm not!" He took his glass and drank my health. The others were busy at the cold buffet and I sat alone with Ciano. Suddenly he said quietly to me: "War will last a long time." I agreed and Ciano remarked that we were the only ones to share this opinion. Here at Schönhof everyone is saying that the war will soon be over.

Then he asked me to tell him about Finland; he was a great admirer of the Finns and loved this vigorous nation. They were an heroic people, only to be compared with the Romans—and the Italians were certainly Romans. I talked of Finland and the great difficulties it was having with National Socialist Germany. Ciano said he could understand that; the National Socialists had to stick their noses into everything. "They are just the same barbarians that they were two thousand years ago."

At one o'clock everyone went to bed. Ribbentrop had had a basket of very fine apples put in my room, and a bottle of apple juice. I found this very thoughtful, as I supposed that the apples and the juice had come from the celebrated Tree of Knowledge.

27th October, 1941

This morning at ten o'clock the shooting began again. There were only three drives. Ciano again had great luck. At three o'clock there was a shooting lunch. After the meal the gentlemen went off to rest. I gave treatment to Himmler, Ribbentrop and Ciano. In the evening Ciano spoke to Himmler about me. He asked him to let me travel regularly to Rome, as my treatment did him a lot of good. Himmler said very amiably: "Of course, any time." If Ciano should need me, then he should apply to Himmler personally, who would let me go to Rome immediately. But he should not direct his request to Ribbentrop; that would mean delay. Ciano thanked him and was very pleased about it.

At half past seven dinner—it was excellent. At the end there was a huge pyramid of ice cream. Then Ribbentrop made a speech. First of all he thanked the guests for coming, next all those who had arranged the shoot so admirably, then he turned to Ciano and said: "My dear friend Ciano, I am happy that you have enjoyed yourself with us. The time is not far distant when our two peoples will live in peace and harmony, as we did during these days at Schönhof. In another year the shooting will be still better, as I have given orders that twice as many pheasants be reared. Next year too England will be convinced that she can no longer conquer the Greater German Reich. Then we will have reached our goal. And in the year 1943, I promise you, the first peace-time shoot will take place at Schönhof. The German Reich will then be more powerful than ever!"

Next Ribbentrop invited all the guests to come out with him to the castle steps in order to inspect the bag. The courtyard was brightly lit with torches; the whole bag lay before us. Eight huntsmen in uniform sounded the retreat. It was solemn and moving.

Early in the morning we go back to Salzburg, Ciano to Rome. Shooting days are over.

Salzburg
28th–29th October, 1941

At the end of the Schönhof shoot I talked with Himmler during the treatment and we went into the question of shooting. I said that I loved it and never felt so well as when out deer-stalking. I became quite a different person when I was in the open air stalking deer for hours on end, and continued to reap the benefit of those days out hunting for a considerable time afterwards.

Himmler replied that that was certainly the best part of hunting, but the real aim of deer-stalking, to have a shot at a wretched deer, went against the grain with him. "How can you find any pleasure, Herr Kersten, in shooting from behind cover at poor creatures browsing on the edge of a wood, innocent, defenceless and unsuspecting? Properly considered, it's pure murder. I've often bagged a deer, but I must tell you that I've had a bad conscience each time I've looked into its dead eyes."

Himmler had intimated this sort of thing to me before. Those who knew him, to whom I talked about it, told me that he had once been a keen sportsman, but after much reflection and under Hitler's influence he had changed his point of view. Nowadays he was very soft-hearted on the matter. Whenever he was invited into the country to shoot, he soon left the others. When they met him again, hours later, he had not once fired a shot. He had passed the time in contemplating the trees or deep in intellectual conversation with the huntsmen about nature and Germanic mythology. Quite recently it had again happened that he refused to shoot, giving as his reason that he didn't want to disturb the beauty of nature and the peace of the woods. He preferred to do his shooting with a camera.

I reflected on these points and resumed the conversation saying: "Men have gone hunting in every age, Herr Himmler. What would happen to the game if it were not kept within bounds? Hunting is also truly Germanic—it's in our blood somehow."

"You can't catch me with such arguments, Herr Kersten," Himmler answered. "If our forefathers went hunting, they did it because they urgently needed game to eat. I approve of this sort of hunting and would also take part in it myself. It was really dangerous too, and they didn't shoot with repeating rifles and telescopic sights from behind cover. That was a proper occupation for men. But what happens today? Fat men theatrically clad in hunting costume, armed with the most up-to-date guns, drive up in their large cars to the hunting lodges. Here they are met by the huntsmen and taken on proper stalking paths, from which every twig has been carefully removed, to shoot some poor roebuck or deer, which has been selected and marked down by the huntsman weeks before. That has just as little to do with the basic Germanic hunting instincts as the banquet which follows, with its quantities of wine and schnaps, has to do with the Germanic drinking party after the chase.

"I often ask myself, what does all this really amount to? Why does a business man, usually so careful of his time, spend three hours to drive at sixty miles an hour to his place in the country, hold a shoot, have a good meal and rush back home again? He could use the time far better on business. It's simply a fashion, the effort to appear other than one really is, dressing oneself up in sporting rig or just going out with a weapon in one's hand and working off one's inferiority complexes. The only one to suffer is the deer, blown to bits without a pang."

"But how can you generalize like that, Herr Himmler?" I objected. "Göring for instance seems to me to be a dyed-in-the-wool sportsman."

"That's certainly what he thinks himself," Himmler answered, "for he shoots everything that comes the way of his gun and can be very unpleasant if his luck is out. The result is that his people regularly pull the wool over his eyes. He thinks that he's deer-stalking in the approved style and selecting his own deer. But the deer has really been marked down a dozen times and it's Göring who is guided to the deer. Or he thinks he has a special gift for boar-hunting, but the boars are driven in front of the guns from an enclosed thicket where they have been well guarded for days. You have to know these tricks.

"No, Herr Kersten, don't talk to me about this sort of hunting. I just don't care for so crude a sport. Nature is so marvellously beautiful and every animal too has a right to live. It's just this point of view that I admire so much in our forefathers. They, for instance, formally declared war on rats and mice, which were required to stop their depradations and leave a fixed area within a definite time limit, before beginning a war of annihilation against them. You will find this respect for animals in all Indo-Germanic peoples. It was of extraordinary interest to me to hear recently that even today Buddhist monks, when they pass through a wood in the evening, carry a bell with them, to make any woodland animals they might meet keep away, so that no harm will come to them.

"But with us every slug is trampled on, every worm destroyed; there are even rewards for killing sparrows, and children are urged to slaughter harmless animals. Naturally I can't make any real change now in war-time. It might be misunderstood. But after the war I will issue the strictest regulations for protecting animals. Children at school will be methodically brought up to love animals, and I will give special police powers to societies for the protection of animals."

"I already see the day coming," I answered, "when hunting too will be forbidden. So I will make good use of the time that remains. But I must seriously consider whether you will still find me here, Herr Himmler, once you forbid hunting and shooting—which certainly won't be difficult for you, as your Führer is also set against it."

"That certainly won't happen to you, Herr Kersten," said Himmler. "You are a foreigner and foreigners will still be free to hunt and shoot. You can go shooting in peace; I won't stop you if it gives you pleasure. The main thing is that you should keep fit. But you will understand my point of view."

"Not entirely, Herr Himmler," I retorted. "You are not quite so gentle when it's only a matter of men. Thousands of men fall daily in the war; you hardly give a thought to that. You regard this slaughter as necessary to the laws of national survival. Isn't there a mass-murder of animals daily in all the slaughter-houses on earth? You must become a vegetarian, Herr Reichsführer, and not allow yourself to touch another piece of meat once you begin to reflect on organized slaughter of this sort. If I had the choice I would much prefer to be killed instantly while grazing at the edge of a wood, than travel for days in the slaughter-truck, and have to wait in the slaughter-yard with its stench in my nostrils, before I was struck dead. You were born a farmer, Herr Himmler, so you will already have had experience in this field."

"Stop, it upsets me to think of it," Himmler answered, "you could put a man off his whole lunch. It's true that you could beat me with logical arguments in this matter, but in spite of that you won't make me believe in the killing of wild animals. I'm ready at any time, moreover, to become a vegetarian, although in contrast to the Führer I'm not one at the moment, if that would in any way help to stop the killing of animals. Even Indian teaching, too, permits eating the flesh of animals whose death was not intended by oneself."

"That's a fine piece of jesuitry, Herr Himmler," I answered, laughing, "from that point of view you can really eat your cutlet with an easy conscience."

How can one reconcile the facts that the same man who pities the fate of hunted animals blandly ignores the fate of men?

XIV

BEGINNING OF THE TRAGEDY

Berlin
11*th November,* 1941

TODAY Himmler is very depressed. He has just come from the Führer's Chancery. I gave him treatment. After much pressure and questions as to what's the matter with him he told me that the destruction of the Jews is being planned.

I know his opinions on that subject and that they have not changed at all. He wanted to expel the Jews, but that did not succeed; in spite of initial success the scheme finally broke down owing to the refusal of other countries to accept them. Now the destruction of the Jews is imminent. I was horrified and replied that it was fearful cruelty to want to destroy men simply because they were Jews. They had a heart as he and I had; hadn't every man a right to live?

After a longer pause Himmler said: "These are the points to consider: the Jews are constantly overturning every system of government by means of wars and revolutions. Not only political, but economic and intellectual revolutions. It's only necessary to reflect on the destruction of commercial honour, the break-up of artistic codes, in short of all those standards which lend stability to a state. This leads to nations being robbed of their material and intellectual heritage and to a general proletarization. But as the proletariat can't direct a state, leadership comes into the hands of the opposite kind of Jews who are against the proletariat. The Jews cause the rottenness on which they thrive. They dominate the entire world through the centres of news, the press, the cinema, art and practically everything else. The damage which the Jews have been doing for centuries—and the future would only be worse—is of a kind so comprehensive that it can only be met by eliminating them entirely.

"It's the destructive Jewish spirit which has caused the lack of unity in Europe; it's the same with all wars and all want. It's a blood-guilt of the Jews which has swallowed up countless millions of victims and will consume more. You can only meet the Jews with their own methods and their own words: an eye for an eye and a tooth for a tooth. The millions of dead for whom the Jews have been responsible over the centuries must be held against them. These interrelated facts have already led to the partial extermination of the Jews by other peoples in the past. Only when the last Jew has disappeared from the world will there also be an end to the destruction of nations—and to war waged as a business concern worth millions; and countless future generations will be saved from mutual slaughter on behalf of the invisible Jewish Empire."

Filled with horror I emphatically conjured Himmler to give up this idea and the plan to be discerned behind it. The suffering and counter-suffering were not to be contemplated. To this Himmler answered that he knew it would mean much suffering for the Jews. But what had the Americans done earlier? They had exterminated the Indians—who only wanted to go on living in their native land—in the most abominable way. "It is the curse of greatness that it must step over dead bodies to create new life. Yet we must create new life, we must cleanse the soil or it will never bear fruit. It will be a great burden for me to bear."

Himmler then quoted the phrase: "Retaliation strides remorseless through the history of the world." It was an historical fact that the Jewish Empire had cost millions of dead, far more millions since the Jews lived all over the world. These dead demanded atonement. Even the old Jewish saying, an eye for an eye and a tooth for a tooth, spoke of this atonement.

"Earlier I had other things in mind," said Himmler, "but the urge to atonement and self-defence overwhelmed me. It's the old tragic conflict between will and obligation. At this moment I'm learning how terrible it can be. Please leave me alone now."

16th November, 1941

In these last few days with Himmler I have been constantly trying to return to the fate of the Jews. Contrary to all his habits he only listens to me in silence. Once he briefly asserted: "You're right, the extermination of peoples is unGermanic. You can demand everything from me, even pity. But you cannot demand protection for organized nihilism. That would be suicide."

Since I labour in vain against the atrocious principle to which Himmler is committed, I have promised myself that I will undertake as many special interventions as possible to rescue Jews, hoping that Himmler will grant a number of exceptions. For if his basic attitude, that the Jews should not be destroyed, but 'only' evacuated (the word 'only' is quite horrible enough), still holds good fundamentally, he must be won over to make as many exceptions as possible.

Above all I feel myself of one mind with the millions of men throughout the world who must hope to prevent or mitigate the coming dangers in every possible way.

XV

HIMMLER'S CARD INDEX OF PRESENTS

Hartzwalde
20th December, 1941

HIMMLER told me an interesting thing today. He possesses a card index of presents. An exact entry is made of every present he gives. He has a reason for keeping a register of his gifts. "First you always have to know whom you have given a present to, so as not to give the same thing twice, and secondly you ought not to give too much, or people become acquisitive." Besides, the character of the recipient can be studied in detail. "Just from the way the letter of thanks is written, you can establish what sort of a person the writer is." Collecting the hand-writings and signatures of the recipients as source material for graph-ology also had its value to him.

I asked Himmler whether I might have a look at this card index. He told me that I should get in touch with Fräulein Lorenz; she was the 'Auntie for Presents' in the SS.

Hartzwalde
21st December, 1941

Today I had a look at the card index. A really fine piece of book-keeping. In it is noted when the recipient was born, what rank he holds in the service, what are his position, rank and number in the Party, how many children he has, the maiden name of his wife, where he lives and how he should be addressed: whether intimately (*Du*), or 'Dear Party-member', or simply 'Party-member', or 'My Dear Party-member' or 'Herr'. In the same way every present which the Reichs-führer receives is also recorded.

I was able to look through the card index a little and establish that most of the presents were of small value. For instance, Christmas candlesticks and plates, SS calendars, porcelain figures from the Allach factory, which is SS property. Ladies most often get half a pound of chocolate or a pound of coffee, tinned sardines, butter or bacon. For Christmas Himmler often bestows half a goose or books.

When time permits, Himmler personally writes brief dedications to these presents, which often amount to a hundred and more. He never misses delivering one present personally, not even in war-time whenever possible: he himself packs the basket of presents for the maid who has worked for twenty years in his home and drives to the house of her parents, in order to show his gratitude by presenting the gift personally.

Fräulein Lorenz also showed me my card and said that I could take the Christmas present assigned to me at the same time.

Now I am at Hartzwalde making ready for Christmas myself. How beautiful it is here in the loneliness of the woods. Here I'm on my 'Finnish island'.

May the coming year bring peace and free us from the fearful nightmare.

XVI

THE FUTURE OF BRANDENBURG

Hochwald
8th February, 1942

IN THE course of conversation today Himmler told me this: the Führer had charged him with resettling a considerable part of the population of Brandenburg after the war. The Führer estimated that after the war Berlin would become a city of eight million inhabitants. But a city of that size needed a green belt for the health of its people. As the land round Berlin had much poor soil, in places even rated in the seventh and eighth categories, it gave a wretched existence for farmers and produced little.

Therefore Hitler had arranged that all soil of this kind, in a 100 kilometre radius of Berlin, should be reafforested. Farmers would have their land expropriated. He had received the commission to resettle the population by villages on good soil in the East. It would happen like this: a village standing on poor soil would disappear; property and houses would be valued by the state, and the owner would receive better soil in the East and buildings erected by the state quite ready for him. Personal possessions would be forwarded by the state to the new living place. Village communities would be resettled as a whole, so that the settlers should not be home-sick for their old home. It was hoped that they would soon feel better off in the new home than in the old. Areas vacated in this way would be reafforested, the buildings torn down or blown up and every memory of them extinguished.

So around Berlin in another hundred years would arise the most beautiful green belt of woods to ensure the health of the people who would live in the metropolis. A few villages on good soil would remain. But in general no village in this sixty-mile zone should be less than six miles from the next. Properties might also remain, if they were productive and if their owners replanted low-category soil with trees at their own cost.

Colonies of villas would arise in these new woodland areas and those living in them and working in Berlin would be able to travel there and back each day. Indeed, after the war Berlin would be so entirely reconstructed that the suburban traffic network would have to be extended.

"In principle," declared Himmler, "poor soil should no longer be used for farming in Germany after the war. We can afford to abandon it, because we will get much better soil in the East. What hard labour is still expected today of farmers who have inherited poor soil! What these men have made of the poor soil of Brandenburg in the course of centuries is an epic of labour, but also a martyrdom. It's become such a habit that not a thought is given to it. But population is always increasing. There's no reason why this miserable state of things should not be replaced by a better. Do you know that Germany in the time of Charlemagne is estimated to have had a population of only six million and now has eighty? From that you see how urgent is a solution to the whole problem."

XVII

WAR WITH RUSSIA

1. *AN OPINION*

22nd June, 1941

WAR with Russia. "This is Germany's mortal hour. The death struggle began today. Germany has lost the war. Nobody can conquer the monstrous space that is Russia. Russia can only be conquered by the Russians themselves, not by people from beyond her frontiers. Hitler was ill-advised by men who understand nothing about Germany and Russia or who want the worst to happen. There were plenty of competent advisers to urge Hitler against this adventure. Hitler could have been the greatest man in the world, if he had never started a war; now he will go down to history as Germany's grave-digger."

My old friend and patient, August Diehn, director of the Kalisyndikat, Berlin, said this to me as I was treating him early this morning.

Diehn asked me about the attitude of Himmler and his entourage. I told him that a mood of victory and confidence prevailed—they were already sharing out the world. Diehn retorted that he had no desire to go on living. All that he had done by hard work would be destroyed by this war. He said that he was particularly sorry for the German people, who had no idea what a guttersnipe they had pinned their faith to. There would be a bitter awakening.

Diehn's actual words were: "These people won't rest until they have turned Europe into a heap of ruins."

2. *A PROPOSAL*

Rome
15th November, 1942

This evening at six I had an interview with a man who had both knowledge and experience of Russia. He declared: "The Germans are going headlong to disaster. The war in the East is lost for them and

126

they are drawing the whole of Europe—indeed the whole civilized world—down to disaster with them. They have committed every conceivable mistake in Russia. Certainly nothing has helped Stalin so much as the Germans' ignorance. Russia can never be overcome by a foreign power, for Russians can only be conquered by Russians. Hitler has succeeded in turning Stalin into a national figure, and the crafty Bolsheviks have known how to make excellent use of this."

I asked: "Can nothing be done then?"

"Oh yes," was the answer, "but only on one condition: the Germans must set up a Russian national army. Of three million Russian prisoners of war perhaps ten per cent are real Russian Communists. These must be separated from the others. But the others will gladly fight for a free national Russia, if it can be presented to them in that light."

I asked for a brief exposition of these ideas and received them in the form of a memorandum.

3. HIMMLER'S AND HITLER'S REACTIONS

Field Headquarters
21st November, 1942

This morning Himmler was in the best of humours. Yesterday's treatment had done him good and he had slept excellently. He spoke with great contempt of Italy; the situation in Russia was rather serious. I regarded this as the right moment and handed the memorandum to Himmler. After a quick glance through it he said: "This is extremely interesting."

After supper Himmler said to me that he had read the memorandum and had spoken to Hitler about it the same afternoon. Hitler had torn the proposal from his hand in a frenzy and shouted as he asked whether now, when he was master of Russia, the victory should be snatched from him. There could be no question of that. The difficulties on the Stalingrad front would be overcome in a few weeks, and then Russia would fall into his lap like a ripe apple. "We are the only people who know the psychology for dealing with Russia" were, it seems, his words. Himmler thought that was an end of the matter.

Apart from this, he told me in detail what Hitler intended to do with Russia. He would incorporate the land up to the River Ob in the Reich. The area between the River Ob and the River Lena he would hand over to be administered by the English; Hitler hoped soon to come to an understanding with the English. England would realize that this war was not being waged against her position in the world, but against the world's enemies, the Jewish Bolsheviks. The United States of America would receive the area between the River Lena, Kamschatka and the Sea of Okhotsk.

Astounded, I asked: "And what would the Japanese get?"

Himmler answered: "They've got North China as it is, as well as the Philippines and the Dutch colonial possessions."

I replied that I regarded it a fearful cruelty to take their colonies away from a small Germanic people, the Dutch, who had built them up in an exemplary way with much toil and industry over three hundred years.

Himmler ironically retorted: "They should have thought about that before. If they had grasped the Führer's outstretched hand and had marched with us, then the Führer would have guaranteed their colonial possessions to them—even if this might have been very difficult in an East Asian world aspiring to independence. But why should we bring unpleasantness and sacrifices on ourselves for so obstinate a people?"

I told Himmler that he should not always speak of Holland with such hatred; he knew how much it hurt me.

Himmler replied: "A statesman must be hard. War is a matter of life and death, and there's no place for sentiment."

I answered that despite this a man might let himself be moved to mercy; that was no crime, but only showed that he had a good heart.

Himmler laughed. "You're quite right. Perhaps one is often too tough."

I took advantage of this favourable moment to put before him a list with the names of 28 Dutchmen, 6 Germans and 4 Norwegians, who were said to be held under suspicion of a crime for which the penalty was death, and asked for their release. Himmler glanced through the list and said: "Really, I oughtn't to do that!" I replied: "I know, but your humane feelings will make you sign a release for these men." To this Himmler said: "For my own sake. But the people don't deserve it." He signed, rang for Dr. Brandt and in my presence gave orders for the immediate freeing of the people on the list.

4. *A HERO'S DEATH AN ESSENTIAL FOR SS LEADERS*

Field Headquarters
21st December, 1942

This morning Himmler was very pessimistic. The fighting round Stalingrad did not seem to be going to his satisfaction. He was very abusive of his SS Leaders. They were too soft and too much affected by the spirit of the Army. Most of them came from the old Army, where they had begun their military careers as officers or N.C.O.s. Himmler thought that his Leaders were more of a burden than a help to the Party. It would be best, he believed, if they were all to meet a hero's death at the front. Then he would be rid of them altogether. After that he could fill the vacant places from the rising generation, which was tough as steel, and he could form and train them in the spirit of Adolf Hitler.

I told Himmler that I found it very interesting to learn his attitude towards men who served Hitler and himself so loyally.

Himmler answered: "Ach, they're not in the least loyal; they only want their reward and see the Führer as the man who'll help them to get it. I'm convinced that after our victory my SS Leaders will put in the most fantastic claims. But I shan't bother about them then." Every SS Führer should have been so devotedly loyal to Hitler, he maintained, that at any moment he would have given his life for his Führer without hesitation.

I asked whether he would hang himself, if Hitler ordered it. Himmler looked at me for a moment, shocked, then said: "Yes, certainly! At once! For if the Führer orders anything like that, he has his reasons. And it's not for me as an obedient soldier to question those reasons. I only recognize unconditional obedience."

I told him that I would not do such a thing if the President of Finland ordered me.

Today I was fortunate enough, after a long treatment of Himmler, to secure the release of 7 Belgians, 6 Luxemburgers, 18 Frenchmen, 12 Frenchwomen, 3 Dutchmen, 2 Norwegians and an Esthonian. They were all to have been sentenced to death for sabotage.

5. POST-WAR RUSSIA

Field Headquarters
15th January, 1944

On the 10th of January Himmler suddenly called me back to headquarters, as his health was not good. After the strenuous weeks I had been through, I should really have liked to pass a few days in comfort in Hartzwalde, where I had arrived with coffee and chocolate from Sweden, luxuries I had long gone without.

Himmler was depressed in mind as well as in health. The state of the Russian Front was causing him great anxiety. Russia was like the hydra in the Greek myth, Himmler declared today: if you cut off its head, seven more grew in its place. "Millions of Russians have fallen in this war, we've taken millions prisoner, but millions more are always being led into the field. In 1931, on her own estimate, Russia had a population of 111 million west of the Urals, and 52 million to the east of them. The Race and Settlement Office of the SS has calculated that these figures have grown today to 125 million and 60 million respectively; and that by 1952 Russia will have a population of at least 200 million. So she grows at the rate of some 3 million a year. To deal with this increase, militarily speaking, we must kill between 3 and 4 million Russians a year."

"If such calculations can be made in an office," I said to Himmler, "then you might have known all this some time ago and you should never have started this insane war."

Himmler answered: "Of course I knew it. And because we knew it we were frightened and saw the danger. But we couldn't know that other countries would attack us from the rear during the very first phase, the Polish one, instead of leaving us to deal with the Russian colossus which threatened the entire world. Still less could we know that the U.S.A. would supply the Russians with the very best weapons. Without American weapons and supplies, Russia would have been overwhelmed by our Blitzkreig and by the violence of our attack, even though the Western powers had senselessly tied our hands. But they had no notion of Russia, still less of the forces which Russia has been setting in motion for years—and as little idea of the changes in Asia which Russia has been deliberately preparing for years.

"If you look at the map, you'll see this overwhelming land-mass. Of course a part of this must be set aside as unsuitable for permanent settlement, particularly the north of Asian Russia. West of the Urals Russia forms a gigantic area from the Caucasus to the far north. Attached to this western area there is the long snake-like stretch of habitable land running across Asian Russia to the Pacific. Therein lies Russia's weakness. So long as that remains, Russia can be conquered—but not later."

To my question whether the Russians might not be able to bring about a change in these extremely strict limits imposed upon them by Nature, Himmler replied: "It's possible. The Russians are masters at that. They have already succeeded in breeding a species of corn which will bear more degrees of cold than any known hitherto. The Russians might also be able to push the limits of corn-growing further to the north. During the fighting in Russia we came up against a plant-testing ground where these experiments had been carried out for years. By an unhappy mischance the special significance of this species of corn was not at once recognized, with the result that the corn was given out to the troops. When this was known, the Führer flew into a rage, for he has a high opinion of these Russian tests. Fortunately this did not happen in an SS unit. If the Russians succeed in extending the limits for corn-growing 120 miles to the north, then Russia will look quite different. It will no longer be a snake stretching out into Siberia, but a compact state extending some 6,000 miles from west to east. The distance from Basel to Königsberg is only 900 miles."

When I remarked that so far the war was not won nor lost, nor in either case would Hitler need to bother himself with the limits of corn-growing, Himmler answered: "You can't calculate like that, for it might happen very quickly. In certain circumstances ten years might be enough, for Russia is staking everything on it, on the extension of her living space: Russia has known for generations that lack of habitable land is her weakness. And for this reason, to make doubly sure, she is also trying to win land or at least definite influence to the south. Russia has made a satellite of the state of Tanu-Tuwa to the west of Mongolia; she has revolutionized Mongolia, so that Outer Mongolia has declared itself a Soviet state, made an alliance with Russia, and opened the doors wide to the Russians. That happened in 1922, but already in 1907 Russia was discussing the partition of Persia with England. Anyhow Russia will be kept out of Manchuria through the pressure of Japan. But if Russia should emerge from this war more or less intact, then the Badmajew Plan will be put into action and Europe may abandon hope."

When I asked what this Badmajew Plan was, Himmler told me to get the papers about it from Dr. Brandt.

XVIII

THE SOLDIER-PEASANTS

1. CONSTRUCTION OF VILLAGES TO BE INHABITED BY SOLDIER-PEASANTS ('WEHRBAUERN')

Field Headquarters, Ukraine
16th July, 1942

I⊤ WAS not possible for me to treat Himmler this morning, as he could not achieve that relaxed state which is the preliminary to a successful treatment. He was still entirely under the influence of a talk with Hitler, to whom he had had an opportunity of exposing his ideas on military peasant settlements.

"You won't understand how happy I am, Herr Kersten." These were Himmler's opening words. "The Führer not only listened to me, he even refrained from constant interruptions, as is his usual habit—a habit, incidentally, which completely destroys one's train of thought, so that one ends by listening to the Führer's views on the subject in question, instead of presenting one's own case. No, today he went so far as to approve of my proposals, asking questions and drawing my attention to important details which I had not considered and which need additional study on my part. This is the happiest day of my life. Everything I have been considering and planning on a small scale can now be realized. I shall set to at once on a large scale—and with all the vigour I can muster. You know me: once I start anything I see it through to the end, no matter how great the difficulties may be."

I asked Himmler to lie down so that I could begin the treatment. He did not even listen to me, but continued: "The Germans were once a farming people and must essentially become one again. The East will help to strengthen this agricultural side of the German nation —it will become the everlasting fountain of youth for the life-blood of Germany, from which it will in its turn be constantly renewed. These phrases opened my remarks to the Führer and I linked them with the idea of defending Europe's living space, which I knew lay very close to the Führer's heart. Villages inhabited by an armed peasantry will form the basis of the settlement in the East—and will simultaneously be its defence; they will be the kernel of Europe's great defensive wall, which the Führer is to build at the victorious conclusion of the war. Germanic villages inhabited by a military peasantry and filling a belt several hundred miles wide—just imagine, Herr Kersten, what a sublime idea!

"It's the greatest piece of colonization which the world will ever have seen, linked too with a most noble and essential task, the protection of the Western world against an irruption from Asia. When he has accomplished that, the name of Adolf Hitler will be the greatest in Germanic history—and he has commissioned me to carry out the task." Here Himmler amended: "That is to say, the Reichsführer of the SS will always supervise the achievement of this gigantic work, which will stretch over decades, and he will be the intellectual force behind it."

Himmler fetched out his papers, maps and plans, on which I saw villages and settlements marked everywhere, small and large farms, forests, but also sites for industry, traversed by a mighty network of streets, which were again linked up with a number of arterial roads stretching across the entire country. Next to it lay a plan marked 'Model of a *Wehrbauern* Settlement'. He put this before me and explained it in detail: "Look, Herr Kersten, here is the ground-plan of a Germanic *Wehrbauern* village, as it will be laid out in the East. Such a village will embrace between thirty and forty farms. Each farmer receives up to 300 acres of land, more or less according to the quality of the soil. In any case a class of financially powerful and independent farmers will develop. Slaves won't till this soil; rather, a farming aristocracy will come into being, such as you still find on the Westphalian estates."

Himmler rummaged anew among his papers and fetched out a scheme for the erection of a training college in the East and read out some specially striking passages. Then he went back to explaining the plans of the settlement: "Here you see the Party headquarters, the combined centre for general intellectual training and instruction, also a meeting place for the farmers where they can relax and find recreation. The entertainment centres of the village are at Party headquarters; here is the village cinema; here is the source of instruction on important agricultural questions; here is the home of the community nurse. The manor house and the Party headquarters will be closely linked. An

SS or Party Leader of merit will occupy the manor house, specially chosen by me on account of his qualities as a man and as a soldier in the war. He will be the Leader of the farming community; on the administrative side he will be the burgomaster, on the Party side the Leader of the local group. We'll achieve a complete fusion of the Party and state and put an end to the unholy confusion that exists at present, so that even Herr Bormann will have no more criticism to make. The Leader of the farming community will at the same time be the military commander of the *Wehrbauern* village."

"Then is it also going to be a military unit?" I put in.

"Of course. That is one of the most important tasks entrusted to these villages of military peasants," Himmler replied. "The organization is designed with that in view. Each village with its forty farms, farmers, their sons and labourers will be roughly the battle-strength of a company, and the company commander will occupy the manor house.

"They'll all be fighting for their own farms and their own hearths; everyone will know that any measures taken have not been ordered by a distant bureaucracy, but by men who possess farms, belonging to themselves, men subject to the same laws as those they administer. The only form of democracy which is suited to democratic men will come into being, a new Germanic allegiance-state, based on settlements inhabited by Germanic soldier-peasants."

2. *FARMERS AND SOLDIERS*

17th July, 1942

"I can imagine the actual settlement being put into effect," was the opinion I expressed on Himmler's statement about the *Wehrbauern*, "but to link it up with the military problem seems to me fantastic. After all we're no longer living in the age of Gustavus Adolphus, who could fight with peasant armies and for whom the most primitive weapons were enough. Today you operate with tanks, flame-throwers, aircraft, etc. In the light of that all this seems to me to be no more than a fine piece of Germanic romanticism."

"I see, Herr Kersten, that you want to be more clever than the Führer, who in fact attaches the greatest importance to science and is always goading scientists on to new achievements. He immediately recognized the importance of my proposals. He has stipulated that every *Wehrbauer* must take his rifle home with him, together with his steel helmet and other equipment. The smallest unit will possess machine-guns, automatic weapons and grenades; there will be tanks at battalion level."

"Will men enjoy always having to go on playing at soldiers?" I put in. "Young men like it well enough for a couple of years, and will even gladly take part in a training exercise, but they certainly won't enjoy being permanently under military discipline."

"Leave us to worry about that," Himmler replied, "we'll soon fix that by psychological methods. It's merely a question of training—which is just what we understand. The greatest interests of the state depend on this question which simply must be solved. An army recruited from a military peasantry is the only one which is really patriotic and ready to fight and die for its fatherland. The civilized townee only considers how best he can wriggle out of the army. Can you really blame him for this? Military training is a laborious attempt to crush the poor devil's individuality; much time and effort are devoted to this. The military peasant, on the other hand, knows what he has to lose and what he's fighting for. Cowards are born in towns, heroes in the country. We only need to create the conditions and a new nation of heroes will arise in the East."

Himmler had again forgotten all the people who were waiting to see him—and also his treatment; I therefore proposed to postpone this until the evening.

"My God, you've given the Reichsführer a long treatment today," Brandt said to me, as I came out of the room.

"Not at all," I answered, "today he gave me a treatment. My head is still swimming with all the talk about military peasantries, sniper units, tank-hunting and anti-parachute formations and so on."

"Don't you think it's a good idea then?" Brandt asked me. "The Führer is taken with it too."

"I won't express any judgment on it," I answered, "but the Reichsführer does not know farmers. He paints himself an ideal picture of a Germanic military peasantry which cannot exist in reality. The farmer is primarily an egoist; he will certainly be glad to take a farm in the East, but if he has to wage war constantly, the Reichsführer will soon find how much opposition he has brought on himself and what resistance will grow up against him. The farmer is wholly occupied with his job of farming, regarding everything apart from that as a waste of time. He will gladly ride and shoot a bit on Sundays, in the way of social activity, but not under military compulsion. What farmers are ready to ruin their own fields by running tanks over them? These ideologies will bring the Reichsführer little joy."

3. HOLY PLACES

19th July, 1942

Yesterday evening I was with Himmler to give him the treatment which had once more been postponed. He began talking about the *Wehrbauern* again. I proposed that he should first have the treatment. That followed. Then he took me back to his map-table.

"There is one question I should like to ask you," I said, "which is much on my mind. I don't see any churches in your peasant settlements. Yet a church is a part of any village—or at least several villages should have one between them. Do you intend to set up parishes?"

"What are you thinking of, Herr Kersten?" answered Himmler. "Spending our good money on churches! We aren't mad yet. Our military peasantry will need no churches."

"How about churches and clergy which care for the peasants now, and what will happen when they want their children baptized? What will you do then?" I argued.

"Then the clergy should find the money themselves and build themselves a church at their own expense. We won't stop them, and apart from that these buildings will later come in useful for us. The more our training takes root and men become infused with our spirit, the less will they depend on the churches—and one day they will be empty. Then we will see to it that the churches remain the property of the permanent farming community. It will be a particular satisfaction to me when we take over these churches and turn them into Germanic holy places. Our training will beat the clergy. You may be sure of that."

4. TRANSFORMATION OF LAND AND CLIMATE

21st July, 1942

Today we continued the conversation about the armed peasantry. I questioned Himmler: "You've even provided space for industry on your plans. Do you then want to establish industrial sites? I thought there was only to be an agricultural population living in the East."

"Yes, Herr Kersten, I had been dreaming of that, but the Führer has other ideas; he wants certain types of industry—reserving the choice to himself—to be installed there. This is a blemish with which we'll just have to put up. The great thing is that the Führer has accepted the master-plan."

Himmler showed me some waste areas of land on the map which were being considered for industry. Then I chanced to notice an expanse which was marked 'eventual forest site'. I asked Himmler about this and let loose a new outburst of enthusiasm on his part: "Think of that, I almost forgot to tell you. We're going to alter the climate in the East completely."

I must have looked rather blank at this, for Himmler went on: "You don't believe it, but it will come about. That is one of the Führer's great strokes of genius. Germanic man can only live in a climate suited to his needs and in a country adapted to his character, where he will feel at home and not be tormented by home-sickness. The great expanses of the East don't attract him; they inspire him with a sort of horror. We can't set up mountains in these areas, but we can plant trees; and that's what we'll do with the part which is of no agricultural value.

"That's the first step. At the same time we'll create a countryside something like that of Schleswig-Holstein. We will in fact erect wind-breaks everywhere, thus breaking up the landscape, and in this way we'll create the kind of living space which suits our character. I have already given exact instructions to my planning offices. They are ready to work out plans for me; the first drafts, which show that it's possible, are already to hand. With wind-breaks the climate alters of its own accord. As you know, completely new climatic conditions arise under the protection of these wind-breaks, in which the rearing of cattle and agriculture thrive extremely well. The protection given by the forests will also play its part. The force of the east wind will be broken. The countryside in the East will not be recognizable in a hundred years' time. It's a work of vast proportions which is coming into being. A new Germanic race will overcome the unfavourable climate and construct a living space adapted to its character."

5. LIVING SPACE IN THE EAST INSTEAD OF COLONIES. AN EASTERN WALL AGAINST ASIA

22nd July, 1942

"Have you enough men for your really super-Faustian *Wehrbauern* plans?" I asked Himmler.

These remarkable statements were his answer:

"The prime requisite is naturally that our people should multiply and possess the strength to colonize this area. But we won't limit ourselves to Germans only, we'll call on the Germanic race in all countries, the Norwegians and the Swedes, the Dutch and the Danes. Wherever we find young and enterprising elements we'll offer them our land in the East under the best conditions and with full protection for their property. And men will come quite voluntarily. This new living space will be the meeting place for all the capable and energetic men of Europe—the greatest concentration of forces for a new European peasantry. Our former colonies will then play a quite unimportant *rôle*. Our colonies are at our own front door; we no longer need the old ones and we'll let others enjoy our former colonial possessions in peace. We're creating a new colonial empire for the motherland in the heart of Europe, in which all Europe's Germanic blood will share a new colonial task. At the same time it's the most effective measure of security, for only in this way can we call a halt to the threatening assault of Asia. If we succeed in this task, then this violent fighting and all its sacrifices make sense, for in the end they'll create security for the Germanic race, even if the English refuse to realize this."

"Will you really let the English and the Americans settle there then?"

"Of course, and gladly," Himmler answered, "if they have the right racial qualifications. The Germanic race is international in character. Then we'll at last attain security, once the entire world recognizes the common basic values of the whole Germanic race; and we'll construct a great Germanic International, to set against the Jewish and Communist one. Today the Germanic peoples are engaged in a long and internecine mutual struggle. In the East there is room for the Germanic peoples of the world to engage in a more noble contest in which they can all realize the special traits of their race; for they will all stand face to face with the common enemy; there will be constant fighting on the frontiers. That is good: it will keep their strength up and prevent them from stagnating or becoming dissolute in prosperity. The assault of Asia will break against the Germanic armed peasantry, who will simultaneously drive the plough and shoulder the musket."

6. HOW ABOUT THE NATIVE POPULATION?

Through Brandt I got a glimpse at a draft of Himmler's order for the treatment of foreign peoples, first drawn up for the Poles, but then extended to all the Eastern territories. As far as I can summarize it, these points were made: Recognition should be given to as many different peoples as possible, which should be placed under their own local administration, in order to stop their uniting against German domination. Good racial types should be assimilated into Germany and kept there. There would only be fourth-rate schools for the rest of the population, where they would be taught to add up and to write their names, to be hard-working and honourable; and the first commandment would be to obey the Germans. Anyone who wanted a higher education for his child would have to send him to Germany for ever.

The rest of the population would provide workers without leaders of their own for great undertakings in the Eastern territories and Europe. The whole procedure might in some cases be cruel and tragic, but in contrast to the Bolshevik extermination of entire nations, which had to be avoided as unGermanic, this was the best and kindest method; at least these people would have more to eat and to live on than before.

23rd July, 1942

I spoke to Himmler about this draft. He explained: Since the irruption of the Mongols in the thirteenth century these peoples had for 700 years been trained to an Asian outlook. They could not be expected to think in a European or Germanic way.

I replied that this was just the reason why these peoples should now at last be allowed to lead their own lives.

Himmler then described the position of Germany and of Europe. Europe had to be united in order to be able to assert itself against Asia, and, besides that, food and living space were needed, which could only be found in the East. But the defence of this territory by military means alone was inadequate; to achieve this, its whole structure had to be altered. The armed peasantry villages would be the means of this. But success depended on the removal of all unruly elements and dangerous obstacles; that was why the foreign peoples would have to be kept in subjection. One guarantee of this was a low standard of education. This would correspond to the standard of education which these peoples had under the Soviets, so there was no question of their being worse off than before.

I replied that they certainly expected something different from the Germans and would be bitterly disappointed.

Himmler answered: "Good racial types and those who show promise of achievement will receive their education here in Germany according to our high cultural standards. But any who are not worth it will have to stay where they are. I'll give you a biblical answer: once a slave always a slave. What are the needs of primitive man? Food and certain kinds of pleasure. These people will have enough work and therefore adequate food and livelihood. Their local habits and customs will be preserved; so that there will be sustenance both for their bodies and their souls. There will be plenty of work—the building programme for the Greater German Reich, arterial roads from the Atlantic to the Urals and the Black Sea, the construction of canals and the regulation of rivers in the Eastern territories, sites for settlements and great building projects in Germany herself.

"All original creation is hard. A man must be tough if he is to charge a decadent Europe with new vitality. If there is anything wrong with our methods, they will be altered. For centuries, incidentally, the English have shown us by their example that you mustn't go too far with the native population if you want to dominate them for the general good of all parties."

XIX

HIMMLER'S TRIP TO FINLAND

Field Headquarters, Ukraine
24th July, 1942

TODAY it was decided that we should fly to Finland. Himmler is going to talk over the Jewish question with President Ryti and Foreign Minister Witting. Bread stocks in Finland will only last another three weeks. Himmler again openly declares that the Finns have to choose between hunger and delivering up their Jews. I appealed to his humanity and to the brotherhood-in-arms with Finland.

Himmler replied: "There are no conditions. Finland must do as we wish."

I answered: "We're still an independent state and can do as we like in our own country. And we are fighting with Germany against Russia."

Himmler closed one eye and replied: "Don't talk nonsense, Herr Kersten. Your independence will only last as long as it suits the Führer's purpose. Germany is the strongest country in the world. No power on earth can overcome us."

"That may be," I answered.

Himmler retorted: "It not only may be, it is so. Even the English Prime Minister Chamberlain realized that when he came to the Führer and begged for peace. You don't think that this wily Englishman would have travelled to Godesberg or Munich if he had not recognized the strength and greatness of National Socialist Germany? For us National Socialists those two visits of Chamberlain's were a turning-point in our history. When we saw that the English regarded us as their equals, the Führer realized that the hour had struck. For Chamberlain's visits were only to give the English time to rearm.

"The Führer considers," Himmler went on, "that this war is practically won already. What fighting still goes on is simply the last convulsions of the conquered. But I'm informed that a strong anti-German feeling is becoming noticeable in Finland."

Himmler gave me a sidelong glance as he said this and added: "If you weren't so afraid of the Russians, you would possibly have preferred the English and would like to eat cheap American tinned food. Anything rather than show sympathy for National Socialist Germany!"

1. DESIGNS ON SWEDEN

Shitomir
25th July, 1942

Today Himmler told me that Hitler was very dissatisfied that he had not occupied Sweden at the same time as Norway. Now it was not so easy to incorporate Sweden, even if she should give Germany a pretext. But Sweden was being very cautious in her foreign policy and would give Germany no excuse for invasion. "We had expected that Sweden would make difficulties about our transit of troops, but she has been very cunning and immediately granted all our demands. Iron supplies flow without any difficulty and there's no trouble on that score. Yet a conflict with Sweden might well arise from Finnish causes, for the north of Sweden is inhabited by Finns."

At first I thought this was a joke but when I realized that Himmler was serious I asked him why he wanted to occupy Sweden.

"In the first place," Himmler answered, "hostility to Germany has grown in Sweden in the last few months. Secondly, it's not right that next to the Germanic Reich of Adolf Hitler there should be a neutral country where the worst anti-German elements can assemble. Thirdly, certain newspapers are attacking Germany; and fourthly, enemy agents have their headquarters in Sweden." Besides all this, Sweden possessed large stocks which would be very useful for the German war-effort. There was therefore more to recommend a move than had been supposed earlier in the year. Swedish stocks would benefit the German war-effort for at least four to six months. If Sweden did not want to fight against Bolshevism, she should at least offer her stocks, for the war was also being fought on Sweden's behalf.

I was thunderstruck when Himmler explained this and replied that we had already thoroughly discussed this question in February. Then he had taken the attitude that it was better to leave Sweden in peace, if only because the iron supplies were flowing so well.

Himmler replied: "Well, we'll discuss the matter further when we're in Finland next week."

2. HIMMLER'S OFFER FOR THE PARTITION OF SWEDEN

Helsinki
30th July, 1942

As Witting and I were standing to one side and talking in the garden of the German Embassy, Himmler suddenly joined us. We walked up and down together, Himmler talking with Witting about exploration of the ocean depths. In the middle of the conversation Himmler broke off, stopped, stared hard at Witting and said: "I think perhaps the moment has come for Germany and Finland to reach an understanding about Sweden; Finland would receive the northern half of Sweden, the areas with a Finnish population and the Norwegian harbour of Kirkenes, while Germany would annex central and southern Sweden to the Greater German Reich." Norway would be annexed in any case after final victory.

Himmler continued, saying that the Führer considered that he had made a great mistake in not occupying Sweden at the same time as Norway, a mistake which could now be rectified. Finland would cause great satisfaction to Germany if she would agree. When Himmler added that Finland would emerge as a greater Finland after the war, Witting observed that Finland had no ambitions in this direction, but was simply striving to live on the best terms with her neighbours.

In reply to this Himmler said that after the war Finland would only have one neighbour, the Greater German Reich. Then Witting explained that the Finnish people would completely fail to understand such conduct towards Sweden, if only owing to the great help which they had received from Sweden in their Winter War against Russia—much less would they be able to approve of such a step. Witting's decisive rejection made Himmler change the conversation and say: "I have only been expressing a few of my private thoughts, believing that they might be of interest to Finland."

Witting answered emphatically: "I don't think so."

Himmler replied: "Then this talk will remain a secret between the three of us."

3. SURRENDER OF THE FINNISH JEWS

While Himmler was at his hotel, and without his knowledge, I got into touch with Witting, the Foreign Minister. We agreed both on the facts and the tactics of the matter. First of all the Jewish problem was to be dealt with by procrastination. We saw two possibilities. The simplest would be to explain to Himmler that, owing to the law of Finland, surrendering the Jews would require the consent of Parliament. At that time however Parliament was in recess and in the normal course of events would not be meeting again until November. Without defining the precise attitude of the Finnish Government, we had to present the matter in such a way as to show that the government was ready—at the request of the Reich—to call an extraordinary session of Parliament.

Then Himmler would have to be made to realize that an event of this kind might arouse political passions unnecessarily in the middle of the war, and might also uncover a number of other not altogether welcome questions. He would have to consider that the Finnish people hadn't the least sympathy with such treatment of the Jews and that handing them over would only lead to a deterioration of Finnish opinion concerning Germany. This would be aggravated by the fact that a number of Jews had heroically sacrificed their lives, both in the Winter War and in the present campaign. No Finn would understand how anyone could be willing to surrender the mothers and wives of such men.

On the other hand, however, the Finns had to consider that Germany could certainly bring pressure to bear on them in view of Finland's food situation. Witting, like Kivimäki, believed that this would be a national catastrophe for Finland. But on this point Finland would in no circumstances give way. In the light of these considerations we decided that Witting should reply on the lines indicated above. It would be my task to urge Himmler in the same direction.

When Himmler, as anticipated, revealed to me the next day that he would now negotiate the Jewish question with the Finnish Government, I proposed that he should trust me, as a Finn, at least to the point of first sounding out opinion in a preliminary talk with Witting and with Rangell, the Prime Minister. Then he could decide on further action in the Jewish question in the light of these talks. This was agreed. I went away and after some time returned—without meanwhile having renewed my contacts with the Finnish spokesmen—and gave him a report on the previous day's discussions.

I put them to him in this way—that both Ministers shared his outlook in principle, but still harboured doubts about the immediate technical procedure. As Himmler could not himself decide on this matter, he at once telephoned Hitler and informed him of the trend of the negotiations. Hitler was satisfied that the Finns seemed to accept in principle and agreed that the question be postponed until November.

4. WITTING'S VIEWS ON HIMMLER'S DEMANDS

Helsinki
1st August, 1942

I sat for two hours over lunch with Witting, the Foreign Minister. He was very pleased that we had succeeded in satisfying Himmler. Witting was horrified by the offer of partitioning Sweden. "What an incredible presumption, that we should provoke Sweden! That we should now turn against the Swedes the very guns which they supplied to us for our Winter War. That's really the most monstrous suggestion I've ever heard!" He expressed himself in the same way over the exacting demands in the Jewish question. "The Finns are a decent people—we would rather share the fate of the Jews! We'll never hand them over."

I asked whether there was no chance of Finland suing for peace through America. Witting considered that there was no chance at the moment. Germany had strong military forces stationed in Finland. "Practically speaking we're an occupied country! The Germans will certainly not withdraw from Finland without a fight."

This morning at eleven Himmler flew to Mannerheim's headquarters to receive the Grand Cross. At four I'm invited to tea with President Ryti. Witting will accompany me.

I spent three hours with Ryti. He is horrified by the German development. He hopes that the time will come when Finland can break away from Germany. "But no conflict just now!" Ryti emphasized to me that Finland had only one desire: to be able to live in peace and independence on its own soil.

On the drive back from Ryti's village to Helsinki Witting spoke very seriously. He considers Finland's situation both delicate and difficult. "It's no easy matter to be allied with National Socialist Germany. You never know where you are!" No move was advisable at the moment, as Finland could not surrender to the Russians. The talk with Himmler, the day before yesterday, in the German Embassy had clearly shown him what perils had to be faced in dealing with National Socialist Germany.

5. *HIMMLER'S OPINION OF PRESIDENT RYTI*

On the flight back from Finland Himmler expressed his opinion on Ryti as follows: "Ryti is an English gentleman; he went to school in England; besides that, he's a Mason. He will never become a friend to National Socialism; he is definitely anti-German. I even consider him a very dangerous man!"

"Why?" I enquired. "I know Ryti to be a very honourable man and a great Finnish patriot."

Himmler laughed. "The word 'patriot' is proof enough that he doesn't understand the Führer. We don't want any local patriots on our side, only men who think and feel in a Greater Germanic manner." In another fifty years the narrow territorial ideals, to be encountered in Finland, would be as adversely judged as those of the small states which had once predominated in Germany; and such petty nationalism soon showed its weakness when faced with antagonists constantly increasing in strength. He had always been very distrustful too of such Masons as Ryti and Mannerheim; now it was clear to him how right he had been.

8th August, 1942

Following his trip to Finland Himmler said this at table today:

In the long run it was impossible to draw the new map of Europe without making plans for the great Swedish people. They would be freed from their isolation and stagnation to form part of the Greater German Reich. "You'll see what forces will be released in Sweden then. The Swedes can play an important part. The fundamental ideals of Gustavus Adolphus, by which Sweden should be brought on to the European stage, will take on new life. If his death in battle had not broken off his plans, he would probably have founded a Germanic Reich from the North Cape to the Thuringian Forest, from the Baltic to the Low Countries; and that would have spared us a great deal."

All great new achievements in history had been accomplished in the midst of violent revolutions and disorders; only then could a new order flourish. Himmler cited Alexander, the Barbarian Invasions, Charlemagne, the Hohenstaufen, the British Empire, Napoleon. "Since the Congress of Vienna Europe, in the narrow limits of her present territories and economies, has lost the memory and the measure of such events. Others, Russia and America for instance, have held to them. The North of the U.S.A. imposed its will on the South in a bloody war and established the unity of the country. The emergence of Churchill has changed things for England, as his vain attempts at self-assertion are losing half the British Empire to Asia and the other half to America. What can Finland hope for? America is far away—too far. And Bolshevism is close at hand—too close."

XX

HIMMLER ON RELIGION

1. *HIMMLER'S VIEWS ON SURVIVAL AFTER DEATH*

Field Headquarters
8th August, 1942

A<small>N</small> SS Leader told me this a little while ago. In the course of his
duties he was Himmler's guest at Tegernsee. Himmler's small daughter
said grace before lunch in his presence. He had gazed at the Reichsführer in astonishment, not being able to understand how he—so
hostile to the Church—could allow prayers to be said in his own house.
It argued some discrepancy in Himmler's outlook. He asked me
whether I had come across any signs of religion in him in the course of
my medical duties. I answered evasively and said I might find occasion
to talk to Himmler about it; I promised myself that I would do this.

My own observations had revealed one or two things which may
be significant. I know for instance that Himmler is extremely super-
stitious: he believes in good and evil spirits. He takes an interest in
astrology, though he does not really believe it to be true; he takes
advice from at least two astrologers, so that he can ponder on what
they say—even if he remains somewhat sceptical. Besides that, he is
always afraid of an invisible power to which he will one day have to
give an account of himself. When he is in poor health, this becomes
very marked. Then he can't get rid of certain inherent fears. He is
particularly afraid of dying in agony.

Himmler is an outspoken antagonist of the Christian and especially
the Catholic religion. This hostility towards Christianity has led him
to take a systematic interest in other religions. He has particular faith
in Germanic religious conceptions, the Indo-Germanic no less than
those of the North. There are not many men in the SS with whom he
can seriously discuss such matters. They take for gospel truth what

their 'King Henry' has to tell them in this sphere and are astounded by his knowledge and by his wide reading. Sometimes he entertains University professors, Germanic scholars of repute; he will argue with them for hours on end, putting forward his own ideas and allowing them to be contradicted—at such times he quite loses his overbearing manner. Brandt assured me that up to the outbreak of the war this used to happen as a regular event. Himmler learnt a great deal from such talks that he would not have heard anywhere else and they often made him very reflective.

The tale about his daughter saying grace frequently recurred to me, and in trying to get to the bottom of it I learnt something from an SS Leader, who expressed Himmler's attitude on these lines: "Everything is still in a state of flux. We're struggling towards a final form of belief. You can expect mature men to take part in this struggle and to share the dangers of having no fixed creed. But it's not right to root children up from their familiar world and make them face the problems of faith before they're fully grown. Let them keep to the old ways so long as the old order survives; they'll come across it every day when they're playing with their friends. Once they're grown up, they can decide for themselves. Faith has to grow of its own accord; you can only clear the way for it, not dictate it."

I had learnt something from occasional remarks of Himmler's about Mohammedanism and from his caustic criticism of the Catholic Church; but to get a true picture of his attitude towards religion I had to master the chief books on which he based it, if I was to be able to argue with him. So I asked Brandt what Himmler had read in this field. He mentioned the Bhagavad-Gita, which he particularly prized for its 'great Aryan qualities', the Eddas, the Vedas and the Rig-Vedas, the sayings of Buddha, the Visudi-Magga, the Book of Purity and some astrological works. I procured those I could from a library and looked through them. After that I felt better prepared.

Today the chance came of its own accord. Himmler is considering a visit to Rome to see Mussolini. Questions of faith, the Church and the Pope arose in the course of our talk. Himmler asked me during the treatment how the Catholic Church might best be described. He did not wait for an answer but declared: "As a joint-stock company from which the chief shareholders—since its foundation and for nearly two thousand years—draw a hundred or a thousand per cent profit and give nothing in return. Insurance companies which always say that it's not in the contract whenever you make a claim are mere novices in the art of deception compared with this gigantic swindle. What makes these profits so masterly is that the capital of the company always remains in the hands of the chief shareholders and is never touched; because the small shareholders, the ordinary run of priests, have no heirs, so that the Church automatically retains the entire fortune."

I asked Himmler, when he spoke so violently against Christianity, which was the predominant factor in Western civilization, whether he felt the same about all religious concepts.

"What do you mean, Herr Kersten?" was his answer. "Surely common sense must tell you that some higher Being—whether you call it God or Providence or anything else you like—is behind nature and the marvellous order which exists in the world of men and animals and plants. If we refused to recognize that we should be no better than the Marxists. It's no pretence, nor concession, as is often alleged against me, but a very serious matter, when I insist that members of the SS must believe in God. I'm not going to have men around me who refuse to recognize any higher Being or Providence or whatever you like to call it."

"Then you do believe in survival after death?" I asked Himmler.

"That's a very delicate question," he replied. "Obviously everything does not end with death, as the materialists assert. But it's very hard to imagine what form such survival will take. Certainly I don't believe what the Catholic Church teaches, either that we go to Hell or rejoice with the angels in Heaven once we've passed through Purgatory. That's a very primitive outlook, not worth discussing. I've often wondered how a modern man can believe anything of that sort, but never been able to understand it. Least of all can I grasp how the fate of a man should be decided for all eternity after a brief life on this earth where so much happens by accident. Only a cruel god could make such a decision. Why did he create men in the first place? In his omniscience why place them in the middle of the immense dangers which they daily have to face—simply in order to damn them for all eternity if they're not strong enough to endure it?

"You're no Catholic, but Catholicism does take Christianity seriously and does think out all its consequences. You can't avoid the impression, however impartial you are, that the whole system has only been invented to secure the power of the Church and of those who hold office in it. You're bound to go in fear and trembling for the salvation of your soul, once you accept its teaching seriously and base your life on it. That's what the Church wants. Get this clear: what you do or don't do in a life which, measured against eternity, only lasts a few seconds, decides your eternal destiny. Viewed from a common-sense standpoint, that's monstrous—but very much to the point when viewed as a prop to the Church's power."

"What form will survival after death take, do you think?" I asked Himmler.

"We should rather enquire how the Germanic and Indo-Germanic peoples envisaged this question," Himmler replied, "then we'll make some progress in the matter. Here I can give you some accurate information. The Indo-Germanic peoples believe in rebirth. Life doesn't come to an end with *one* experience of it. The good and evil deeds which man does on this earth affect his next life in the form of his Karma, which is not an inexorable fate, but one which he can control and alter. The Germanic belief entails no surrender to divine grace, but the knowledge that what you have done on this earth will witness for you or against you, inescapably. But you have a chance to alter your fate by your own efforts in a new life."

With these words Himmler seized his 'Vade-mecum', a little collection of memoranda for his guidance, and read me out the following quotation from one of the Indian books:

" 'As his wife, children and friends welcome a man who has been long away from home, so on the threshold of another life, when he has finished with this one, his good deeds await him like friends welcoming a dear friend.' "

"And what about his evil deeds?" I enquired. "For if they are all to be reckoned up in detail, they can cause him great anguish. Divine grace seems to me preferable to this sort of reckoning."

"In this life you have to pay for everything, so why shouldn't you be presented with a bill in this field too?" Himmler answered. "You can settle up, even if you need one or two more lives to do so."

"But aren't you often frightened yourself, Herr Reichsführer, when you reflect on the things you sometimes have to do, which one day will be debited against you?"

He replied with great seriousness: "You oughtn't to look at things from such a limited and egotistical point of view; you have to consider the Germanic world as a whole—which also has its Karma. A man has to sacrifice himself, even though it is often very hard for him; he oughtn't to think of himself. Of course it's pleasanter to concern yourself with flower-beds rather than political dust-heaps and refuse-dumps, but flowers themselves won't thrive unless these things are seen to. I try to reach a compromise in my own life; I try to help people and do good, relieve the oppressed and remove injustices wherever I can. Do you think my heart's in all the things which have to be done simply from reasons of state? What wouldn't I give to be Minister for Religious Matters like Rust and be able to dedicate myself to positive achievements only! I've often considered whether

I won't suggest to the Führer after the war that he should separate the post of Reichsführer SS from that of Chief of Police. The Führer's already moving in that direction, since he has appointed the Reichsführer SS to take charge of the Armed Peasantry settlements and all colonization in the Eastern territories. Perhaps this post could be amalgamated with that of Minister for Religious Matters. That wouldn't be a bad solution; I should be able to devote myself entirely to positive achievements. But the present state of things both at home and abroad demands the fusion of Reichsführer SS and Chief of Police —that too is a Karma, which I must come to terms with and turn to my own use."

I was astonished to hear Himmler so frankly admit how close was the connection between his religious conceptions and his personal destiny; and I wanted to put more questions to him. But Himmler shook his head. "Wait, I've got something else to read you first." He took the Bhagavad-Gita, of which he was particularly fond, saying that he never moved without it, and quoted the following passage, which I asked leave to copy down: 'It is decreed that whenever men lose their respect for law and truth, and the world is given over to injustice, I will be born anew. I have no desire for gain. . . .'

"This passage is absolutely made for the Führer," Himmler declared. "He rose up out of our deepest need, when the German people had come to a dead end. He is one of those brilliant figures which always appear in the Germanic world when it has reached a final crisis in body, mind and soul. Goethe was one such figure in the intellectual sphere, Bismarck in the political—the Führer in the political, cultural and military combined. It has been ordained by the Karma of the Germanic world that he should wage war against the East and save the Germanic peoples—a figure of the greatest brilliance has become incarnate in his person."

Himmler uttered these words with great solemnity and effect. Now it became clear to me why Himmler had sometimes pointed to Hitler as a person whom men would regard in centuries to come with the same reverence that they had accorded to Christ. Himmler saw in him not simply a figure who had to be surrounded with the aura of religious myth because this was useful in the struggle against the Church—but rather a figure from another world of the sort that always rose up to bring help in times of crisis. It all fitted in with the legends of the Holy Grail and the story of Parsifal. If Himmler dwelt in this world of the imagination he must also have regarded himself as the reincarnation of some great figure in Germanic history.

I asked him about that and he put me off with the answer: "One is reluctant to discuss one's personal *rôle* in such matters. I've often reflected on it. But I've not yet come to any conclusion."

Today I had a long talk with Brandt about this last point; he informed me that he knew for a fact that the Reichsführer regarded himself as a reincarnation of Henry the Lion. He knew more about his life than almost anyone else and viewed his settlements in the East as one of the great achievements in Germanic history. Himmler was aware and by no means displeased that he was known as 'King Henry' or 'The Black Duke' among his own followers. Himmler had made a very impressive speech about Henry the Lion at the Brunswick celebrations to honour his memory. Brandt found it quite in order that a man should model himself on such an illustrious figure—and all the better if he went so far as to identify himself with the model.

2. REBIRTH IN THE FAMILY

12th September, 1942

The following incident led to a continuation of my talks on religion: An important SS Leader had quite openly come out against the Christian conception of life after death on the occasion of an SS man's funeral. He declared that the SS were opposed to this and that the only form of survival was in one's children and grandchildren, just as our ancestors only lived again in us, to be at last extinguished with us. One of the SS Leaders present on this occasion had told me about it and I asked Himmler whether this represented the attitude of the SS correctly.

"By no means," he replied. "The only reason why I don't join issue with such statements is because the majority of my men aren't yet ready for the sort of religion we have been discussing. It would only confuse them. Besides, it's a good thing for us if they do believe that, as it will encourage them to bring as many children into the world as possible—because nobody can bear being quite forgotten. It's a very human weakness, but you have to take it into account. Of course such beliefs are childish. Just consider how little comfort an honest man would find in living again in his children, should these happen to be worthless or even criminal. The idea only makes sense when it's linked up with reincarnation, so that you believe that you're reborn in a greater family, as the Germanic peoples did."

"Do you yourself believe in that sort of reincarnation?" I asked Himmler.

"I'm not going to answer that," he said, "but the idea of re-incarnation in a larger family proves that the Germanic peoples did believe in reincarnation and made it a part of their religion. Nor am I alone in my belief in reincarnation. A number of great men have shared it. Consider Goethe's celebrated remark to Charlotte von Stein: 'In some distant past you were my sister or my wife.' You can see what's behind it. Think of Richard Wagner, Hölderlin or Schopenhauer. The same thread runs through the whole of German intellectual life. You have only to observe what care the Church takes to obliterate every trace of it—that shows the strength of the forces lying dormant there. The time will come when they'll be brought forward into the light."

3. *THE STRUGGLE AGAINST THE CATHOLIC CHURCH*

Rome
17th October, 1942

Himmler has been in Rome since October 14th, his aim being, so he told me, to pacify Mussolini and the Italian Government, since strong anti-German feelings had become apparent in that quarter. He is very impressed by the power of the Catholic Church, which he cannot help noticing every day. Since he sees in the Church the embodiment of every trait most alien to the Germanic spirit, he is no longer the dispassionate observer with whom one can discuss religious matters. He's irritated, regarding the Church simply as an enemy whose every manifestation is a direct challenge to him, and he reacts accordingly. He's dominated by the old phrase, '*Ecrasez l'infâme*'.

"Have you seen these priests with their red robes in the streets of Rome? Yesterday I met twenty of these Lord's Day bandits. They all spoke German. That infuriated me. Millions of Germans are engaged in a heroic struggle for Germany's and Europe's freedom—and these pitiful creatures are strolling about Rome in their women's clothes; they're blood of our blood, yet we have to look on without doing anything about it."

Before I could reply at all, Himmler went on: "Have you any idea what these German priests are up to? Outwardly they seem to be perfecting themselves in their religious exercises, but in reality they're a highly efficient intelligence service—I know that for a fact. There's no point in underlining it. When they've got some important information to impart, they shut themselves up like hermits and memorize it until they know it by heart—and beyond that they have their bibles ready to hand for sending messages in code. Ten or twenty bibles of the same type taken across the frontier by priests of every sort give away a mass of information, and nothing can be done about it—they've got more helpers all over the place."

I asked Himmler whether he had been inside any church in Rome and seen the touching faith with which people prayed and sought for answers to their petitions.

"Certainly," said Himmler, "the Church is very skilful in making use of popular credulity and want, for the purpose of increasing her own power. The lesser clergy may even themselves believe that it's purely a religious matter. That goes to strengthen the Church, for unless these priests—largely recruited from among the peasants and unaccustomed to deceit—had faith they would not be in a position to impart it. But the higher clergy know well enough that it's all a matter of power and that Christianity simply occupies the front of the stage to conceal the struggle for power."

"But, Herr Reichsführer," I put in, "I've read the Bhagavad-Gita, which you so prize, and other Indian writings and found in them much the same teaching as Christianity offers in the Sermon on the Mount. The Ten Commandments recur in a slightly different form in Buddhist doctrine, in the Vedas and the Rig-Vedas. There's no doubt that the spirituality is the same, except that Christianity adds belief in a personal God who judges men after their death. It's the actual putting into practice of this teaching which would really make a difference. If all nations or even a few let themselves be wholly guided by the Ten Commandments or the Sermon on the Mount, what would happen? At once peace on earth would be assured for ever."

"That's true enough," Himmler answered, "and I've nothing against Christianity in itself; no doubt it has lofty moral ideals. But we have to be on our guard against a world power which makes use of Christianity and its organization to oppose our own national resurrection by methods of which we're everywhere conscious. You have only to read history with your eyes open. In every crisis you'll trace the influence of two great world powers, the Catholic Church and the Jews. They're both striving for world leadership, basically hostile to each other, only united in their struggle against the Germanic peoples. We've already removed one of these powers, at least from Germany; the time will come to settle accounts with the other after the war. At the moment, unfortunately, our hands are tied; diplomatic caution demands that we should mask our real feelings, but it won't always be the same. Then we'll unfrock these priests—neither their God nor their Virgin Mary will be able to do a thing for them then.

What I'd like best would be to liquidate the clergy here in Rome and settle accounts with the Holy Father."

"But you're surely not opposed to the Virgin Mary, Herr Reichs-führer?" I objected.

"No, not at all. To link womanhood with religion is a noble idea. It suits our Germanic outlook. In ancient Rome it was virgins, the Vestals, who guarded the sacred flame in the Temple of Vesta; and many peoples used to honour their 'wise women'. I'm very touched myself when I see how women and children bring their troubles to the Virgin Mary."

We were interrupted, as Himmler had to confer with Ciano; he assured me that he was getting to dislike occasions of this sort more and more. "I detest these talks which lead to nothing and where each knows that the other is only deceiving him," said Himmler, as he took his departure. "I admire the wisdom of those Indian religions which insisted that kings and high state officials should withdraw and meditate in a monastery for two or three months every year. One day we'll institute something on those lines." Then he added, laughing: "How do you think Ribbentrop or Ley would take to monastic life? I would just like to see Ley's face if he was offered sour milk and black bread for nourishment and the Bhagavad-Gita to sustain his soul."

4. CHOOSING A NEW FÜHRER IN CONCLAVE

Rome
20th October, 1942

Himmler: "On the Führer's death we'll choose a new Leader in much the same way that the Pope's elected; it's a good system which has stood the test of time."

Astounded, I answered: "Then there's something good about the Catholic Church?"

Himmler replied: "Naturally we'll make use of anything that is good and do away with the bad. We'll take the healthiest branches from the tree of history and graft them anew on the trunk of Germanic National Socialism." After the war there would be a Senate for electing a Führer which would include: all Gauleiters, ten of the chief Party officials, ten of the chief SS Leaders, five of the chief SA Leaders, and the Reichsminister. The best man among them would become the new Führer. It was the finest system a Herrenvolk could have for electing its Führer. The Senate however would have other tasks and become a permanency.

XXI

CIANO

Rome
27th November, 1940

HAVING accompanied Ribbentrop to Rome, I'm also to give treatment to Count Ciano and Buffarini, the Minister of the Interior. I'm living as the Italian Government's guest at the Grand Hotel. Everybody's very considerate and friendly, probably because I'm a Finn.

12th December, 1940

I received a great honour today, the Cross of Commander of the Order of Sts. Maurice and Lazarus, presented by Count Ciano, in the name of the king.

It seems to me that there's some hostility towards Germany among the Fascist leaders. Ciano has told me that the Italians are afraid of the Germans. They never know what the Nazis will do next and consider that National Socialism is a poor imitation of Fascism, based on a misunderstanding. Ciano is glad that he can speak frankly with me, as I'm a Finn.

Rome
3rd May, 1942

Arrived here today with Irmgard, at Ciano's urgent request. Some time ago he asked Himmler whether I would come. At first Himmler was indignant, saying: "These Italians should keep their belly-aches to themselves." They were useless as soldiers and only a drag on the Germans—and a pack of lying Jesuits to boot. "When it's a matter of fighting they usually keep away, but they always know where to come to cure their belly-aches."

157

Rome
6th June, 1942

As usual, it was necessary to prolong the treatment. My departure has been postponed until today. I discussed with Ciano and Buffarini, the Minister of the Interior, whether I should return to Rome in the autumn. Buffarini advised me to take apartments in Rome, gradually break my German connections and transfer to Italy. Sooner or later Italy would have to make a separate peace, and it would be convenient for me if I were already installed in Rome. Buffarini's final words were: "Leave those cold-blooded Germans and come to us."

Rome
13th October, 1942

The Italian Government is giving a big reception for Himmler at the Hotel Ambassadore. Ciano has also invited me. All the Fascist Party Leaders and every member of the Italian Government are coming.

After the meal Buffarini and I joined Himmler and Ciano, who told Himmler what extraordinary benefit he had derived from my treatment. Himmler replied that he didn't know how he'd be able to live without my help. "Kersten's treatment is quite unique," he said, "he is a great magician, a Buddha, and we all have reason to be grateful to him. He's succeeded where all other doctors have failed in immediately overcoming my stomach pains and enabling me to get down to my work." Himmler went on: "The only reproach I have to make him is that he won't accept any recognition or honours." Ciano laughingly replied: "Then we Italians must be proud that he's accepted the Maurice Cross from us."

All this was very disagreeable to me. I said that satisfying my patients and helping those who stood in need was the only honour I desired.

Himmler then said: "Our Buddha often causes me great anxiety, however. He comes to me with a list of names in his hand and asks me to release men who are opposed to the war and to the Führer's great conceptions. Most of them are Dutchmen, Jews and German traitors. And he's so incredibly obstinate and persistent that I always have to give way to him."

Ciano laughed and said: "Yes, nobody can refuse Kersten any-thing." And Himmler added: "Our Buddha is well aware of that and that's why he always returns to the charge."

Rome
13th November, 1942

It's marvellous to be back in Rome. If only I didn't have to go back to Germany. Life is so beautiful in the Eternal City. Count Ciano is ready to help me transfer to Rome. But I doubt whether anything will come of it, Himmler is too angry with Italy. But I'll do my best.

Ciano was in a very pessimistic mood today and said: "Allies very silly. Why land in Africa? Why not in Genoa? Then for Italy war is over. Now a long war and many Italians have to die for those barbarous Germans. Most unpleasant."

I asked Ciano why Italy did not make an end to a war in which she stood to gain nothing.

Ciano answered: "No go. Too many German armies here and spies. Nothing doing. Germans know everything."

I found this very disturbing. Poor Italy, lovely Italy. I said that it might not be so bad. The Nazis could not hang all the Italians. Ciano laughed and said: "Himmler won't hang me. I'll see to that. Barbarians always want to hang everything. Mussolini trusts the Germans too much. Ribbentrop's crazy. Germans have no sense of humour. Always bad-tempered. You must come to Rome, Kersten. There's sun here and people are gay."

Then we discussed my return to Rome in April, when I would try to stay longer. Ciano answered: "Splendid! Wonderful! Welcome! Bring your family too."

XXII

HIMMLER'S ORIGINAL PLAN FOR THE
SOLUTION OF THE JEWISH PROBLEM

Munich
10*th November,* 1942

HIMMLER has informed me that the Italians would make a separate peace. The traitor Ciano had sold Italy to the Allies. It was only Ciano's connivance which had made possible the Allied landings in Africa. Ciano was the worst of traitors. "You may be sure, Herr Kersten, that the day is coming when the Führer will have Ciano hanged." Himmler got very excited and had a recurrence of his stomach pains. At the moment his health is once more in a bad way. The Allied landings have clearly dealt him a shrewd blow in the belly. "Can you understand why the Allies should land in Africa?" he enquired. I replied that I had no knowledge of politics. Then Himmler went on: "There would have been some logic in English and American landings in Greece. Then perhaps we could have come to an understanding and joined forces against Bolshevism, the enemy of mankind. But the Jews, who are Bolshevism's main support, dominate America and England. There's no chance of an understanding while they remain in control."

"Is that your own opinion or the Führer's?" I enquired of Himmler.

"It's one we share," he answered.

"Why don't you use neutral channels to seek an honourable understanding with England and America?"

"There are domestic reasons against that, for it would shake the prestige of the National Socialist Party and the Führer would prefer anything to that. The Party must survive the war without any loss of influence—it is the backbone of the nation."

In the course of further conversation Himmler declared that the Allied landings in Africa had temporarily delayed progress on the Eastern Front, since the position in Africa was still obscure. The Führer considered that he would have the African campaign under control within three or four months. Then he would be able to concentrate all his available forces on dealing the Bolshevik hordes a death-blow.

Since the landings in Africa the Führer had given orders for proceeding ruthlessly against the Jews. I said that I couldn't understand this inhuman campaign against the Jews, who were all entirely defenceless, being shut up in concentration camps. Himmler replied: "I've got to do it." I retorted: "History will condemn you as the greatest Jew-baiter of all time."

A few minutes later Himmler said in a tired voice: "Ach, Kersten, I never wanted to destroy the Jews. I had quite different ideas. But Goebbels has it all on his conscience."

I gazed at Himmler in astonishment. "Tell me what you mean."

"Some years ago the Führer gave me orders to get rid of the Jews. They were to be allowed to take their fortunes and property with them. I made a start and even punished excesses committed by my people which were reported to me. But I was inexorable on one point: the Jews had to leave Germany. In 1938 Roosevelt had enquiries made about our intentions with regard to the Jews. We let him know what our intentions were: to remove all Jews from Germany, allowing them to take all their property with them; foreign investments were to take the place of industrial property in Germany. We even set up an emigration office for Jews and a committee to arrange the economic issues involved, presided over by a high official in the Ministry of Commerce. The Jews could have led an exactly similar life abroad. We asked for Roosevelt's support in executing the entire project. We never received an answer to this request. Shortly afterwards the Counsellor of our Paris Embassy, vom Rath, was murdered by one Grünspan, a Jew. In spite of that I went on helping the Jews to get away. But our magnanimity was ignored and the world started an infamous campaign against us. Underground political forces were set in motion to start a war, and they succeeded. Our economic and political troubles increased. Jews were behind them all. Up to the spring of 1940 Jews could still leave Germany without any trouble—then Goebbels got the upper hand."

"Why Goebbels?"

Himmler replied: "Goebbels' attitude was that the Jewish question could only be solved by the total extermination of the Jews. W^L."

Jew remained alive, he would always be an enemy to National Socialist Germany. Therefore any kindness shown them was out of place. My view was that it would be enough to expel the Jews. In 1934 I had proposed to the Führer that he should give the Jews a large piece of territory and let them set up an independent state in it. I wanted to help them. We made enquiries in a number of different quarters, but no one wanted to have the Jews."

I asked whether he had been thinking of Palestine.

"No, Madagascar. It's an island which has good soil and a climate which suits the Jews."

"But Madagascar's a French possession."

"We could have had an international conference and arranged matters with France. But things turned out differently. Then finally the war came and brought with it circumstances which sealed the fate of the Jews."

Field Headquarters
9th June, 1944

Today I had a very long talk about the Jews with Himmler. I said that the world would no longer tolerate the extermination of the Jews; it was high time that he put a stop to it. Himmler said that was beyond his power; he was not the Führer and Adolf Hitler had expressly ordered it. I asked him whether he was aware that history would one day point to him as one of the greatest murderers on record, because of the way in which he had exterminated the Jews. He should think of his reputation, not sully it with that reproach. Himmler replied that he had done nothing wrong and only carried out Adolf Hitler's orders.

Then I asked him what were his personal feelings on the matter. He replied that he would give a great deal to avoid having to carry out these orders. He would also employ special units, not the Waffen SS. In this connection Himmler regretted that his Madagascar plan had not come into operation before the war. An independent Jewish state woud have been the proper solution. It would have been a home for Jews from every land and Germany would have finished with them for ever. But unfortunately foreign powers, agreeing for once with Goebbels, Bormann and their followers, had put a stop to this programme.

I told Himmler that he still had a chance to stand well with history by showing humanity to the Jews and other victims of the concentration camp—if he really disagreed with Hitler's orders to exterminate them. He could simply forget certain of the Führer's orders and not carry them out.

"Perhaps you're right, Herr Kersten," Himmler responded, but he also added that the Führer would never forgive him and would immediately have him hanged.

I looked at him in astonishment and enquired: "Is your position as weak as all that? If so, I would seek out colleagues in the Party and get them to join in convincing Hitler that the extermination of the Jews is sending Germany back to the horrors of the Middle Ages."

Himmler replied that he had nothing to reproach himself, nothing on his conscience. But he would not be able to talk to anybody on this subject, it was too dangerous; there was no one he could trust. As we parted he said: "We'll discuss this again in a few days' time."

I made use of this opportunity to give him a list of men who had been condemned to death for sabotage: six Dutchmen, three from Luxemburg, four Norwegians, three Danes and two Belgians. I asked Himmler to pardon them and he consented.

Field Headquarters
16th June, 1944

Today I had another long talk with Himmler about the Jews and the gypsies, in which I urged him to abandon the policy of extermination and let them go to a neutral country. If that proved impossible, I begged him to grant them better treatment at least. In the end he agreed to this and said that he was also prepared to let certain categories of Jews and others in concentration camps go to a neutral country, provided this was done in complete secrecy. For Hitler had come to regard the extermination policy as his own idea, since Goebbels and Bormann, who really originated it, had so talked him over.

I asked Himmler to inform Berger, Brandt and Schellenberg of his magnanimous decision, as they were all three reliable and would be able to help carry out his humane ideas. Luckily Berger was already in conference at Field Headquarters and in another hour Schellenberg was coming to receive treatment from me. Himmler agreed to my proposal and said he would lunch with us on the following day. It would be for me to bring the talk discreetly round to the subject. All three of them were bitter antagonists of Goebbels, Bormann and their people, so it would be sound strategy to let them take part in the scheme, as there was no danger of their trying to thwart it. I expressed my pleasure by telling Himmler that now he was really behaving like a great Germanic Leader. . . .

Field Headquarters
Sunday Evening, 17*th June,* 1944

Berger, Brandt, Schellenberg and I were invited to lunch with Himmler today.

Himmler declared that the Reich and the world would have been spared a great deal if only his Madagascar plan had been taken up. Unfortunately in 1941 the Führer had made the fateful decision to exterminate the Jews, misled by Goebbels, Bormann and their followers. But he, Himmler, had recently given much thought to the matter and decided on a different Jewish policy. He was also prepared to let the Jews go abroad: I, who had made certain proposals to him, believed that Sweden would be ready to open her frontiers to them.

When Schellenberg enquired whether he could inform interested parties in Switzerland of this change in policy, Himmler agreed provided that his own name was kept out of it. These talks had to be kept extremely secret, as they were in direct contradiction to the Party programme.

Himmler added that he had two reasons for this change of policy. Firstly, extermination was a dirty business; and secondly it aroused a good deal of ill-will, as innocent people abroad were too stupid and too ignorant to realize the necessity for it.

XXIII

REPORT ON HITLER'S ILLNESS

Field Headquarters
12*th December,* 1942

THIS was the most exciting day I've had since I first began treating Himmler. He was very nervous and restless; I realized that he had something on his mind and questioned him about it. His reply was to ask me: "Can you treat a man suffering from severe headaches, dizziness and insomnia?"

"Of course, but I must examine him before I can give a definite opinion," I answered. "Above all I must know the cause of these symptoms."

Himmler replied: "I'll tell you who he is. But you must swear to tell nobody about it and treat what I confide to you with the utmost secrecy."

My answer was that, as a doctor, I was constantly having secrets entrusted to me; it was no new experience for me, as the strictest discretion was a part of my professional duty.

Himmler then fetched a black portfolio from his safe and took a blue manuscript from it, saying: "Read this. Here are the secret documents with the report on the Führer's illness."

The report comprised twenty-six pages and at a first glance I realized that it had drawn freely on Hitler's medical record from the days when he lay blinded in the hospital at Pasewalk. From there the report went on to establish that in his youth as a soldier Hitler had fallen a victim to poison gas; he had been incompetently treated so that for a time he was in danger of blindness. There were also certain of the symptoms associated with syphilis. He was released from Pasewalk apparently cured. In 1937 symptoms appeared which proved that syphilis was evidently continuing its ravages; and at the beginning of

165

1942 symptoms of a similar nature showed beyond any shadow of doubt that Hitler was suffering from progressive paralysis. Every symptom was present except for fixity of vision and confusion of speech.

I handed the report back to Himmler and informed him that unfortunately I could do nothing in this case, as my speciality was manual therapy, not mental disease. Himmler enquired my opinion about what could be done in such a case. I replied by asking whether Hitler was receiving treatment. "Certainly," Himmler answered. "Morell is giving him injections, which he asserts will check the progress of the disease, and in any event maintain the Führer's ability to work."

"What guarantee is there that this is true?" I put in. "There's no acknowledged remedy for progressive paralysis in the present state of medical science."

"Of course I've considered that too," Himmler replied, "but if you have to choose between two doctors, of whom one gives up and says that the disease is mortal, while the other asserts that he can cure or at least check it and keep the patient fit to work for years, what do you do then? This is no ordinary patient, but the Führer of the Greater German Reich, which is occupied in a struggle of life and death—that can only be won with the Führer, for he is the only person whose powers are equal to the task; he mustn't fail us."

Himmler was very excited; he went on: "We must try every medical means to keep him going. I refuse to believe that this is the end, that the Führer's mind will give way, the mind that has such mighty achievements to its credit. There is always a chance. It often happens, when doctors lay down the law, that Nature proves stronger and defeats them, so that the patient recovers whom they have abandoned as a 'hopeless case'. When I reflect how the Führer was sent to us by Providence, I just can't believe that there's no way of saving him from the consequences of syphilis. And now along comes Morell and declares that he can help the Führer. There's nothing in the facts of the case to contradict him, for when he's had the injections the Führer is astonishingly clear and logical, and his thoughts are as original as ever they were in the old days. Now tell me, what would you do, Herr Kersten?"

Himmler answered for me and went on: "I know what you're going to say: that in spite of all this he should have a thorough examination in a mental hospital. In any other case I would say the same, but with the Führer it's just not possible, quite apart from the fact that he would never consent to it. You have only to consider what sort of an effect that would have on the German people, let alone abroad. You can't imagine that it could be kept a secret—within a few days the foreign intelligence service would have the exact story, even if we were to pretend that it was some other illness. The German people and every one of our soldiers would learn about it from the enemy radio. We would bring down on ourselves the most disastrous defeat imaginable. That's the reason why I've decided to trust Morell and let him have his way. I'll see to it that nothing happens. The great thing will be if he manages to keep the Führer going until we've won the war. Then we'll see, and the Führer can retire for a well-earned rest."

With this Himmler took the documents from me, put them in the black portfolio again and locked them in his safe—not without once more impressing upon me the need for absolute secrecy.

As I was going Himmler told me: "You realize now what anxieties I have; things aren't always easy for me. The world regards Adolf Hitler as a strong man—and that's how he must go down to history as well. The Greater German Reich will stretch from the Urals to the North Sea after the war. That will be the Führer's great achievement. He's the greatest man who has ever lived and without him it would never have been possible. So what does it matter that he should be ill now, when his work is almost accomplished?"

Many things were now clear to me, though my mind was still dazed by all that I had heard. First of all I wanted to ascertain how many people knew the secret. So I discreetly approached Brandt to ask what he knew about the secret documents in a blue manuscript, comprising some twenty-six pages.

Brandt went pale with horror. "Good God, did the Reichsführer talk to you about that? You don't know what danger you're in. You, a foreigner, to have knowledge of the greatest state secret in our possession!"

I calmed him down and learnt from him that the facts were known only to very few men apart from Himmler, among whom were Bormann and probably Göring. Then I wanted to find out who had drawn up the report. Brandt said that he ought not to tell me. The man in question had considered it his duty to inform the Reichsführer and had recently had a long interview with him at Field Headquarters. I also enquired how long Himmler had known the facts of the case. Brandt declared that some rumours had always been circulating, but Himmler had violently rejected them until the appearance of this report, which had been written by a man with a very deep sense of responsibility, a person about whose integrity there could be no question. Then Himmler, after a great deal of reflection, had no longer dared to doubt the facts. Brandt conjured me not to broach the subject again even with Himmler.

19th December, 1942

Today I discussed the report on Hitler's illness with Himmler again, despite Brandt's warning. Himmler himself gave me an opening by enquiring whether any way of helping Hitler had occurred to me in the meantime. I pointed out to Himmler that they might try a malaria cure, on the Wagner-Jauregg's lines; that all exertion should be avoided, but it was most urgent that treatment should begin at once. I insisted on the dire threat to the entire German people, having at their head a man who was suffering from progressive paralysis —worse still in war-time and under an authoritarian system which forced him to make the gravest decisions on his own responsibility. I explained to Himmler that the illness might affect the mind by weakening the judgment and impairing the critical faculty, by producing delusions and especially megalomania; it might afflict the patient physically in the form of headaches, insomnia, loss of muscular force, trembling of the hands, confusion of speech, convulsions and paralysis of the limbs. I was quite unable to comprehend how he could choose the easy way and leave Hitler's treatment to Morell; he was taking a fearful responsibility on himself by permitting that orders be issued—and accepted as quite valid, which were in fact dictated by a man suffering from a severe illness. There was no means of telling whether such orders were issued in a lucid interval or under the direct influence of the disease—yet they might decide the fate of millions. Now that he knew the facts how would he receive the Führer's orders in future? Would he accept them and decide in every case whether they emanated from a sound mind or not?

As Himmler made no reply, I became more open and told him that he ought to regard Hitler as a sick man and get rid of the idea that he was the same Führer as he had known hitherto. Only a man of entirely sound mind could occupy the post of Führer. He had no need to recognize Hitler as Führer, once that condition was lacking.

Himmler answered wearily, shaking his head: "I've considered all that. Logically, you're right enough, but actually the situation is quite different. I told you yesterday that we'll lose the war once the Führer drops out. You must realize that we can't change horses in midstream. Our people would never be able to bear the shock."

"I just don't believe it," I objected. "The Führer has surely appointed a successor for such an eventuality who will come forward and take charge. It's relatively simple to make people accept things under an authoritarian system. You've got a propaganda minister too who's adroit enough to find the right way of presenting the matter. The Germans—and certainly the Allies as well—will see in Hitler's departure a chance of the peace for which they long."

"That sounds all very fine," Himmler replied, "but this is the crux of the matter—the Führer's will only envisages his death and makes no provision for a successor in any previous eventuality. Fierce quarrels over the succession would immediately break out between the army and the Party which would have a quite disastrous effect on the situation at home."

"But you've still got the SS, Herr Reichsführer," I retorted, "and Göring has his Luftwaffe! If you lay the facts of the case before a number of important generals, explaining to them that the Führer is a sick man and that he's got to abdicate in the interests of the nation as a whole, they'll gratefully recognize it as a most statesmanlike act on your part. If you were to add, Herr Himmler, that the rapid attainment of an honourable peace will be the new Führer's first duty, then you would command general support. In northern countries at all events Göring is regarded as the man for the job. There would be no difficulty about that, provided he has no ambition to copy Hitler in directing the war himself, but is content to leave it to a general, so long as the emergency lasts. But it's for you to make the first move."

"That's just it, Herr Kersten. I can't make a move against the Führer—I who am Reichsführer of the SS whose motto is 'My Honour is my Loyalty'. Everybody would think that my motives were selfish, that I was trying to seize power for myself. Of course I could get a medical opinion to justify my action, but everybody is aware how easily such opinions can be procured. Appearances are against me. You've got to have experienced the Führer's force of conviction and the way he has of presenting matters. Medical opinions are nothing in comparison, even those of the greatest authorities. What doctors regard as the Führer's clearly defined symptoms can just as easily be interpreted as the effects of fatigue and exhaustion, from which he can recover. The disease of which they really form part is only apparent when he's properly examined by specialists. But a thorough examination would only be possible if we took action, and that would be to attack the Führer's whole position and authority. And what if the diagnosis happened to be wrong? It wouldn't be so bad in the case of an ordinary person; he would simply go back to his business. But a Führer could never again assume responsibility for the Reich. I would have done untold harm to my people and got rid of the Reich's greatest man, who is still capable of the most grandiose ideas—and all because of a doctor's suspicions."

"Something more than mere suspicion," I replied, "according to that report. It states factually that the syphilis was contracted over twenty years ago and that the symptoms only disappeared after the acknowledged treatment for that particular disease."

"Perhaps," Himmler answered, "but you have overlooked spontaneous cures, admitted by medical science even in the case of cancer. Syphilis *need not* lead to progressive paralysis; the body can triumph over the infection. There's more likelihood of that in the Führer's case, for he neither smokes nor drinks, is a vegetarian and leads an entirely regular life. It's only because the Führer once suffered from syphilis that the doctors want to relate his symptoms to paralysis. The idea would probably never have occurred to them if they hadn't known that. But the possibility remains that the body has overcome the infection and that this is really no more than sheer exhaustion—not to be wondered at in view of the Führer's more than human labours. In these circumstances I cannot decide to take so drastic a step."

"But what will you do then?" I asked Himmler. "Will you simply let the matter alone and wait for Hitler's condition to get worse and worse? Can you endure the idea that the German people have at their head a man who is very probably suffering from progressive paralysis?"

Himmler reflected for a moment and then replied: "It has still not gone far enough; I'll watch carefully and it will be time enough to act once it's established that the report is correct."

That's how the talk concluded. I received the impression that Himmler really meant what he said; I only doubt whether he's capable of being objective in his observation. He regards Hitler as the greatest figure in the history of Germany, and depends so intimately on him, being used to executing his orders without question. I told Brandt that we had again discussed the report on Hitler's illness and made no bones about letting him know my views. He agreed with me and pointed out that Himmler could not attend to the matter, because Bormann had recently come between him and the Führer. The best of plans were meaningless unless Himmler could win over Bormann. But Himmler was much too weak with Bormann; his worst mistake was that he never used the power which he really possessed. Himmler was always at pains to live on the best of terms—at least outwardly— with those who were close to the Führer and able to influence him. He would never let it come to an open conflict with Bormann, nor give the latter a chance to shake Hitler's confidence in his loyalty. One had to recognize that clearly and not build up any false hopes.

Hartzwalde
4th February, 1943

I had a long conversation today with SS General Berger, who's in charge of the SS Head Office. He referred to rumours abroad that Hitler was suffering from syphilis and progressive paralysis; and he wanted to know whether I had heard anything of the sort during my trips abroad. I replied that I was reluctant to discuss the subject, but did recollect something of the kind. Berger said that Himmler's hints had been so obscure that he was still in doubt of the truth. He only knew for certain that Hitler had been gassed in the first war; he had heard nothing about the syphilis. There were some signs to indicate it, such as extreme irritability, but they might have a different origin. Berger was well enough aware of the disease's effect on varying age-groups, having observed numbers of men in his own unit. He had not been able to notice any of the typical symptoms in Hitler. It was possible that the gas had brought out some hereditary syphilitic infection. Anyhow it was risky even to allege that Hitler had syphilis.

"Yes, and very dangerous!" I replied. "Better not talk about it." I said that I had never examined Hitler, had never even seen him from close to, and had no opinion on the matter.

"Himmler's hint gave me a lot to think about," Berger answered. "Has he been taken in by some malicious rumour? Or is it really so? Or . . .?" Berger ended very seriously: "You're right. It's a dangerous subject—and very obscure. We'll keep our mouths shut and behave as if we had never raised the matter."

XXIV

THE DUTCH RESETTLEMENT PLAN

Berlin
1*st March,* 1941

AT SIX o'clock this afternoon Dr. Brandt let me have a look at secret documents about resettling the Dutch in eastern Poland. They comprised forty-three typewritten sheets in a yellow cover; they were signed by Hitler, countersigned by Bormann, and marked secret.

Their contents may be summarized as follows: The whole population of Holland, estimated at eight and a half million, was to be resettled by stages in eastern Poland. The first to go would be three million 'irreconcilables'—an expression which embraced all those who were likely to remain hostile to Germany even after she had won the war, together with their families.

The resettlement plan was a closely guarded secret, known only to very few. Details had not yet been worked out. But it was generally known that certain Dutch trade groups would be transferred to the East, farmers, market gardeners and others. The larger plan existed, however, for it was on paper and I had read it myself. The more limited scheme for transferring farmers and others has then to be regarded as the first stage of a more comprehensive resettlement. It served to camouflage the real plan which had to be kept secret for the time being, so as not to provoke world opinion against it prematurely.

Himmler alleged that a sudden impulse of Hitler's had produced this idea of resettling the entire Dutch population. There had been riots in Amsterdam in February 1941. Himmler was with Hitler when the news came through and told him, whereupon Hitler fell into a rage and broke out: "I'll resettle the lot of them. I'll make an end of these parasites." There and then he dictated the order for the resettlement.

10th March, 1941

I'm putting up a fight for Holland. The Dutch people's impending doom upset me so much that I couldn't sleep at all last night. In the last few days Himmler has been very unwell—always a favourable circumstance when trying to get him to do something. All this time I've repeatedly told him that he is trying his nervous system too severely, and that he can't expect to assume responsibility for resettling the Dutch without suffering for it. And surely it was an almost impossible strain on the Reich's transport system to attempt the transfer of over eight million men right across Germany in the middle of the war? They would block the lines of communication and impede the movement of troops. The flight of civilians in France had shown the sort of thing that would happen. It might occur just as easily in Germany, especially as the Dutch were not so highly disciplined as the Germans.

Himmler retorted that they would soon learn. So then I tried a different argument and said that it was beyond my comprehension how a man as highly intelligent as he could embark on so rash a proceeding as this one of resettling the Dutch. As his doctor it was my duty to warn him against the risk of undertaking so much extra work—it was more than his weakened physique could stand. I will continue to influence him in this direction.

6th April, 1941

Departure from Berlin for the Führer's headquarters at Bruck an der Mur in Styria. Himmler is beginning to give way a little on the Dutch resettlement question.

Himmler has been very ill in the last few weeks and he depends on me a great deal. My treatment is not proving as effective as before and Himmler is reduced to despair. I keep on telling him that he's putting too much strain on his nervous system and that I can't guarantee the success of my treatment unless he will take more rest. Himmler is begging me to do everything in my power, as he can't give up now. It would be such a terrible blow for Hitler. I go on retorting that he must obey my orders if he wants me to make him fit for work. Above all he mustn't take more responsibility on himself. The end of the war would be time enough to resettle the Dutch. Then it could be done without any trouble. Today I told him that if you put ten amps on a circuit made for six you're bound to blow a fuse.

16th April, 1941

At last Himmler is willing to postpone resettling the Dutch until after the war. His stomach cramps have grown so much worse that I was summoned to him three times today to treat them. The last time was at ten o'clock at night. He lay exhausted and twisted with pain on his chaise-longue. When I came into the room he just said: "Please help me, I can't bear any more pain."

"Yes, I'll help you," I replied, "but you must also listen to me and do what I consider best for your health. If you refuse, however, I'm afraid the day is coming when I'll no longer be able to help. I have a unique knowledge of your nervous system and of what you can stand and what you can't."

"I'll do anything you like," Himmler cried, "only stop these stomach-aches."

The pains yielded to a brief treatment and Himmler was visibly relieved. I made him see that the cramps had been provoked by over-work. That couldn't go on. He ought to leave the inessential and concentrate only on his most important tasks. He would have to postpone resettling the Dutch until he was better. Such a vast scheme was best put off until after the war. If he went on like that, he would have a breakdown one of these days. And then what would history say of him? That Himmler was one of those fools who let their work get on top of them.

"No, history shan't say that of me," said Himmler. "But what then do you advise?"

"Go straight to Hitler," I replied, "and tell him that it's not possible to resettle the Dutch at this time; that it must be put off until after the war. Both on account of the strain on rail transport and the regrouping of the Waffen SS which it would entail." (The Russian campaign was already planned and Himmler had to reorganize his Waffen SS.) Himmler replied that he would talk to Hitler the next day; he already had an appointment with him about another matter. But it was essential that he should be free of his stomach pains, otherwise he would not be able to go to the Führer. I've promised him that he'll have no pains tomorrow.

17th April, 1941

This morning I was back with Himmler by ten o'clock. He had slept well and was free of pain. He said that he was very grateful to me. The treatment over, I once more exhorted him to postpone resettling the Dutch until after the war. Now he has gone to Hitler.

18th April, 1941

Today Himmler informed me that Hitler had stated, both verbally and in writing, that the Dutch resettlement plan should be postponed until after the war. Himmler's words were: "Now I've carried out your wishes and got your Dutch a reprieve from the Führer. It's quite right that I should reserve my health for more important tasks. Apart from that, we've no transport to spare for the resettlement. But I will have to make a start on it as soon as the war is over."

I'm back at Hartzwalde at last. I gathered a bunch of snowdrops and crocuses in the garden and placed them in front of the picture of the Queen of Holland and Prince Henry on my writing table—a silent greeting to Holland.

XXV

THE NEW BIGAMY

1. *THE EXPERIMENTAL STAGE*

Salzburg
4th May, 1943

MOUNTING losses on the Eastern Front were causing Hitler great anxiety, Himmler told me. For they were consuming Germany's man-power and it was evident that they had to be replaced if the German people were to control the areas they had conquered. Therefore the Führer had decided, the moment the war was over, to make compre-hensive changes in the existing marriage laws and to introduce bigamy.

In its first stage this would not mean the general abolition of monogamy, but the right to contract a second marriage would be granted to holders of the German Cross in gold and holders of the Knights' Cross, as a special tribute to heroism in battle. This right would next be extended to holders of the Iron Cross First Class and to those who held the silver and gold clasps awarded for service in front-line fighting. This would embrace the majority of those with proven fighting qualities: it was of the utmost importance to the Reich that they should transmit these to their children. At the same time this would provide an opportunity to gather information on the practical results of bigamy. Then it could be decided whether to abolish mono-gamy entirely or to reserve bigamy only for those already mentioned, so that bigamy would come to an end when those entitled to it died out.

2. *EXISTING MARRIAGE LAWS IMMORAL?*

"My personal opinion," Himmler added, "is that it would be a natural development for us to break with monogamy. Marriage in its existing form is the Catholic Church's satanic achievement; marriage laws are in themselves immoral. The case-histories of monogamy so often show up the woman as thinking: 'Why should I take as much trouble with my appearance as before I was married? I've still got my status, which my husband can't alter, whether I indulge his whims and care for him or not, whether I dress to please him or not, whether I remain the woman of his dreams or not.' But with bigamy each wife would act as a stimulus to the other so that both would try to be their husband's dream-woman—no more untidy hair, no more sloveliness. Their models, which will intensify these reflections, will be the ideals of beauty projected by art and the cinema.

"The fact that a man has to spend his entire existence with one wife drives him first of all to deceive her and then makes him a hypocrite as he tries to cover it up. The result is indifference between the partners. They avoid each other's embraces and the final consequence is that they don't produce children. This is the reason why millions of children are never born, children whom the state urgently requires. On the other hand the husband never dares to have children by the woman with whom he is carrying on an affair, much though he would like to, simply because middle-class morality forbids it. Again it's the state which loses, for it gets no children from the second woman either."

3. ILLEGITIMATE CHILDREN

Himmler declared that there were many sides to this problem and went on: "This double standard expresses itself characteristically in the status which middle-class convention accords to the children born of such affairs, whom it calls illegitimate. It stipulates that they are no relation of their own father and his family. That in fact is the law—that a bastard and his father do not count as relations. Nature is robbed of her rights simply in order to keep up appearances in middle-class society. The father has no chance to do the most natural thing in the world: treat the child as his own and occupy himself with its upbringing. It's not his child in law, but the child of a woman who has no connection with him except for the fact that he gives her money. He's not allowed to marry the child's mother either, seeing that he's already married. The law calls it 'concubinage' if he lives with her and the police have to intervene in the disturbances caused by open scandal. Information of this kind is constantly being laid against my own people.

M

"A man in this situation has no access to his child. He's up against the law again if he wants to adopt the child, so long as he has children of his own or even has the possibility of having them. In other words, the law is in direct contradiction to our crying need—children and still more children. We must show courage and act decisively in this matter, even if it means arousing still greater opposition from the Church—a little more or less is of no consequence."

4. *A MATTER OF HABIT? THE 'DOMINA'*

Field Headquarters
7th May, 1943

While discussing bigamy with Himmler I used this argument: "You'll arouse the fiercest opposition among women, and that can't be a matter of indifference to you. Woman's present status in Western civilization depends on the institution you propose to overthrow. Do you really think that wives will accept a legally recognized rival without a struggle?"

"The first wife would keep special rights. She would have the title of 'Domina', which would be the official term. The second wife will know that beforehand. It's a matter of habit too. After a generation or two it will seem quite natural that a man should have two wives instead of one. We'll also grant the first wife the right to separate from her husband if she can't get on with the second wife, though he will have no obligation to support her after that. Why shouldn't polygamy work as well with us as it does in other countries?"

"Germany is not Asia," I objected. "You must remember that a city or small country town where people live in not more than half a dozen rooms will be the usual background for your bigamous marriages. I pity from the bottom of my heart the wretched husband who has daily to listen to and smooth down the quarrels of his two wives and their various children, with each mother championing her own offspring. The neighbours will also have something to say and the dear relations on both sides—just think, two mothers-in-law. In my opinion it would be easier to win the Knights' Cross than to endure that for long. You must create a special award for bravery under this domestic fire. The result will be that the poor tormented fellow, twice a husband, will leave his two legitimate wives to seek the rest and relaxation which he can't find at home in the arms of yet another woman."

5. THE MATERIAL BACKGROUND

Himmler laughed. "You exaggerate, of course; naturally the Führer has also given his mind to this aspect. His instructions as to what is requisite for bigamy are quite clear—that any man who has a right to it also acquires an estate. We'll have no difficulty about that, for the war has given us some excellent estates of this sort in the East. The troubles which would no doubt arise in towns quite disappear in rural surroundings, where everybody has to work hard at a clearly defined task. Bigamy will be easy there."

"Then one of the wives will be the mistress and force the other to be her maid. That's one of the oldest laws which you can do nothing about," I retorted. "That's why I admire the old Vikings who took the trouble to solve this problem properly."

"I can't recall the facts at the moment," Himmler answered, "tell me about it." He was always very interested when talk got on to Germanic customs.

I related to him how the monogamous principle had always prevailed on the Vikings' manors in Iceland, as with all Germanic peoples. The wife had remained undisputed mistress of the bastards whom the husband begat on the maid—and of the maid herself. This right had never been questioned. The Vikings had known very well what they were about. "You have at least to leave the status of the first wife untouched when you're dealing with circumstances such as that. She may put up with her husband's carrying on with another woman, but she'll never surrender her status as the lawful lady of the manor. Besides, you don't suppose that women are guided by ideologies and the needs of the state, Herr Himmler, to the point of letting such things affect the commanding position they have always held? Defence of her children and the struggle against a rival are among the oldest laws in this matter. A wife wants sole rights and sole control of her children for herself. She sees any other woman as a rival who will dispute these rights and whom she must eliminate. The rival on the other hand will be only too pleased to accept the ideological and political necessity of bigamy, in order to force her way into the existing marriage. But here again the old law obtains, for she does this to make a place for her own children—in other words, she too is struggling against her rival. No ideologies will help you here, the best of rules and regulations are no good. You ought to seek advice from women and hear their opinions, before you start setting up such laws as these, instead of leaving the task to men who, however honest they are, will be quick to see bigamy as a social necessity, simply in order to legalize their own intrigues."

Himmler seemed vastly amused. "I've never heard you talk like this before, my dear Herr Kersten. You sound just like a suffragette. Have you been listening to an apostle of women's rights? Of course there's something in what you say, but you don't understand how much can be done in this field by the power of education and a propaganda that's really to the point. Consider this: only a few years ago a bastard was still regarded as a disgrace. A man was afraid to admit that he had an illegitimate child. In the SS I've systematically gone about defying existing laws and explaining to my men that children are always a great blessing, legitimate or not. What's been the result? Now my men tell me with shining eyes that they have just had an illegitimate child. Their girls regard it as an honour, not a disgrace, in defiance of the law's present attitude. You can read announcements of these births any day in the *Schwarze Korps*. Aren't these the results of education?"

6. THE 'LEBENSBORN' (MATERNITY HOME FOR UN-MARRIED MOTHERS)

Himmler continued: "Here's another case in point. My first aim in setting up the *Lebensborn* was to meet a crying need and to give unmarried women, who were racially pure, the chance to have their children free of cost. There they could pass the weeks before the birth of their child in agreeable surroundings and quietly await the great event. You can hardly realize how much it means to a woman, who used to be cold-shouldered and insulted because her child was illegitimate, to enter a home where she can relax spiritually and physically, receive medical attention and feel that everybody is glad about the child she's going to have. At first the *Lebensborn* was regarded with middle-class disapproval and distrust. Now it enjoys the greatest respect. It accords protection and spiritual succour to those who give birth to illegitimate children. Even married women have their children in the *Lebensborn*; nowadays they account for fifty per cent of the confinements. But no difference is made between married and unmarried women—they're all addressed by their Christian names, without any Fräulein or Frau tacked on. So none of them knows who is married and who isn't. This is genuine love of one's neighbour. It ought to be brought home to those clerics who go on about unmarried mothers in the pulpit and quite ignore how they are turning people against the unfortunate women. Even women who don't belong to the Party, even brunettes, they're all taken in, not just the blondes. Only thoroughly inferior specimens are refused admittance and left to the old-fashioned lying-in hospitals."

7. 'CONCEPTION-ASSISTANTS'

9th May, 1943

We continued our recent talks and, to my astonishment, Himmler explained that he had gone even further in this matter. "Privately I let it be known that any unmarried woman who was alone in the world but longed for a child might turn to the *Lebensborn* with perfect confidence. The Reichsführing SS would sponsor the child and provide for its education. I was well aware that this was a revolutionary step. According to the existing middle-class code an unmarried woman has no right to long for a child. She has to wait respectably until the man comes along who'll grant her desire. If he fails to appear, she must simply accept her fate. Generally she doesn't find the right man or is unable to marry on account of her work, but she still wants a child. I realized this and I've given such women the opportunity to have the child they want. The woman receives assistance, has the happy experience of being a mother and for the first time plays her full part in the life of the community, while the state receives a valuable addition to the nation. For you can imagine that we only employ valuable and racially pure men as 'Conception-assistants'.

"I waited eagerly to see how much use would be made of this service. At first of course nothing happened, but each year brings some improvement—and you'll see what we shall make of the scheme once the war is over. Our propaganda will be subtle and unobtrusive, but highly effective: it will become a point of honour with every woman, and her duty to the Reich, if she's still childless at the age of thirty, to have children in this way. That will be the *Lebensborn's* finest hour! Things will have reached such a pitch one of these days that nobody will object when we make it no longer voluntary but compulsory by law. Anyhow our initiative has already broken down the prejudices that used to exist. That's why I'm confident that we'll have the same success with bigamy and overcome every sort of psychological difficulty that stands in the way. There is one purpose behind all these measures, bigamy, assisting the birth of illegitimate children and as a necessary consequence putting them on the same legal footing as those born in wedlock. This purpose is to safeguard and improve the racial qualities of the Greater German Reich, so that it can accomplish its great tasks both in the centre of Europe and against the increasing avalanche of Asian peoples."

11th May, 1943

When I watch Himmler expounding, I constantly have the impression of a scholar, yet also of a prophet deeply convinced of what he says. He paces up and down the room, then when he comes to some very important point halts in front of me and fixes me with a compelling stare through his glasses, in order to give more effect to what he's saying. At such moments it is easy to understand the great influence he exerts over his staff of Leaders, awkward and hesitant though he often appears. An outsider, only noting his extremely donnish and bespectacled appearance, would find this hard to believe.

8. *HISTORICAL INSTANCES*

As so often, Himmler went back into history for instances and declared: "Every country in Europe can show examples of rulers who have had a second wife whose children have been respected and placed on the same footing as those of the first wife. Charlemagne was a case in point. The Emperor Arnulf was an illegitimate child, as was Dunois, the famous Bastard of Orleans, and even William the Conqueror of England. It was the habit with princes, simply because they could afford it. Nor was it the practice only for a brief period; it endured from the rise of the Germanic states to well past the Renaissance, until it finally became the accepted thing in royal families. Many who can afford it still do the same thing today, but in the old days it all happened quite naturally without any attempt at concealment, while nowadays it's all hushed up.

"What bitter deceptions await the girls and women who are disposed to do the same thing in all honesty nowadays! Once this instinct is accepted as natural, all that can be avoided. Didn't Goethe say: 'Man is polygamous by nature, woman monogamous.' Why? Because a man's real sexual instincts extend over a wide field, whereas a woman's protective instincts for her children incline her to monogamy. There are often material grounds for this, but where none exist the idea of sin intervenes, because the Church needs it, and this idea is the surest way of overcoming man's strongest instinct."

14th May, 1943

A mirage, startling in its bold splashes of colour, hovers over this group of talks on 'Bigamy'. It arises from a one-sided view of history and an ideology no less one-sided. One fact may help to elucidate it— Himmler's great-grandfather was an illegitimate child.

XXVI

THE BURGUNDIAN FREE STATE

Salzburg
6th March, 1943

HIMMLER told me that Hitler had in mind the foundation of a new state as soon as the peace treaties were under discussion. Burgundy was to be reconstructed in a modern form; it was unique, and in its possibilities one of the richest states there had ever been. The new state would include: the old Burgundian possessions, in the north, Artois, Hainault and Luxembourg; Lorraine, Franche-Comté and the old Duchy of Burgundy; in the south, Dauphiné and Provence; to these would be added Picardy, including Amiens, and Champagne, including Rheims and Troyes. This new state of Burgundy would have access both to the English Channel and to the Mediterranean. Hitler had not yet decided on the capital, but the claims of Rheims and Dijon were being considered. German and French would be the official languages. The state would be governed by a Reichs administrator and a Chancellor. Léon Degrelle, leader of the Belgian Rexists, was being considered as the first Reich's administrator, since he had so distinguished himself at the front. Burgundy would be an independent state within the European Reich, having its own laws, its own army and government, its own currency, stamps and honours. The celebrated Order of the Golden Fleece would be revived; its Grand Master would be a French SS Leader.

The state would have to be so constituted that it entirely eliminated the contrast between possessions and destitution—the hallmark of Marxism. Thus it would embrace Burgundy's newly emerging nation in one social community. The civil service would be drawn from the local population. Specialists and advisers could be taken from the

European SS, should the Chancellor consider that necessary. These SS Leaders would then acquire Burgundian nationality as well as their own. The aim was to turn Burgundy into a model state, an example to all the other countries in the world.

I protested that Burgundy would be a state dominated by the German Nazi Party. Himmler asserted that this would not be the case, for Hitler had expressly stipulated that no German Party authority would have the right to interfere in Burgundian affairs. There would be a Burgundian embassy in Berlin and a German one in Burgundy.

Himmler had once again worked himself up into a mood of enthusiasm: "I'll see to it that Burgundy is permeated by the philosophy of the SS, so that the model state of the Führer's dreams will come into being."

7th March, 1943

We returned to the subject of Burgundy. Himmler said: "Throughout her history, France has been attacking Germany. Just look at the frontiers on a map from the year 919 to 1919. In these thousand years France has grown a third larger, always at Germany's expense. She has employed violent and incendiary attacks—you have only to consider the Palatinate and the burning down of Heidelberg Castle. She has used trickery, she has broken treaties, she has waged war. To be sure the essential blame rests with the German princes, who after the decline of the Hohenstaufens destroyed the unity of the Reich and with it the unity of Europe. But France betrayed Europe! At the peace treaties of 1648, which concluded the Thirty Years' War, it was France which insisted on conditions which not only maintained but prolonged the chaos of centuries in Germany. For France then asserted that this chaos was 'a dispensation of Providence'. The French have constantly caused destruction in Europe; they have an acquisitive instinct and they fear for what they call their security, which only shows their guilty conscience towards Europe."

I protested that the arguments on the French side were not very different, that Germany had always been a menace to France. Himmler's reply was: "Just read what Moltke said about the French when discussing the surrender at Sedan. That's the best description of how France has acted towards Germany over a thousand years. And you can't say anything against Moltke, for he came from Denmark—your beloved Scandinavia."

8th March, 1943

When we continued our talk about Burgundy, I enquired what would be left to France. The state of Burgundy would mean a loss of territory such as she could hardly endure; that would cause trouble.

Himmler replied: "The Führer is sick of the idea that France, with her hysteria and degeneracy, should occupy the same place in the Europe of the future, at the side of Germany, as she has held in the past. The French ruling class have made trouble and bloodshed for Germany over the centuries. Until the decline of the Hohenstaufens, and later, the Reich held territory which included the towns of Marseilles, Lyons, Besançon, Verdun, Cambrai, Arras and Dunkirk. Burgundy will acquire all the territory that France has annexed unjustly. Burgundy has an historic right to that. The spirit of European unity must replace the old selfish and separatist attitude in the rest of France. That too is a product of history. Frenchmen of the better sort, who have recognized Hitler's greatness and the need for a new order in Europe, can acquire Burgundian nationality. The others can have the rest of France, which will be known as Gaul."

When I remarked that only an Asiatic conqueror would think of treating an old and civilized people in this way, Himmler declared that the Gauls had asked for it and deserved nothing better. Gaul would, moreover, be a free state and could decide whether to federate with the Reich or remain on her own.

XXVII

KERSTEN MOVES TO SWEDEN

Stockholm
2nd October, 1943

I TRAVELLED to Stockholm on the 30th of September, 1943. During my stay I visited the Swedish Foreign Minister Günther, who had followed with close attention my efforts on behalf of the so-called Warsaw Swedes. He himself was working out a vast rescue scheme for Scandinavians and representatives of other nations under arrest in the Third Reich, thus following Sweden's humanitarian and neutral traditions. We discussed these matters and came to the conclusion that I might be useful to the Minister in his work. I received from the Swedish Government the first lists of Scandinavians and other nationals who were under arrest in Germany; I was to endeavour to secure their release.

First of all, however, I had to talk Himmler over, so that he would put no obstacles in the way of my own and my family's departure for Sweden. I would certainly have met with a refusal if I had expressed my wish without giving reasons which appealed to Himmler personally. But how was I to set about it? I consulted with the Finnish Ambassador Kivimäki, to whom I always went when I had some delicate matter to discuss. The upshot of our conversation was that I should inform Himmler that I might shortly be obliged to give up treating him, for I was going to be called up as a doctor in the Finnish Army. But there was a way of getting round the summons. In view of my relations with the Reichsführer SS the Finnish Embassy was prepared quietly to arrange matters so that I could treat Finnish soldiers who were convalescing in Sweden. This would also make it possible for me to travel to Himmler's headquarters and continue the course of treatments.

As by this time the tension between Germany and Finland was already becoming noticeable, after some reflection Himmler consented to my moving to Sweden. On the one hand he did not want to lose me, whatever happened, and on the other he wanted to avoid any sort of friction with Finland at that time.

I moved to Stockholm on the 30th of September, 1943. Since I flew to Sweden as a Finnish courier with dispatch boxes, I was able to take some of my secret papers with me without any danger.

Stockholm
3rd October, 1943

Today I visited the Graffman family at Danderyd near Stockholm. Frau Graffman comes from Holland and her parents are patients of mine. It's delightful to find Dutch acquaintances here so unexpectedly. Holger Graffman is a Swede and a very decent man. Today an American, Abram Stevens Hewitt, came to coffee. He is Roosevelt's special representative here in Stockholm. I am fortunate to have found a man in close touch with America. Perhaps an opportunity will arise to help Finland towards making peace. But it must be peace with honour. I had a long conversation today with Hewitt, who also speaks German, so that we can understand each other very well. He would like to receive treatment from me, as his health is not very good. I will be very glad to do that and will start right away tomorrow. A very satisfactory Sunday. . . .

I'm living at the Belfrage Pension in Stockholm. Here I've got to know a charming couple, Baron and Baroness von Delwig. He is related to the Hoppenhof Delwigs, whom I often met as a child. Memories of old Livonia come back to me.

PEACE TALKS WITH MR. HEWITT

Stockholm
12th October, 1943

Mr. Hewitt and I get on very well together. We are both of the opinion that this terrible war must be brought to an end. But Hewitt is right in saying that the world refuses to make peace with a National Socialist Germany. However, my first thoughts are for Finland; and

Finland and America are not at war. Hewitt believes that it is quite possible that President Roosevelt may intervene to arrange peace between Finland and Russia, as America still has great sympathy for Finland. I told Hewitt that Finland is not altogether bound to National Socialist Germany, and that the Finns themselves dislike National Socialism. It was only despair over our Winter War with Russia which made us Germany's allies. Hewitt said that he could appreciate that and was prepared to act as an intermediary. But Finland had to make the first move. I told him that I was going to fly to Finland in a few days' time, in order to make a report about Germany, and that I would also take the opportunity of mentioning my talks with him. For it's my sincere wish that Finland should break away from the Axis powers and make peace. Probably I'll fly to Helsinki on the 15th of October.

Stockholm
24th October, 1943

Today being Sunday I again called on Graffman at Danderyd. He is a very intelligent and far-sighted person. We talked about the military situation. He said that Germany will not and cannot win the war, because American technology and aircraft production are on a scale that will overwhelm Germany. I agreed but stated my conviction that Germany could last for another couple of years. But Graffman disagreed and believed that Germany would break up in another six months. What would happen then, I enquired. Graffman said that it would at least be an end of Hitler's Reich, but there would be dark days for Europe, and for that reason the sooner peace was made the better. I replied: "Yes, that's what I think and hope. In my opinion, the West underestimates the danger from the East." Graffman said that he did not underestimate this himself. That's why it was so urgently necessary to make peace in good time.

I enquired whether we couldn't speak to Hewitt about it. Graffman replied that Hewitt would be coming to Danderyd in about an hour's time, when we could discuss the matter together. But nobody would make peace with Hitler; the *régime* had to go first. I said: "That may be possible. I can talk to Himmler about it, for I think that he's ready to discuss matters." Hewitt came at six in the evening and we began our talk the moment he arrived. He too recognizes the danger from the East. I offered to fly to Himmler to explore the possibilities of peace. Hewitt declared that the first demands which the U.S.A. and England would make were the evacuation of all occupied territories, abolition of the Nazi Party and the SS, with free and democratic elections to follow under American and British control; abolition of the Hitler dictatorship; and the leading Nazis to be secured in concentration camps. Those responsible for war-crimes would have to stand their trial. The German Army would have to be reduced to a point where it could no longer be used as an instrument for aggression.

I told Hewitt: "I think that Himmler might possibly accept these conditions, provided that an exception is made in his own case and his personal freedom guaranteed." Hewitt and Graffman agree that we must discuss the whole idea in detail. Hewitt will sound American opinion. We must clarify the offers and demands to be made in the next few weeks. Then Hewitt will fly to America and discuss the matter with Roosevelt.

Here follows the copy of a letter written to Himmler from Stockholm on the 24th of October, 1943, and sent by way of the Finnish diplomatic bag:

Dear Herr Reichsführer,

I am taking advantage of this Sunday evening to communicate to you proposals which might have the greatest significance for Germany, for Europe, even for the entire world. What I offer is the possibility of an honourable peace.

I have an American patient here in Stockholm; his name is Abram Stevens Hewitt (he is not a Jew) and he is in close contact with the American Government. He is here on a mission and working for the American Foreign Minister Stettinius. We have had many discussions together and, in view of the ever mounting destruction caused by the war, we have worked out proposals for peace talks. I beg of you not to throw this letter into your waste-paper basket, Herr Reichsführer, but receive it with the humanity which resides in the heart of Heinrich Himmler. In centuries yet to come the gratitude of the entire world will still be yours. It is not easy for me, as a Finn, to conduct peace negotiations on behalf of Germany. I ask you, therefore, to send somebody to me here in Stockholm who enjoys your entire confidence, so that I can introduce him to Mr. Hewitt. Please don't hesitate, but decide at once, Herr Reichsführer—the fate of Europe hangs on it.

Herr Schellenberg seems to me the person indicated, as he also speaks English.

Lose no time, I beg of you, Herr Reichsführer. Every day wasted means that thousands of Germans, English and Americans must die, every day brings greater destruction.

I send you the seven points which I have worked out with Mr.

Hewitt and Herr Holger Graffman, another of my patients. They may serve as a basis for the peace talks which will follow:

1. Evacuation of all territories occupied by Germany and restitution of their sovereignty.

2. Abolition of the Nazi Party; democratic elections under American and British supervision.

3. Abolition of Hitler's dictatorship.

4. Restitution of the 1914 German frontier.

5. Reduction of German army and air force to a size excluding the possibility of aggression.

6. Complete control of the German armament industry by the Americans and the British.

7. Removal of the leading Nazis and their appearance before a court charged with war-crimes.

These points are acceptable to all parties and I beg of you to seize this favourable opportunity, Herr Reichsführer. Fate and history itself have placed it in your hands to bring an end to this terrible war.

Yours respectfully,
Felix Kersten.

Stockholm
25th October, 1943

I was in Finland from the 15th to the 19th of October. The new Finnish Foreign Minister Ramsay had asked me to report to him. I informed him that Germany's military situation was desperate and that she could only last another couple of years at the outside. I thought that a complete collapse would then follow. I considered it absolutely necessary that Finland should now put out peace feelers, in order to escape from German pressure which could no longer be so severe as before. I also told Ramsay that in Stockholm I could establish contact with Roosevelt, should he so desire, as his special representative there, Mr. Hewitt, was a patient of mine; and I could act as go-between. I advised Ramsay to conduct these negotiations, however, through Gripenberg, the Finnish Ambassador in Stockholm.

Ramsay was very pleased about this contact and commissioned me to put Gripenberg in touch with Hewitt. This took place yesterday. I also told Ramsay that Himmler had still not been able to forget the Finnish Jews; he had questioned me on this matter again and said that he had instructions from Hitler to go into it. But in order to gain time I had at once offered to go into it myself. Ramsay commended me for this and asked me to do what I could to quieten the authorities in Germany when I went back there. I told him that I would proceed in this matter exactly as before.

I spent two hours over coffee with President Ryti on the 16th of October. He's very worried. German pressure on Finland is still strong. He knows that Finland needs peace, but can't see how to get it. Thank God we're not at war with America. That's his great hope.

Stockholm
1st November, 1943

Peace talks with Hewitt and Graffman are progressing well. Both of them see the danger threatening in the East. Graffman said: "Once Europe's economy is shattered it will be at the mercy of Communist Russia."

A few days ago I wrote to Himmler about my meeting with Hewitt and asked him to send Schellenberg to Stockholm. It's of the first importance that he should see Hewitt. I can't intervene in peace talks between America and Germany, since I'm a Finn. I am in a state of tension, wondering whether Schellenberg will come.

I've been twice with Hewitt to see Gripenberg. Hewitt has great sympathy for Finland's difficult position.

Stockholm
9th November, 1943

Schellenberg has arrived in Stockholm. I've introduced him to Hewitt and they get on well together. It's my sincere wish that this contact will lead to peace.

Hochwald
4th December, 1943

This morning I tried to make Himmler realize that it was time for him to come to a decision about my negotiations in Stockholm with Hewitt and Graffman. I told him: "No country in Europe is getting anything out of this war; it's time it was stopped." The moment had come for him to decide.

Himmler replied: "Ach, don't torment me, give me time. I can't get rid of the Führer, to whom I owe everything." Then he went on: "It was he who gave me the position I now hold—and am I now to use my position as Reichsführer to overthrow the Führer? It's quite beyond

me, Herr Kersten. Try to understand. Read the pledge of loyalty which
I have taken as my motto. Am I to ignore all that and become a
traitor? For heaven's sake don't ask that of me, Herr Kersten."

My reply was: "I'm not asking you for anything. But the German
people and Europe await your decision. You're the only man who can
make it. Don't hesitate, Herr Reichsführer, grant peace to Europe, if
you really want to appear before history as a great Germanic Leader.
In Stockholm Mr. Hewitt is waiting for your decision, so that he can
take it to Roosevelt. Seize your chance—it never comes a second
time."

Himmler replied: "The conditions that Schellenberg put before me
are hardly acceptable. Consider the sacrifices we have made, Herr
Kersten. Are they all to be in vain? How can I take the responsibility
for that when faced with the Leaders of the Party?"

"You will have no responsibility towards them," I retorted, "for
they will have ceased to exist. But if you now follow the path
of peace, you will received the German people's gratitude and
Europe's."

"I've carefully studied the letter you sent me from Stockholm,"
said Himmler. "The conditions are hair-raising. But perhaps one might
discuss them if the situation became really grave. However, one
condition is quite unacceptable: that we should accept responsibility
for certain war-crimes which are no crimes in our eyes. For everything
that's been done in Germany under the Führer's *régime* has been
carried out with a due regard for the law."

Even the annihilation of the Poles and the Jews, I enquired.

"Certainly, that also assumed a legal form," Himmler said
"Because the Führer ordered the annihilation of the Jews in Breslau in
1941. And the Führer's orders are the supreme law in Germany."

After a time Himmler added: "I've never acted on my own
initiative, I've only carried out the Führer's orders. So neither I nor the
SS can accept any responsibility."

"Then who in your opinion is responsible?" I enquired. "Hitler?"

"Certainly," Himmler replied. "I'm quite prepared to admit that.
If anybody must be held responsible, then it's the Führer. But that's a
legal question and I know nothing about the law. So there's no point
in our discussing the matter."

I said that I nevertheless had to discuss my peace talks in Stockholm
with him. Himmler took from his wallet the letter I had sent from
Stockholm outlining the peace conditions. "H'm, evacuation of all
occupied territories," he said; "that's a very hard condition. You
should reflect that the conquest of those lands has cost us some of

Germany's best blood, Herr Kersten. But if it has to be, I might be able to agree to it. Then, for instance, you've put here—recognition of the 1914 frontiers. Mr. Hewitt is not going to leave us with very much. For security's sake we must extend a hundred miles or so further east than that.

"Democratic elections in Germany," Himmler went on, "under American and English supervision. I've no objection to that. Removal of the Führer and abolition of the Party? What am I to do about that?"

"It's your affair what you do about it," I replied, "but it's got to be done. For the Allies will never come to terms with the Party nor with the Führer."

"Yes, that's the bit that's hardest to swallow," Himmler retorted. "It means cutting the ground from under my own feet." He reflected. "And then this piece of nonsense," he cried, very much upset: "I'm to include in the peace terms the Allies' right to hold Germans responsible for what they're pleased to call war-crimes. That's complete madness, Herr Kersten. We Germans aren't criminals, we've committed no war-crimes. We're a decent people who have fought honourably. Perhaps it's not a crime that the Allies in the last few years have been reducing our towns to ruins. Can't you realize that in the event of a German defeat Russia—and possibly ten years later America—will dominate Europe?

"Next on your list comes reduction of the German Army to a size which will make aggression impossible. What does Mr. Hewitt mean by that? Are we to go back to an army of a hundred thousand? We could offer no resistance to the Russians with that. Germany needs an army of at least three millions if she is to protect Europe from the East."

A few minutes later Himmler said in a tired voice: "I can't come to a decision today. Hewitt will be in Stockholm for a few days longer. Your proposals aren't unacceptable to me, except for the one about responsibility for alleged war-crimes."

I asked Himmler whether I might let Hewitt and Graffman know that he, Himmler, was agreed in principle.

"Ach, wait a few more days," Himmler replied. "I've got to think it over. I realize that this war is a disaster for everybody. And if I can do anything to stop it, I will. But America must also show some signs of goodwill."

This talk between the Reichsführer SS, Heinrich Himmler, and myself took place on the 4th of December, 1943, at Hochwald, the Field Headquarters in East Prussia. The talk began early in the morning at a quarter past nine and finished at ten minutes to eleven.

Hochwald
9th December, 1943

I've been trying hard all day to bring Himmler to make peace. It has become a real battle between us. Himmler always falls back on the argument: "I can't betray my Führer. Everything that I an , I owe to him. I was nothing before he put me in my present position. And now I'm to leave him in the lurch—it's a terrifying thought."

Gradually Himmler calmed down and realized that something had to be done. This morning at a quarter to ten he said that he had come to the end of his inner conflict and was ready to negotiate with Hewitt for peace on the basis of my proposals. But he wanted it to be understood that Germany was neither defeated nor in a state of collapse, and that her military strength was unimpaired. Still, he was prepared to take this step in consideration of the world's need for peace. However, he demanded that America should make an effort to understand Germany and should show signs of good faith.

Himmler commissioned me to let Hewitt know, but considered it essential that the utmost secrecy should be observed concerning the negotiations.

Field Headquarters
13th December, 1943

When I returned to Himmler this morning, I told him that the moment had come to bring peace to Europe and her tortured peoples. "Have you already forgotten our recent talks?" I asked him. "Must you still concern yourself with trivialities?"

"Ach yes, you're quite right," Himmler replied, "I've got too much on my mind. And I've got no colleague I can really trust, who could take the constant burden of routine off my shoulders. And if I think there is a man who could represent me, then he goes too far and behaves like a bull in a china-shop."

"And who is now demanding that you should kill all prisoners of war out of hand," I added, "so as to blacken your name for all time."

"You're mistaken," Himmler replied. "None of my Leaders has discussed that with me; that's my concern. A few days ago the Führer spoke to me about it—it was his idea."

"And don't you realize, Herr Reichsführer, that such ideas can only issue from a sick mind?" I asked.

"I've no right to consider that, Herr Kersten."

"You've got to consider it," I replied, "And now you must take action to prevent Adolf Hitler from heaping more disasters on Europe."

"Yes, yes, yes, you're right, I know it, I know it, I know it," Himmler replied. "I never stop thinking about your negotiations with Hewitt. I've told you that I'm agreed in principle. This morning, too, the idea came to me whether it might not be better to invite Hewitt here. It doesn't matter whether he flies to America from Stockholm or via Germany and Lisbon. Then we can quietly go over the proposals in detail. And he would be in a better position for discussing them with Roosevelt."

I agreed that this was a good idea, but considered that it might give Ribbentrop a chance to intervene.

"Certainly not; there's no danger of that," said Himmler. "We'll let Hewitt fly in without a visa and keep the Foreign Office out of it. The best way would be for you to fly to Stockholm with an authorization to say that the gentleman who flies back with you is entitled to cross the frontier without showing his papers. Then you go with Hewitt to Hartzwalde and I'll meet him there. We'll provide for his departure to Spain in the same way."

I agreed that this was the best way to discuss matters with Hewitt, but asked Himmler to choose another man, as this was entirely a matter between Germany and America, nor did I desire any active rôle in politics. Schellenberg would be the man for the job. Besides, Schellenberg had made a very good impression on Hewitt, who would also agree to this choice.

"Do you really think it's better that Schellenberg should go to Stockholm instead of you to invite Hewitt?" Himmler enquired.

"Certainly, Herr Reichsführer," I replied. I had made contact with Hewitt in order to be of service to Europe. And in this case I regarded myself simply as a doctor who prescribed a medicine to cure his patient. But it was the patient himself who had to take the medicine. That was not the doctor's job.

"Yes, yes, that's true enough," Himmler agreed, "I'll send for Schellenberg and discuss it with him. We would be able to agree on all conditions except for this damned war-crimes business—the Americans must drop that. It goes against our German honour." Those were Himmler's words.

When I had written down this conversation, I went to Brandt and told him how matters stood. Brandt was glad that Himmler was at last prepared to end the war. He said that for a long time the Führer's orders had seemed to him to be getting more and more peculiar. How splendid it would be if we got peace. He would then immediately emigrate from Germany. Brandt asked me: "And where will you go after the war?" "To Holland," I said, "where I belong."

Gut Hartswalde
22nd December, 1943

This morning I was able to secure the release of 6 Germans, 8 Dutchmen, 4 Esthonians and a Dane, all of whom were due to be shot.

Postscript

Some time passed before Schellenberg went, and when he finally reached Stockholm he was unable to make contact with Hewitt, who had left for Washington, as the time-limit agreed upon had already elapsed.

XXVIII

SETTLING WITH THE DIEHARDS

Hochwald
20th June, 1944

HIMMLER told me today that he had been talking with Hitler last night about those diehards who find fault with everything and are too stupid to grasp the magnitude of the Führer's achievements for Germany, while they themselves only prejudice and weaken the German position. "They are a national disgrace," he declared, "and among them are millions who are aiding the enemy unawares and undermining the National Socialist state. They're doing a good job of work for the Jews. But in spite of them the German nation, which is fundamentally decent, will win through to the victory which has cost it so dear. But those who are a national disgrace will have no share in that victory. For it's the Führer's express wish that we should proceed relentlessly against them as soon as the war is over. They deserve no pity."

"But who are these men you call a national disgrace?" I interjected.

"They're the reactionaries and the men in the old city corporations. They're to be found on their country estates, in their factories, businesses and offices making capital out of the disasters that fall on decent National Socialists. We'll have a thorough clean-up after the war, oust these men from their country estates and their factories, remove them from their posts, withdraw their concessions and destroy the basis of their existence."

I protested that men of this class were nevertheless doing their duty at the front. "There will be nothing to reproach in our treatment of those soldiers and their families who have stood the test," Himmler replied. "But it's by no means unusual to find that soldiers from this class have little stomach for fighting. The Führer declares that the majority of the old officers' corps are anti-National Socialist. In other

198

words—they're traitors. And after the war traitors will have no right
to live. The Führer's patience is at last exhausted."

I protested that I could only regard it as a monstrous crime if men
of this sort, who could be counted by the million, were to be struck
down simply because they thought differently from Hitler, but were in
other respects Germans and men of honour. Himmler only replied
that the Führer never committed a crime. He, Himmler, and the best
elements in the nation were convinced National Socialists and daily
gave thanks to Providence that it had accorded them the great good
fortune to be allowed to serve Adolf Hitler, who was the greatest
German of all time. He would be happy to sacrifice his life for him at
any moment—hundreds of thousands had already given their lives for
this ideal.

"Now just take a look at these diehards: all over the place they're
quietly carrying out sabotage and crimes against the nation. You need
only consider one case: an industrialist had invented a brilliant new
means of transport which would ensure a safe passage to Africa without
any danger from torpedoes. He constructed one of these transports at
his own expense—tens of thousands of marks—and offered the
prototype to the appropriate committee. But there were diehards ready
for sabotage sitting on this committee and they had a similar transport
constructed at a different shipyard, ostensibly according to this same
design. But the speciality of their design was that it included a fault in
construction. This second ship was sent on its trial trip and was
naturally a failure. Then the committee announced that the whole
system of construction was unsound, so that there was no need to try
out the prototype, as that too would be unpracticable. The result was
to abandon the construction of these transports. With the further
result that the Africa Corps was never provided with the right transports, the African campaign was lost, and thousands of German
soldiers perished in consequence. The diehards are responsible for their
death. Thousands of these diehards are engaged in sabotage all over the
place.

"They sabotage the production of new weapons and aircraft; they
draw up grandiose designs for wooden barracks without shelters which
are destroyed by bombs; they misdirect trains carrying munitions and
machinery, so that in one place munitions pile up and go to waste
while in another there are neither munitions nor fuel, with the result
that our tanks can neither move nor use their guns and the front can
only be held by throwing away more lives. These diehards are responsible for the deaths of untold thousands."

"I just can't believe it," I replied. "These are either products of the imagination or items invented by interested parties, police spies who have got to say something to earn their pay."

"Interested parties?" said Himmler. "I've got evidence, some of it evidence from people who don't even belong to the Party, let alone the Gestapo—men who are simply horrified at the fate that has befallen their own sons and brothers. If the diehards were to kill one of us who're at the head of affairs, that wouldn't be nearly so bad as these cowardly and insidious methods of theirs. They are killing tens and hundreds of thousands of men who are young and trusting, simply in order to get at us, to do us harm and undermine our position. They're climbing over the heaped-up bodies of men who've died fighting for Germany.

"Are they fools enough to think that the Soviets are so humane that they should contribute to their victory? I'm praying for the day when I have the chance to settle accounts with these murderous and reactionary swine. And I'll avenge every murdered man a thousand times over. I refuse to discuss this subject. Not even with you, Herr Kersten."

XXIX

HIMMLER AND THE 20TH OF JULY

Hochwald
20th July, 1944

DURING the treatment this morning Himmler told me that the Americans were at present having great trouble with the Russians. Serious conflicts were going to arise between them which would eventually have a decisive effect on the future course of the war.

In the morning I also had time for quite a long walk and after lunch I went to rest. Suddenly there were shouts of alarm. Sturmbannführer Lukas, Himmler's driver, burst into my sleeping car crying: "Attempt on the Führer's life! Attempt on the Führer! But the Führer still lives, nothing has happened to him, he's safe! We have just come with the Reichsführer from the *Wolfschanze.*"[1]

I at once put on my shoes and overcoat and went to the Reichsführer. The guard on his quarters had been doubled, but with my pass I was able to get through. I entered Himmler's office without knocking. He was standing by his desk; I looked at him for a moment and saw that he was arranging and destroying certain papers. Then I asked him: "What's really the matter, Herr Reichsführer?"

Himmler answered me without looking up: "A bomb was thrown at the Führer. But Providence has saved him."

I enquired whether he had any further information.

"The attempt was made by a Colonel in the Wehrmacht," he replied. "Now my hour has come. I will round up all the reactionary gang and have already given orders for the traitors' arrest."

"Whom do you propose to arrest? Are you so sure of who they are? I hope you won't get hold of the wrong people, Herr Reichsführer." Himmler further consulted his papers. "How was it really possible

---

[1] The Wolf's Lair, the name of Hitler's secret headquarters in East Prussia. *Tr.*

for such an attempt to have been made, Herr Himmler," I asked, "without your intelligence network and your secret service knowing anything about it? Won't they be greatly blamed? Isn't there a special small organization whose sole task is to guard Hitler—how can they have failed?"

Himmler made no answer, only burrowing more deeply into his papers. but I questioned him again: "Do you remember, Herr Reichsführer, that some eighteen months ago you showed me a report about the Führer's illness? In view of that, wouldn't it have been better if he had been killed? At that time you assured me that you would see to it that nothing went wrong. Yet in the meantime you were unable to prevent things happening which were obviously wrong. You should have acted then. Now another has acted for you. Look at the matter in this light before you set in motion the machinery which will destroy men whom you call traitors."

Himmler had stopped rummaging among his papers and he regarded me with a horror in which anxiety was also visible. "What's that you are saying, Kersten? Is that your real opinion? You oughtn't to think that, still less say it. By preserving the Führer Providence has given us a sign. The Führer lives, invulnerable—Providence has spared him to us so that we may bring the war to a triumphant conclusion under his leadership. My place is now at the Führer's side where I will be relentless in executing his orders. I am flying immediately to Berlin. You had better wait at Hartzwalde until I summon you."

Himmler took up the last of his papers and went.

I stood alone in his office gazing at the desk which had been emptied of its secrets.

XXX

SWISS ACTIVITIES ON BEHALF OF THE JEWS

Hartswalde
3rd August, 1944

I RECEIVED a visit today from an old patient of mine, Frau Direktor I. of St. Gallen. She told me that a group of Swiss industrialists was joining with the International Red Cross in a scheme to get some twenty thousand Jews out of concentration camps in Germany into Switzerland and send them to the South of France, where they would be interned under Swiss supervision until the end of the war. Frau I. asked me to intervene with Himmler in support of the plan.

4th August, 1944

Today I got into my car and drove to Himmler. He was already aware of Frau I.'s activities. Various efforts in this direction had been attempted both with him and with the Foreign Office, but all had been frustrated because Hitler was utterly opposed to them. Himmler strongly urged me not to trouble him again with this affair. I asked him, however, to see certain Swiss gentlemen about it, among them a Federal Councillor. When I persisted in asking him not to refuse and thus wreck the Swiss scheme, he closed the conversation with these words: "It's beyond my comprehension why you exert yourself so much on the Jews' behalf. Surely you don't think that a single Jew will thank you. One day you will learn to know the Jews."

Hartswalde
29th November, 1944

Shortly after my arrival in Hartzwalde, on the evening of the 28th of November, 1944, I received another visit from Frau I. at my place here.

She informed me that certain German gentlemen, so she supposed, were negotiating in Zurich for the release of the Jews, charging fifty Swiss franks a head for ordinary Jews and five hundred for prominent ones. The Swiss were ready to pay the sum involved in spite of the disgust which this behaviour had aroused.

When I questioned Himmler about these activities, he first of all said that he knew nothing about them. He had recently had a visit from a Swiss and had received him on the strength of my introduction. A few days later he admitted to me that it was true that money had been demanded and that Schellenberg had knowledge of the affair. The money was to be used to buy tractors wanted for agriculture, necessary for supporting and feeding the Jews. I tried to convince Himmler that this transaction could not be justified on moral grounds. After I had won over Obergruppenführer Berger to my point of view and he had put in a word about it, Himmler at last took a stand against the demands for money. Meanwhile five of the twenty million Swiss franks originally estimated had already been deposited faithfully. Schellenberg, who was entrusted with the matter, was to be responsible for handing over the amount to the International Red Cross.

Triberg (in the Black Forest)
2nd December, 1944

I spoke to Himmler again today about releasing the Jews. He was hesitant, but did not actually refuse. He had hopes of victory, which is a good omen. "We'll drive the English and the Americans into the Channel," he informed me. He enquired how many Jews did I really want to have released and sent to Switzerland. I replied: "Twenty thousand, men and women."

"Good God, I can't do that," Himmler replied. "Do you realize that you're giving Goebbels enough rope for the Führer to hang me!"

I made an appeal to his Germanic humanity. At the end of our conversation Himmler said that I should be satisfied if he were first to release two or three thousand Jews into Switzerland. But he wanted to sleep on it. What concerned him most was that the world Press should not interpret this a sign of weakness on Germany's part. There would be no further releases from concentration camps if that should happen. It was particularly difficult to release Jews who were under arrest because of Hitler's deep-rooted hatred for them.

Postscript

Shortly before my Christmas trip to Sweden on the 21st of December, 1944, I wrote to Himmler about this matter:

Finally I would like to remind you, Herr Reichsführer, about your conversations concerning the Jews. I requested you to release twenty thousand Jews from Theresienstadt so that they could go to Switzerland. I was sorry to hear you say that you could in no circumstances consent to this, but you added that as a first step you were prepared to let between two and three thousand Jews go to Switzerland, and were disposed to discuss the matter with me further, provided that the world Press did not interpret this as a sign of weakness on Germany's side. I also think that it would be to Germany's advantage not to have to feed this number of men.

When I fly to Sweden tomorrow, it will be with a lighter heart, knowing that you will keep your promise to me in this matter.

The release of 2,700 Jews granted me by Himmler and their dispatch to Switzerland followed in February 1945.

XXXI

THE SECURITY SERVICE (SD)

1. TALKS WITH OHLENDORF

(a) Treatment of Foreign Peoples

Field Headquarters
28th August, 1943

I HAD an interesting encounter today. I met SS Brigade-führer Ohlendorf. His appearance is prepossessing on the whole—a man of medium height, distinctly nordic in type, with intelligent eyes and an aquiline nose. I had plenty of time to observe him properly as he was sitting and working continuously with a pile of documents in front of him. We got into conversation over lunch. When he heard that I was a Finn he questioned me about my country and its people, then turned to Esthonia and Latvia. He expressed opinions about the way to treat the occupied territories which were in flagrant contradiction with the policy really being followed in them, as it had been described to me by friends from Finland. I referred to the Ukraine and the methods that Koch employed there. His face darkened with anger as he told me that I was not to think that this policy found general acceptance. Speaking quite openly, he cited examples to show the devastating results of Koch's methods. He was going to discuss the subject with the Reichsführer again that very day.

Then he told me that he had been in the Crimea and had a chance to demonstrate there how much better results could be obtained by different methods. He was proud to be able to number Tartars from the Crimea among his friends. If not conviction, then policy alone should dictate such behaviour; such methods as Koch's only played into the hands of the enemy by arousing resistance and disgust.

I enquired from Brandt about Ohlendorf and learnt that he was head of the Security Service inside Germany, a man with a will of his own and very definite views who gave the Reichsführer a lot of work, because he was a most inconvenient person who always spoke the truth regardless of consequences.

(b) *Ohlendorf's Economic Views*

Field Headquarters
29th August, 1943

Ohlendorf has still got to wait to consult with Himmler. Today we discussed Fascism. He informed me that National Socialism and Fascism were totally opposed to each other. When I expressed my surprise at this and enquired how it was that even National Socialists were always talking about the Fascist state, he replied that this was a great mistake and a dangerous one. Fascism began by deifying the state and refusing to recognize those human communities which were based on nature; but National Socialism was itself based on those natural communities and on the men who belonged to them. The state was no more than a way of developing these communities and the human personalities within them. He had been in Italy himself and made a thorough study of Fascism. For the German people it was a vital question whether the Italian and Fascist idea of nation and state should triumph, or the National Socialist.

As he had mentioned the realization of one or other of these views, I asked Ohlendorf whether there were then different movements at work inside National Socialism itself.

"Certainly, that's already being debated," he told me. "There are men who have a great deal to gain from the Fascist divinization of the state and who would like to put the Führer himself in the place of God. Then they would be able to issue the divine commands as representing the nation and satisfy their own desire for power without any trouble. They all talk of the totalitarian state, which is simply a new version of the old absolutist state—in which they would be absolute and irresponsible masters."

"Does Himmler share those views?" I enquired, very curious to know how Ohlendorf would answer.

"He should be entirely opposed to the Fascist conception of a totalitarian state, if only from his knowledge of the Germanic state and his respect for Germanic ideals. He has only to look at the Germanic community or at the feudal state with its mutual obligations to realize that the totalitarian state is unGermanic. Of course it's not easy to accept the communal idea with all its consequences when you've got power—and the police force—in the hollow of your hand; and it's even more difficult when that's going to bring you into conflict with men like Göring or Ley."

"Have they the same outlook, that you can link them together like that?" I asked Ohlendorf.

"By no means," he replied with the serious expression which was natural to him, "but they both make use of the authoritarian system for very different reasons. Göring has a big business outlook; he wants to keep National Socialist economic policy and the German economy firmly attached to the capitalist system, rather than assist National Socialist communal ideals in gradually developing their own economic institutions. On the other side Ley's collective measures threaten to destroy those small and medium-sized businesses which are independent and the real social basis of the Germany economy; Ley is trying to absorb them into his Workers' Front. But then what's the difference between National Socialism and Bolshevism?"

I asked Ohlendorf to explain further as the whole subject was quite new to me.

"Different conceptions of the state and the nation are visible in their economic consequences," he went on. "Germany's historic tradition is to maintain small and medium-sized businesses which are free and independent, existing on numerous different levels. Then the healthy survive and the inefficient are eliminated simply as the result of economic laws. What we require is self-responsible vital development within the framework of the community—and this in every department of life, of which economics is one. The alternative idea, which the Fascists hold, is that it's the state which assigns tasks and dignity both to the individual and to the nation. In the economic field this means that the state assumes the management of industry. And what's the result of this? Small and medium-sized businesses which are independent are closed down on the plea of state necessity, because from a business point of view they will naturally produce much more under the control of Göring or Ley."

Never before had I received such a lecture on economics and the state. At the same time I was astounded at the frankness with which Ohlendorf had spoken.

Field Headquarters
30th August, 1943

In case he should be again kept waiting for Himmler, I made an appointment with Ohlendorf for the evening, in order to hear more on this interesting subject. I asked him whether the phrase 'Self-government in Industry', which I heard so much about, represented his ideas on communal responsibility.

"Far from it, we've quite misunderstood each other there," Ohlendorf replied. "That means the loss of all authority on the part of the state, whose task it is to bolster the individual business man's personal responsibility. It involves the leaders of industry taking over powers which should belong to the state. They are clothed with the state's authority while entirely lacking any objective status, for they are themselves competing in the same field. They simply use the state's authority in order to secure the best terms for themselves and eliminate all unwelcome competition. This kind of self-government in industry is simply exploiting the state by typically capitalist methods; it's bound to bring the community to the edge of destruction. It also undermines any confidence in the state's objectivity. It further compels all those who regard this process as harmful to accept methods of graft, if they don't want to go bankrupt."

"How does Himmler regard this development?" I asked Ohlendorf.

"He's against monopolistic state capitalism in itself, but he doesn't understand enough about economics. His experts are too clever for him when they explain that all this has been made necessary by concentration on the war. Besides that, he's got a staunch upholder of capitalism in his own circle, Pohl, who is doing all he can to build up an SS industrial combine. He gets support from the Reichsführer by explaining to him the advantages to be gained from institutions which will be a kind of legacy to the SS in future generations. But the basic conceptions involved go considerably further than the Reichsführer's little pet theories."

Unfortunately I was unable to continue this conversation because Ohlendorf was called away to make his report and then departed. I was as much impressed by his clear reasoning as by the frankness with which he expressed his ideas. I mentioned this to Brandt, who told me: "There's nothing to be said against Ohlendorf, nor his behaviour, but he doesn't know how to cope with the Reichsführer. Really to get into contact with him, he ought to bring him a rune-stone from time to time and chat with the Reichsführer about Germanic ideals. Instead of that he's very cold and superior in his manner as he goes into some matter of which the Reichsführer obviously has little knowledge; he makes the gloomiest prophecies with a deadly serious face. The Reichsführer calls him 'the dull Prussian', or when he's in a bad temper 'the defeatist' or 'the intellectual'—different ways of expressing the lack of ease he feels in his presence. He feels that Ohlendorf is continually watching over him like a second Reichsführer who always knows better and has the ability to propound detailed arguments on any subject. Himmler can't bear that and they're always at loggerheads in consequence."

2. HIMMLER AND THE SECURITY SERVICE

Hartzwalde
2nd September, 1943

Ohlendorf asked if he might have a talk with me. When I agreed he told me that he found himself in a very difficult position. Gauleiter Koch had read the Security Service's reports on the devastating effects of his activities in the Ukraine. He had used them as grounds for a complaint to Himmler about Ohlendorf's sharp criticism of his harsh policy there. Koch asserted that Himmler's Security Service was going against the Führer and high officials of the Reich who enjoyed his confidence. At the same time Goebbels was launching a frontal attack against Ohlendorf's position as head of the Security Service.

It was the Security Service's function to present an impartial picture to leaders of the Party and the government, to show the effect of their measures on every department of life, the economic, the cultural, the administrative, the legal and others. It was the Service's special task to point out when these measures aroused opposition. Under a dictatorship this was of prime importance, as no opposition was voiced in Press or parliament. The Security Service had to reveal the sort of things that come out in open discussion under a parliamentary *régime*. Ohlendorf had done this in the case of Goebbels' demonstration in the Sportpalast. Selecting from the mass of material faithfully reported to him by his observers all over the Reich, he had pointed out that the demonstration had been generally discounted and dismissed as a piece of ostentatious display. Ohlendorf acknowledged that this report was not very discreet, but it was accurate and, viewed from a higher standpoint, it was also necessary. Goebbels had thereupon ordered the suppression of the report which in any case had only gone to Lammers and Göring.

The Reichsführer, who was not very at home with Ohlendorf personally, instead of supporting him, was on the verge of becoming openly antagonistic. It was essential for him to get on better terms with the Reichsführer as soon as possible.

Ohlendorf then asked me whether I wouldn't use my influence with Himmler to help him. With a sly smile he added: "You'll also be assisting your own people. For my conception of nations as entities with a life of their own leads me to work for the independence of the Ukrainians, the Esthonians, the Latvians, the Lithuanians, the Walloons and the Flemings, so that they may preserve their own culture and administration. I'm trying to save them from centralization and colonial exploitation, as well as from the harsh policies of men like Koch. Unless I've been misinformed, that surely accords with your own humanitarian impulses. You're trying to do the same thing on a small scale by assisting individual cases. I'm striving for a fundamental solution to the whole problem. Then the individual cases will solve themselves."

I promised that I would think over his request and let him know my decision.

Berlin

4th September, 1943

I told Ohlendorf today that I was still somewhat undecided. In the first place I had no desire to be wittingly involved in the affairs of the Security Service, nor to be watched by Ohlendorf's intelligence agents. He assured me, however, that it was only a question of a special, factual report and of his personal position. "I could not have asked a favour of you," he said, "if I had thought that you approved of Koch's methods in the Ukraine."

"But why don't you go to Himmler direct?" I asked Ohlendorf. "He must surely be glad to get accurate information from you, so that he can form an impartial picture of the real situation in Germany and the occupied territories."

"So I used to suppose," Ohlendorf replied. "But so many things play their part in this which an outsider can only grasp with difficulty. The Reichsführer believes that whatever the Führer ordains is for the best and a boon to Germany. When objective reports from the whole Reich state how the people react to certain measures—for example how they criticize a speech of the Führer's—then the Reichsführer refuses to believe them. He wants to know the names of the men who drew up the report of those who made these unpleasant remarks, so that he can hold them responsible. According to him the German people simply don't understand the Führer, or else are not sufficiently developed for his ideas.

"The Reichsführer has immense faith in victory. He does not look at the reports put before him from the standpoint of how best to eliminate these evils which are an obstacle to victory. He is much more inclined to regard them as the work of doubters and defeatists, who are using these reports to express their own miserable ideas. I don't think there's another intelligence service in the world which has such a hard time as we have, constantly at loggerheads with our own chief and endangering our own existence simply because we insist on making objective reports."

"You're surely exaggerating, Herr Ohlendorf. It's surely only a conflict of temperaments—yours and Himmler's are so radically different."

"I'm not exaggerating in the least, Herr Kersten. Just ask Brandt—you and he get on so well together—to show you the letter which the Reichsführer wrote to Kaltenbrunner criticizing me over the Koch affair. It was a warning to me, for it described my reports as unnecessary and threatened the closing down of the entire internal intelligence service. Do you think that my people and I got any pleasure out of that? What the Reichsführer really wants is an intelligence service which will please him by issuing optimistic reports, reflecting his own views of the situation. That's not possible, for the more critical the situation becomes, the gloomier become the reports which are simply a reflection of it. Then the Führer will get a clear picture of the situation from the Reichsführer and issue the necessary orders. All that is needed on the practical side is an organization to break the resistance of those who offer open or concealed opposition to those orders. The Gestapo exists for that. The individual opponent is not the concern of the Security Service's home intelligence branch. We only enquire into the causes of opposition and it's our job to indicate the measures taken by the Party or the government which arouse it. The Security Service insists on the greatest objectivity in its reports. It gives a picture of the situation which is photographically exact; it acts as the government's conscience, revealing the situation in every department·of life and showing the effect of every enactment."

"So you've nothing to do with the Gestapo?" I replied. "It's the first time I've heard that, I must say, Herr Ohlendorf. I, and my friends too, have always thought that your people were Himmler's police spies."

"That would be simple—I'd have no need then to sit here and ask you to help dispel the clouds which are gathering over me."

Field Headquarters
7th September, 1943

Ohlendorf has appeared at Field Headquarters to make his report. As a sequel to what he had told me, I took the chance of asking him how he came by material for his intelligence surveys. The system would have to have something in common with the Gestapo, otherwise he would not acquire such material.

"Of course we've got our confidential agents everywhere," he replied, "but they're not employees who denounce the head of their firm; they're in every calling and every walk of life; they report to us how the situation stands in every field and they don't get a penny for doing it. We scan these people very carefully and we reject anything that springs from mixed motives, more especially anything that might arise from a desire for self-advancement. Isolated reports and individual names are of small account. We regard them only as symptoms and make use of them to build up a general picture, so that a mosaic of impressions becomes a valid survey of the entire Reich. It's no concern of ours whether the man who makes the report is a member of the Party, nor whether he's a German or a foreigner. Our only interest is in the accuracy of his information.

"In places where such information is hard to come by, we infiltrate our own men to make a survey. Yet on the whole we're in the happy position of being able to record that confidence in us is growing, as the only organization able to offer an objective report on the situation and on the effect of Party and government enactments throughout the Reich. That is proved by the number of those who voluntarily contribute to our reports—and they come from every level of the population and from every walk of life. If only the leadership would make use of this intelligence system as a conscience to test all its enactments, I would regard my life's work in this field as accomplished; and I intend to develop it further regardless of the opposition."

"Does the Reichsführer no longer let Hitler see your reports, then?" I enquired.

"That's just the trouble. The Higher Command receives daily and hourly reports of the exact situation on all fronts and makes its dispositions accordingly. The same ought to apply to the home front. The Führer and high officials in the Party and the government ought to know about every measure's effect without regarding this as a personal attack on them. But apparently it's going to be another generation before we can get this idea accepted. It wouldn't be so bad in peace-time, but now we're engaged in a life-and-death struggle. Until now anyhow only Goebbels, Göring, Lammers and Bormann received my reports on the home front. But Bormann always keeps them from the Führer. This is absolutely fatal, since they deal with the home front, for which the Party is responsible. I've told you about my recent experience of Goebbels' reactions. The Reichsführer, who as head of the intelligence service is the proper person to do so, doesn't dare to lay my reports before the Führer, even when he believes they're true."

I couldn't help smiling, so fantastic did the whole situation appear to me. "You smile incredulously," Ohlendorf retorted, "but it's the truth. His behaviour is dictated by purely tactical considerations. He would of course make bitter enemies of some important people whose support he needs in other fields. His whole character is against doing that—I know him well. He prefers to give way and try other methods of dealing with difficulties, but he's only partially successful. Such tactics mean that necessary decisions on important matters are post-poned and finally forgotten owing to the pressure of other great events.

"Apart from that, the Reichsführer considers that the Führer ought not to be troubled with matters which might interfere with his lofty conceptions and arouse his displeasure. You surely know how every-body close to the Führer is constantly striving to keep any unpleasant news from reaching him. The Reichsführer is no exception. De facto, he holds the power in Germany, but he makes no use of it. It's a drama, a real drama. I'm worried to death as I see what might be done—and nothing happens. I'm convinced that if the true situation was revealed to the Führer, then measures would be taken. What wouldn't I give to be able to put before the Führer the overwhelming mass of material which we possess about the situation on the home front."

Berlin
15th September, 1943

Ohlendorf visited me today, once more asking me to intervene with Himmler. I expressed my astonishment that he should be so frank with me, when I was a foreigner; I had never before encountered such frankness from a person in his position. Ohlendorf answered me in his disarming way: "Why shouldn't I be frank with you? Even if you were a member of the enemy intelligence, a thing one never knows, I would be telling you nothing new. You're already well aware of the weak points in our system. You're always among the Reichsführer's people too and have been able to form your own impressions. Frank-ness is the best kind of discretion, and as you already know how matters stand, this is the right way of going about it."

"And what am I supposed to do for you, Herr Ohlendorf?"

"Really it's very little, but it may prove very important. Just tell the Reichsführer that you have become acquainted with me. Tell him what you think of me and above all talk him out of that idea of his that I'm a pessimist and a defeatist. To have such a reputation interferes with my work, especially in my position, where I'm being sniped at from all sides. I'm quite prepared for him on my own ground—my professional duties. But when you're constantly coming up against a brick wall, unable even to approach the Reichsführer, then professional work becomes impossible. But only do it of course if you're really convinced—I don't like this way of doing things. It goes against the grain and I'm only making this move on behalf of the cause for which I'm fighting."

Ohlendorf rose to his feet and took his leave. He behaved like a gentleman in all our talks and gave a very good impression of himself. What mistakes one can make—for I had always regarded the Security Service as a vast organization which Himmler directed himself, an extension of himself, an invisible counsellor. Instead of that I had heard from the head of this intelligence service himself what great difficulties he had with his own chief, who refused to make use of the instrument placed at his disposal.

3. HIMMLER ON OHLENDORF

Field Headquarters
18th September, 1943

I told Himmler today that an interesting colleague of his, Brigade-führer Ohlendorf, had become a patient of mine.

"I'm glad of that," he replied. "I hope you'll be able to help him; he has trouble with his liver and gall-bladder. His reports are always gloomy; he has the pessimistic outlook which goes with physical suffering. Liver and gall troubles always have that effect on the mind."

I replied that this surely arose from the work he had to do; there was nothing wrong with his liver, nor his gall. He was simply over-worked and his nervous system upset by constant worry.

"To be quite frank, my dear Herr Kersten, I don't care for the man," Himmler responded. "He has no sense of humour, he's one of those unbearable people who always know better. Having his gold Party-badge and being one of the first recruits to the SS, he regards himself as the Galahad of National Socialism and thinks that all is lost when things happen which conflict with its ideology. He's like a school-master watching over me to see that I do things properly. Yet he hasn't the slightest idea of tactics. If I were to listen to him, I would have to take official action over every one of his reports and make bitter enemies on all sides. His pet idea is that I should let the Führer see his reports. But they're usually so pessimistic that this is quite out of the question; they would only impair the Führer's capacity for action."

"Supposing they are true?" I suggested.

"That doesn't matter," Himmler replied. "Details which are unhelpful must be kept from the Führer, however important they may appear. His task is to lead us to victory; I must keep from him anything which might interfere with this task, even if Herr Ohlendorf does not share this view. But if you'll only restore Ohlendorf to health and strengthen his nervous system, he'll soon be looking at the world through different eyes. Tell him that I consider it a very good idea of his to take treatment from you."

4. OHLENDORF ON HIMMLER

Hartzwalde
24th September, 1943

"We've made some progress, if the Reichsführer believes I've done something sensible," Ohlendorf laughed when I told him about my talk with Himmler. "More than that, the Reichsführer has perfectly expressed to you his opinion of me. I always provoke the anti-Prussian sentiments of the Bavarian in him, though he may not be aware of it and in his speeches even commends Prussian toughness and discipline, Frederick the Great and the 'Soldier King'. It's true that I'm a Prussian and it's for the Prussian sort of order that I'm striving. I'll grant that the real cause of the persistent differences between us lies, as the Reichsführer says, in the fact that I have no gift for tactics. Unless it has clearly defined institutions with definite tasks assigned them, no state can function properly. New tasks should be handed over to the appropriate body as they arise. If the right men are not in the right jobs, then the men must be moved. The Reichsführer has different ideas. He frequently entrusts new tasks as they arise, to individuals, instead of giving them to bodies which already exist for them: often several men will be given the same job. He calls that tactics. This leads to every sort of confusion and contradiction, abilities are wasted and respect for authority destroyed.

"In doing this, he's really copying the Führer, who inherits from his early struggles a preference for these personal appointments and distrusts government institutions. It should be the Reichsführer's job to unify the state's powers and so guarantee its internal order. In fact he's really organizing disorder. The logical result of this principle is that while power seems to be concentrated in an authoritative dictatorship, in reality it is dispersed over a host of people, each one of whom asserts that he's the only responsible authority. But he has neither the time, nor the ability, nor the knowledge required to supervise and control all the tasks assigned him. So numbers of independent and divided authorities come into being. The government's dictatorial powers quite lose their value.

"In my reports I'm always trying to make the consequences of this principle clear to the Reichsführer, especially to point out to him its devastating effects in war-time. When I call things by their names, he thinks I'm improperly criticizing the Führer's methods or showing my lack of tactical sense. When the Reichsführer entrusts an unsuitable person with tasks which would be much better performed by existing institutions, then it's not the immediate tactical situation which I consider, though from such an angle this solution might have some point. What I'm trying to do is to foresee its future consequences.

"I'm horrified when I reflect that one more new post has been created, which can only be an obstacle to the efficiency which specialists can alone provide; it prevents any effective leadership; it gives rise to painful reflections and questionings, moreover, and arouses forces against it which should really be helping, not hindering it. I'm horrified when I reflect on the time that has to be devoted to correcting the results of such mistaken decisions. I'm quite unable to regard such organizing methods from the standpoint of the Reichsführer's personal policy. You couldn't run a real business on the Reichsführer's principles, let alone a state. You own an estate, Herr Kersten. You would understand my worries if you were to run it on the same lines as we run the Reich."

I was unable to say much by way of answer to all that. I had already heard from other sources the things that Ohlendorf had told me, though I had never seen them in quite such a vivid light. Nor had I realized that the portrayal of this disorganization in his reports had made him one of the sharpest critics of the government's inefficiency. Now at least I could understand the universal outcry against such an intelligence service and realize why Himmler regarded him as a schoolmaster always at his elbow.

I asked Ohlendorf whether he still wanted to become a patient of mine. "Yes, I'm quite decided on that," he replied. "But tell the Reichsführer that your treatment is having its effect, my nerves are improving and my pessimism vanishing. Then perhaps he will take my reports more seriously."

After that we had supper together. Ohlendorf drank a great deal of coffee. My enjoyment of our conversation was disturbed by the fact that he used the phrase 'Isn't that so?' at least once in every sentence. It got on my nerves and I began to count the times he used it. I counted seventy-three in the course of half an hour. He also made very frequent use of the phrase 'I must explain that to you'.

Hartzwalde
14th June, 1944

While I was waiting for Himmler yesterday, I met Ohlendorf once again. He came across to me at once, greeting me with a smile. He looked very unwell. I asked whether he was worried and on what sort of terms he was with Himmler. He told me that so far he had been able to wangle things, but at the moment he was faced with another critical situation. Ley had already forbidden officials of the German Workers' Front to co-operate with the Security Service. That had not been too much of a blow, as he had been expecting it, but now Bormann had turned against him. Bormann had threatened once before to checkmate him by telling the Führer how pessimistic his reports were. Now Bormann had forbidden all Party officials, together with all those they appointed, to co-operate with the Security Service. That was a severe blow. Apart from the fact that it meant losing important sources of information, he was now in open conflict with Bormann and had constantly to expect further attacks against himself. He stood in great need of support from Himmler.

I enquired whether his reports were still not allowed to circulate.

"You can judge of that," he replied, "from the fact that Bormann prevents any report from reaching the Führer, and you already know what Himmler's attitude is. Since so many have been forbidden to co-operate, I have had to cut down my weekly reports on the situation to some extent, while I find out what in fact the situation really is. I still manage to get some information from various sources and my own position as deputy Secretary of State in the Ministry of Commerce is very helpful. But now my hands are more or less tied and there is not much that I can do."

I could not help smiling when I reflected that this intelligence service was being thwarted and prohibited in Germany, though the country was engaged in a struggle for its very existence. Yet this service was giving the facts about the war's effects and offering the

Leaders a true account of the reaction to their own measures; but every means was being used to prevent these reports from reaching the men at the top. I asked Ohlendorf whether he wouldn't prefer to give up in face of such a hopeless position.

He told me that he was not able to reconcile that with his own conscience. He was doing his duty. Even if most of his work went into Himmler's waste-paper basket, perhaps enough would penetrate to make the Reichsführer reflect. He hoped too that the situation might develop in such a way that people would turn to him as the person who was best informed, and he had to hold himself in readiness for that.

I next enquired why, with his conviction, he did not go direct to the Führer with his reports in person. He answered me with great seriousness: "I have my place in the hierarchy. That means that my department's reports go to the man above me; the person properly appointed is responsible for their reaching the Führer. How can I, who have always stood for discipline and against arbitrary behaviour, break discipline and behave in an arbitrary way myself?"

It is the truth that Ohlendorf is a Prussian, and certainly not the man to act on his own initiative.

5. THE CREATION OF THE SECURITY SERVICE

Gut Hartzwalde
18th June, 1944

As a sequel to my talks with Ohlendorf I asked one of his closest colleagues how it was that so many men in good positions co-operated with the Security Service; for so I had been told.

He informed me that Heydrich had laid the foundations of the Security Service in 1933. Heydrich had a special gift for persuading outstanding personalities to help with his intelligence service. He had expounded his ideas on building up an intelligence service to some ten or twenty men of this type. What he argued was that, apart from the Bolshevist intelligence system, which had to be rejected on ideological grounds, two types of intelligence service were possible in Europe. First of all there was the French system, named after Fouché, which made use of police spies and paid agents. Then there was the British Secret Service. Every decent Englishman is ready to aid the Secret Service, regarding it as his obvious duty, without requiring any special obligation. British power was really based on the Secret Service, for the best informed have a great advantage over others. That was true both of commercial competition and of politics—and in England the two were very much the same thing. Perhaps that was why England had such a gift for intelligence work and understood its requirements. The SS had adopted as its ideal this English view of intelligence work as a matter for gentlemen. Himmler knew that opinion would be against him, for the Germans disliked any kind of intelligence service, regarding it as an organization of informers. Heydrich considered that it was his duty to overcome this prejudice and asked for Himmler's help in this.

"And was he successful?" I enquired. "Extremely so," I was told. "Heydrich succeeded in removing the psychological difficulties which stood in the way of an intelligence service, so that it came to be regarded as an honourable task. The example of England was particularly effective, as the power of the Secret Service is universally respected. It is always important to have an ideal."

Fundamentally it is not really difficult to win men to your way of thinking, once you understand their mentality. Heydrich seems to have been an adept in this art. It's a matter of catching them, then the law of inertia will keep them where you want them.

XXXII

THE DEFECTION OF FINLAND

Hartzwalde
5th September, 1944

THE radio announced this morning that Finland was asking the Russians for an immediate armistice and had broken off diplomatic relations with Germany. I had seen this coming.

In the afternoon I went to Molchow to see Kivimäki. Molchow is near Altruppin in the Ruppin district, fifteen miles from Hartswalde. The Finnish Embassy was evacuated there, after being bombed out of Berlin.

The Minister, Kivimäki, received me with the words: "I'm glad you've come. Now I'm interned in Germany and not allowed to leave this spot. How are things with you?"

"I'm managing all right. Himmler's stomach-cramps are sufficient guarantee that nothing will happen to me or my family. Himmler's health is very bad just now and I'm sure he will send for me in the course of the next few days."

When I got home, I learnt that a summons to headquarters already awaited me. I was to go to Himmler on the 8th of September.

Hochwald
8th September, 1944

I reached here in a sleeper at ten in the morning and was immediately summoned to Himmler. He was still in bed and in great pain. The Koran lay on his bedside table. Himmler received me with these words: "You Finns are a fine lot. You're just a bunch of traitors. I'd like to know what Mannerheim and Ryti have had to offer to the English and the Russians for this breach of faith. They must have paid

221

a big price for their future security. But the Finnish people have been handed over to the violence of the Russians." He was sorry that he had not had these gentlemen removed sooner and made Finland a Germanic country, as had happened in Norway under Quisling, a man who was really worthy of respect. When a year ago Mannerheim had withdrawn the Finnish battalion from the Waffen SS, that would have been the moment to act and eliminate the whole Finnish Government.

I made no answer, just letting Himmler talk. He got so excited that his stomach-cramps became worse. "Why are you sitting there looking so indifferent? You should be helping me—I can't bear this pain any longer."

I gave him treatment and succeeded in relieving him. Himmler became more friendly and asked me whether I had had a good journey and how my family were. Then he said: "Now that Finland has broken away, you're on the Allied side and an enemy of Germany's."

I laughed and said: "One often moves faster than one thinks, Herr Himmler. If we are going to observe the letter of the law, I should not have given you this treatment."

Then Himmler laughed too and said: "You and I mustn't quarrel over politics. I'm truly grateful to you for keeping me free of pain for all these years. There must be peace between us."

I asked Himmler to arrange that Finns living in Germany be decently treated. It was true that Finland had reached the limits of its strength. Himmler ought never to forget that out of a population of only three and a half millions Finland had sacrificed 60,000 on the field of battle.

Himmler conceded my further request that I might retain German entry and exit visas for my family and myself. Hartzwalde was to remain an extra-territorial area. The conversation ended with these words from Himmler: "Now Russia will slaughter the Finns. For you can't expect that any will survive."

XXXIII

TALKS WITH GENERAL COMMISSIONER LITZMANN

Field Headquarters, Hochwald
10th September, 1944

I'M living this time in a hotel that has just been built and have a bathroom of my own. Field Headquarters has grown in the meantime to the size of a large village. SA-Obergruppenführer Litzmann, General Commissioner for Esthonia, is quartered close by. The orderly told me that Himmler had sent out an urgent summons for Litzmann, who has nevertheless had to wait for five days already without being received. Being acquainted with Litzmann, I called on him yesterday to pay my respects.

Though pleased to see me, he had only sad news to relate. The Russians, armed with the latest American equipment, were pressing onwards to their goal, while German officials were fighting a paper-war against the Esthonians, issuing orders which were overtaken by events by the time that they appeared, so that the Esthonians were being driven into a frenzy.

I asked Litzmann whether he had expected anything better from the Party leadership. "Yes," he replied, "God knows that my father and I had other ideals when we joined the Party."

At one o'clock I went with Litzmann to the restaurant car for lunch. There was pea-soup and plenty of pork, with an apple each for dessert. In the afternoon I took coffee with Brandt, who told me that Himmler had been pacing about all night unable to sleep. It had been a fearful shock to him that Finland had broken away.

"What else should the poor Finns have done? Was it their duty to fight for Germany to the last man?" I enquired.

Brandt showed sympathy with Finland's position. In the evening I invited Litzmann to my room for a cup of Swedish coffee. He has still not been received today.

223

We talked about Esthonia. Litzmann told me how enthusiastically
the German troops had been received in Esthonia. Every Esthonian
had shown his gratitude and welcomed them as liberators. This lasted
for a long time, until the Party leadership forcibly changed the
Esthonians' attitude and succeeded in turning friends into enemies.
"It's beyond one's comprehension how it was possible."

I asked why he had not made a stand against it. Wasn't he General
Commissioner for Esthonia?

"Ach, I'm only a figurehead. I have nothing to say in the matter.
The real authority is the Reich Commissioner for the Eastern Territories
in Riga, who issues orders each one of which is more foolish than the
last. If I dare to protest against them, it all comes back on to me and
I'm called a reactionary. The other authority there, the Leader of the
SS and of the police in Esthonia, countermands all my orders and gets
the Esthonians' backs up every day. I often feel that these people are
Germany's worst enemies, not the English and the Americans. I'm
ashamed, I have to blush, every time I think of Esthonia. The
Esthonians have so much sense of dignity and honour, and they're
such a hard-working people. We could have made them the best of
friends if we had only treated them with humanity and intelligence.
After I had held my position in Esthonia for a year, I submitted to
Heinrich Himmler proposals that I had worked out in which I underlined the importance of an enlightened policy in Esthonia. My proposals were:

"1. Restoration of independence to Esthonia.

"2. Abolition of all Russian decrees.

"3. Restitution of Esthonian frontiers as they were on the 31st of
December, 1939.

"4. Alliance with Esthonia as an equal partner.

"The same thing should have been done with Latvia and Lithuania.

"Himmler received me and enquired whether I had taken leave of
my senses, as my programme entirely contradicted the Führer's
declared policy with regard to the treatment of foreign peoples in the
East. That policy had been laid down once and for all and could not
be altered. He warned me as a friend that if I was to express such ideas
openly, the Führer would only regard them as an act of hostility to
the government. Then he would no longer be able to protect me. So
I saw in what quarter the wind lay."

"And is the German treatment of Esthonia any more sensible
now?" I enquired.

"Orders are being issued, each one harsher than the last. The
Ministry for the East makes the orders, the Reich Commissioner

carries them a stage further; the next day they're made still harsher and the day after that they're revoked. The SS and police chief in Reval enacts quite arbitrary measures which, if I complain enough about them, are revoked by the Reich Commissioner. A fortnight later Himmler will promulgate them in a still harsher form. The Esthonians are saying now: 'The Germans are just as bad as the Russians.' "

Hochwald
11th September, 1944

Himmler is feeling better again today and he gave me a lecture on wealth and morals. Wealth was the greatest of evils; comfort made men lazy, covetous and cowardly. It was not the homes of the rich, but those of the poor, which fostered the spirit of heroism. That was why he was glad to have been born poor and to have no great possessions. He had only one ambition: to die poor. History should never say of him that he had enriched himself with this world's goods. It was the most disgraceful thing to use one's position to enrich oneself. "I admire the way they dealt with thieves in the Middle Ages—by cutting their hands off."

I answered, laughing: "A good many men would lose their hands nowadays."

"Why not?" said Himmler. "After the war I'm going to do all I can to restore German standards of honour. I grant you that morals have declined as a result of the war, but that's the same everywhere."

Then I brought it to Himmler's notice that Litzmann had been waiting for days to be received by him.

"That's true," said Himmler; "I'll receive him at once. Things are very bad in Esthonia; the Russians are driving hard for Reval."

Litzmann was received by Himmler at eleven o'clock. He parted from me with these words: "The Reichsführer is placing a special aircraft at my disposal and I'm flying to Reval immediately. The Russians are outside the town. Himmler has given me orders to mobilize everybody available, men, women and children, to keep the Russians off until the German relieving forces arrive. I can rest assured that the Führer will not abandon Esthonia to its fate. The Reichsführer has also made me a present of an automatic, the latest design—it takes a thousand rounds. I'm afraid I'll arrive too late. Good luck! Perhaps we'll meet again. Of course I'll go to the front and fight in the ranks. The Esthonians will never be able to say that a Litzmann was a coward."

Litzmann flew from the Rastenburg airfield at a quarter to three.

XXXIV

THE SCANDINAVIAN RESCUE CAMPAIGN OF 1944 AND THE RELEASE OF DUTCH PRISONERS

I HAD a number of interviews in the autumn of 1943 with the Swedish Foreign Minister Günther. We had drafted the broad outlines of a plan to secure the release of Norwegians and Danes who were under German arrest. The strictest secrecy was observed over my visits to Günther. I pointed out that our worst obstacle was that we could expect no relaxation in German policy, as this might be interpreted as a sign of weakness.

I was back in Stockholm in April 1944. Günther always showed the warmest interest in the fate of Sweden's Scandinavian neighbours and was making this the object of his policy; I told him everything had been prepared on my side to initiate the Swedish rescue campaign. Goebbels and Kaltenbrunner were against it, and also Ribbentrop. On the other hand there were signs that Himmler was prepared to give way. I had told him that I had a mandate from Günther and had received the impression that Himmler had come to the conclusion that there had been enough bloodshed.

The first stage of the plan that Günther had worked out for the release of the Scandinavians was to get the Norwegians and the Danes out of the German concentration camps. Whenever possible they should be sent to Sweden, who took upon herself the obligation of interning them until the end of the war. If this could not be arranged, Sweden was also ready to construct properly enclosed camps, where the prisoners would be guarded until the end of the war by the Swedish police. Sweden would also guarantee that they did not return to Norway and Denmark before then. The advantage of this plan was that the prisoners would be removed from areas where there was danger of bombing, could be clothed and properly looked after in Sweden; and their minds would be freed from the most oppressive sense of confinement.

Günther said that although his own sympathies were on the side of fighters in the Resistance, he could quite appreciate that National Socialist Germany would want to prevent these enemies of hers from returning to fight in the Resistance against her. If none of these Swedish proposals was acceptable to Himmler, at least it had to be arranged for the Scandinavian prisoners to be assembled in a part of Germany where they were out of danger from bombing. Sweden would then be prepared to feed them and supervise their health arrangements. The best way would be for this to be done under the auspices of the Swedish Red Cross. In the summer of 1944 I returned to Germany with a mandate to discuss these matters with Himmler.

After long negotiations Himmler rejected the first two sets of proposals, but said that he was prepared to view the third more favourably. Within these limits it might even, if necessary, be made acceptable to Hitler by emphasizing the Germanic angle.

I took this reply to Günther myself in the September of 1944. The Swedish Foreign Minister spoke to me early in November of the same year about the possibility of aiding Norwegian students and Danish policemen, together with a large number of Norwegian and Danish women and children who were in German concentration camps. Günther asked me to make clear to Himmler that Sweden was prepared to take over these people and intern them until the end of the war. I informed Günther of my relations with Baron Nagell and of the efforts I was making on behalf of the Dutch. "We'll gladly assume responsibility for all those you get released," he replied.

On the 28th of November I flew into Germany and two days later met Himmler at headquarters. I talked about all these different questions while giving him treatment, but first of all encountered resistance. After long-drawn-out negotiations extending over seventeen days, I succeeded in getting Himmler to release fifty Norwegian students and the same number of Danish policemen, as a first step. I received the assurance that later it might be possible to release a larger number of Norwegian and Danish women and children, provided that the previous releases had not been interpreted by the world Press as a sign of weakness on Germany's part. There were to be further negotiations on the total numbers to be released.

Himmler emphasized on this occasion that the German railways would not be able to provide transport for these people; there was no rolling-stock available for this purpose. I asked Himmler to provide transport himself for the men who were being released just then, to give them the chance of spending Christmas with their families. Himmler promised to give orders to Kaltenbrunner on this point,

In view of the Swedish Foreign Minister's co-operation over such a wide field—he had undertaken to look after all those whose release I was able to secure—I made a special effort to intervene with Himmler on the largest possible scale.

I had already intervened on behalf of the French interned in German camps in September 1944, when I wrote to Himmler as follows:

27th September, 1944

Dear Herr Reichsführer,

Though our aircraft was attacked on the way, I landed safely in Berlin yesterday, and tomorrow I'm flying back to Stockholm. At the same time I would like to thank you for recognizing Gut Hartzwalde as extra-territorial and I hope to have nothing more to fear from Kaltenbrunner.

Now I want to broach a subject which lies very close to my heart. Though France is no longer under German occupation, there are still thousands of French men and women in your concentration camps, being treated as if they were slaves, though patriotism is their only crime. Has Germany no longer a conscience? What sense or logic is there in this? I think that you have been ill-advised, Herr Reichsführer, and by men whose only aim is to fish in troubled waters. I know that you are only carrying out the orders of others and so I call on your magnanimity in the name of humanity and history: release all French, Belgian and Dutch prisoners.

On my side I am able to state, from my talks with the Swedish Government, that it is perfectly possible for all those who are released to go to Sweden and be interned there until the end of the war. I am also convinced that Switzerland would assume responsibility for a proportion of these men. I appeal not to the Reichsführer SS, but to the man Heinrich Himmler. Where there is a will there is also a way, nor will history forget your humane behaviour.

I was very upset by the conversations we had recently about Finland. I think it was very wrong of you to speak with such venom about my Finnish friends and the Finnish Government. They have only done their duty, as you do yours. Finland had reached the limits of her strength and had to make peace; she could not go on any longer. Apart from that, Finland was suffering under German pressure. In these last years she has fought with a heroism which can only be admired against greatly superior forces. But three and a half million Finns could not go on fighting against two hundred million Russians. As a reasonable human being you must realize that. In my opinion my Finnish homeland did the right thing. And I am quite convinced that she will come to an understanding with the Russians.

There are between two and three hundred Finns living in Germany, professional men. I beg of you to protect them and see that they are properly treated.

I will be back in Germany in November to give you treatment. I very much hope that you will grant my request for the release of the French, Belgians and Dutch.

Yours respectfully,
Felix Kersten.

Triberg, in the Black Forest
8th December, 1944

The last few days have been very exciting and strenuous ones for me. Himmler is constantly saying that he is in great difficulties with Hitler and that Bormann is preparing to stab him in the back. It is treason to the Führer to release men just now. These people in concentration camps, on whose behalf I—Kersten—would intervene, were criminals and enemies of the state, people with whom he had nothing in common. In recent years he had unfortunately released far too many men from concentration camps at my request; I ought not to bother him any more now. Quite apart from that, he had so little time at his disposal, for he had to concentrate on final victory and the use of the latest weapons which would astonish the world. Secret weapons would spell victory for National Socialist Germany.

Himmler told me to return to him in another hour. In the restaurant car I encountered Berger, who was foaming with rage because Himmler had passed to him Hitler's orders to have English and American officers shot. Berger said that he refused to do that under any circumstances, even if it meant the sacrifice of his own life: he would rather shoot himself than prisoners of war. Hitler ought to do the shooting himself, if he had the courage.

Gut Hartzwalde
8th December, 1944

The German offensive against the West is going successfully. Himmler explained the situation to me: "Our offensive has been worked out in detail by the Führer in person. We have only to maintain this rate of advance and by the 26th of January we'll have reached the

Channel coast. Then our troops will be free to drive the Russians out of Europe. We have purposely weakened the Eastern Front and flung all troops available against the West. It is of no significance whether the Russians advance another three hundred miles or not. The great thing is that we should make a clean sweep in the West."

In the name of humanity I begged Himmler for the release of 5,000 Dutch from concentration camps, women, children and civilians in the first place. Himmler at first refused and took the opportunity of once more airing his views to me about the Dutch. They were almost as bad as the Jews, traitors to Germanic ideals.

I gave him a forcible answer: that the Dutch had been for centuries an independent and sea-faring people; once theirs had been the greatest navy in the world. It was natural that they should defend their freedom. They were also the embodiment of the qualities recommended in SS training courses—resolution, bravery, refusal to submit to the enemy and loyalty to the fatherland.

Himmler replied that I was completely distorting the facts. The Dutch had forfeited the right to call themselves a Germanic people, once they had taken up arms against the Germans.

"I'm glad there's nobody here to take down what you say," I retorted, "he might give posterity a peculiar idea of your Germanic conceptions."

"It's impossible for me to release five thousand of the Dutch for you," answered Himmler. "How could I justify it to the Führer? It's certainly true that thousands of the Dutch are fighting bravely on our side in the Waffen SS and that they are not all traitors. But those in the concentration camps certainly are."

Germany would have 5,000 less mouths to feed, I went on, ignoring these diversions, if he released these Dutch prisoners I asked for. Was he quite indifferent to the fact that historians five centuries hence would be commenting on Heinrich Himmler's lack of generosity towards a small Germanic people?

I secured the release of 1,000 Dutch women, together with Norwegian and Danish women and children, students and policemen, and Himmler's consent to the transference to Switzerland of 800 Frenchwomen, 400 Belgians, 500 Polish women and between two and three thousand Jews.

21st December, 1944

Before returning to Sweden, I confirmed the agreement reached in the following letter:

Dear Herr Reichsführer,

Thank you very much for your letter dated 12th December, 1944. I arrived safely at Hartzwalde. Obergruppenführer Berger was kind enough to have me brought here in his car. Tomorrow morning I am to fly back to Sweden and I am very·pleased to be able to take back with me the three Swedish gentlemen, Herr Widen, Herr Haggberg and Herr Berglind, whom you released at my request.

This extremely complicated affair is now finally settled, and I thank you whole-heartedly for saving my Swedish friends' lives. But I was always confident that you would help me in this, nor was I mistaken.

I would also like to thank you for your great consideration and to confirm the agreement we reached on the 8th of December.

First of all you promised me to release a thousand Dutch women who are interned in German concentration camps, if the Swedish Government is prepared to accept them and provide transport for them.

You further agreed to release Norwegian and Danish women and children interned in Germany, if Sweden will take them. Sweden must also provide transport for all these people. You told me, Herr Reichsführer, that you were willing to allow Swedish buses into Germany for this purpose, but not more than a hundred and fifty of them. Sweden is to provide food, rolling-stock and personnel.

You promised me at the same time to release the first fifty Norwegian students and the same number of Danish police. Yesterday I went to see Obergruppenführer Kaltenbrunner to discuss the transport of these released prisoners. At my request Schellenberg accompanied me, as I did not want to be alone when dealing with Kaltenbrunner. The latter told me that he had already received your order to release the Norwegians and Danes mentioned above; and he promised me to see to it that they would be able to spend Christmas with their families. I am very grateful to you for fulfilling my request so rapidly, Herr Reichsführer, and I hope that you will now also decide to let the remaining Norwegian students and Danish police return to their homes as free men. After all, they too are Germanic. If you would prefer it, Sweden is also prepared to intern these men, who have been so tried by fate, until the end of the war. Your promise to view these men favourably gave me particular pleasure. And I hope that when I next come to give you treatment, you will release all Dutch, Danes and Norwegians.

I am convinced that Sweden will take them all and history will not forget this magnanimity on your part. I will go to Foreign Minister Günther and inform him of our agreement as soon as I arrive in Sweden. I take it that Günther will empower Richert, the Swedish Ambassador in Berlin, to negotiate with you or those you delegate. I beg you to extend every facility to the Swedish representatives, Herr Reichsführer, and to make with them the same binding agreement that you have made with me. Please put no difficulties in their way. I would very much welcome it if you would employ Schellenberg in these talks.

Finally I should like respectfully to remind you, Herr Reichsführer, of our talks about the Jews. I asked you to release twenty thousand Jews from Theresienstadt so that they could go to Switzerland. Unhappily you said that you could not possibly do this, but were prepared to let between two and three thousand of them go. You would then consider further negotiations with me favourably, provided that the world Press did not represent it as German weakness. In my opinion it would also aid the German food situation, to have so many men removed to neutral countries.

I will fly to Sweden with a lighter heart tomorrow, knowing that you will certainly keep to what you have agreed with me.

With best wishes,

Yours respectfully,

Felix Kersten.

XXXV

HIMMLER'S IDEAS ON ENGLAND

HIMMLER had no personal knowledge of England and was little versed in English politics, which was strange in a man with such pronounced historical interests. It is true that he had some knowledge of one or two English institutions, and of the recruiting of the English aristocracy, but the real trend of English history escaped him. He could not understand a sea-power, which has its own traditions, but viewed all military matters purely from the standpoint of strategy on land, while politically he viewed England as a Germanic people related to Germany. The importance of commerce to the English nation was also an idea quite alien to him. Like most National Socialists he put politics above economics. Such an idea was understandable from the point of view of internal policy in time of war, but it threw no light on a people for whom politics and economics were inextricably connected.

Himmler spoke with enthusiasm of the Greater German Reich which was to come, protected by England's mighty fleet, while the Reich in turn guarded England with its land power and guaranteed the security of her colonies. He quite overlooked the fact that the whole aim of England's traditional policy was to prevent domination of the Continent by any great power—which meant that England was bound to fight against any kind of Greater German Reich; it was both her policy and her tradition. Himmler saw the hidden hand of the Jews in what was really England's long-established policy towards the Continent, and believed that they were keeping the two Germanic nations apart. Himmler was of course strongly influenced by Hitler in his ideas of England.

Himmler entirely failed to understand the relations between England and America, nor did he realize the predominance of America's political position in relation to England. The whole American way of thinking was so alien to him that he could not even begin to understand it.

Once more I select a few of the most significant among the conversations I have recorded.

Friedenau, Berlin
6th February, 1940

Himmler was in a very good humour today. He told me that the Führer had had very welcome news about the position in England. The people there did not want a war and everything pointed to the fact that England would soon be putting out peace feelers, which would certainly not be rejected but welcomed as an expression of Greater German solidarity in that quarter. The Führer would be magnanimous in his treatment of England. Germany had no intention of weakening England's position as a great power. On the contrary, England was to be one of the corner stones in the new Germanic Europe. England and Germany had a common destiny in the Germanic brotherhood. Conflict between the two peoples could not be justified from a Greater Germanic point of view.

England had her historic right to existence as a great power no less than Germany. There was enough room in the world for both of them to live together in peace. Co-operation would have to replace the hostility which used to exist; its advantages were obvious. Germany could protect England with its land power and safeguard her colonial possessions, while England could place at Germany's disposal the protection of her mighty fleet. Together they formed a block proof against every attack and extending into the heart of Europe, an example of Germanic strength. It was a mistake to regard the English as a commercial people and to argue the stock antithesis between soldiers and shopkeepers. The English were a Germanic people, no more commercial than the Germans. The First World War had shown them capable of heroism in battle. Assertions to the contrary were only made to provoke an artificial hatred. But a phrase from the First World War had been far more devastating in its effects: 'England is our only enemy'. That was quite to misinterpret the position, for the real enemy lay in the East. It was a tragedy that at present Germany should have to fight against her Germanic brothers once more. Every shot fired against England affected the Führer like a blow on the heart, but the situation would soon change now.

I would have liked to give a push to this flimsy ideological construction, but there was no chance, as Himmler's time was short and he was frequently interrupted during the treatment.

Berlin

8*th February*, 1940

Himmler returned today to the future relations between England and Germany, and in particular he pointed out the significance of an understanding between 'the Germanic land-power and the Germanic sea-power', in its effect on world leadership for the white races.

I enquired whether he was quite clear in his mind whether the English did not view Germany in the light of Greater Germanic ideologies, but rather from the aspect of the traditional English policy towards the Continent. To prevent the formation of blocs and to preserve the balance of power was the constant aim of English policy. England's tradition was quite against the creation of a Greater German Reich. He ought to be very clear about that, for it was the basis of any valid judgment on English policy.

Himmler strongly denied my arguments. The bonds of race were the great reality. If it was true that race affected both individuals and peoples, then all other factors were dependent on that; it even decided whether nations were to be friends or enemies. Real enmity between peoples of the same blood was quite out of the question. It was only a matter of family quarrels, such as happened even between brothers; it only required common sense on both sides to put a stop to them.

Once more I disagreed and pointed out that family quarrels and civil wars were often the fiercest. Besides he could hardly ignore the traditional course of English policy simply because it did not fit in with his ideology.

Himmler replied: "This English balance of power which you make so much of had some meaning a century or more ago; nowadays things are different. National Socialism has opened the eyes of nations to the real laws which govern their life, nor will England be able to overlook them. She will realize that a strong Germanic Reich is in her interests, for she will be able to rely on any agreements she makes with it and these will afford her greater security than playing off powers against each other on the Continent."

"The English have constantly gone to war to preserve their traditional policy," I replied, "and have never been dominated by feelings of racial kinship."

"It is only a small group in control, with the Jews to back them, who have done that," Himmler answered, "not the English people themselves. That is the group which has stirred up hostility between Germanic nations and shed Germanic blood for its devilish schemes." England would have to get rid of her Jews, that was the preliminary to any understanding between Germany and England. When the Führer made peace with England, he would demand the expulsion of her Jews. England had so many colonial possessions that it would be an easy matter for her to place one of them at the Jews' disposal. "You will live to see England and Germany in peaceful competition with each other, my dear Herr Kersten. Adolf Hitler, Führer of the greatest Germanic land-power, will be received on a state visit to London by the King of England, Führer of the greatest Germanic sea-power; and as equal partners they will conclude a just peace to protect the Germanic race throughout the world."

It was hard to find an answer to anything so fantastic. I could only say: "But you're still at war with England and nothing is yet concluded. You are overlooking the tenacity which the English always display once they have decided on war. Meanwhile you have struck the English some shrewd blows; the matter won't be decided quite as easily as all that."

"But what fighting there has been is of no consequence, Herr Kersten; reasonable Englishmen will think nothing of it. If the news we have received is true, then we will soon make further progress. Perhaps destiny required that we should go to war with England, simply in order to prove that we desire nothing except real peace and agreement on both sides."

Hochwald
9th February, 1942

Himmler had more to say about England today. I reminded him of our talk about the traditional English policy and asked him who had been proved right. He said that England must be aware of the dangers to be expected from a victorious Russia, if she really held to her balance of power policy. She would find in the Greater Germanic Reich a reliable partner and they would be able to rule the world between them.

That might be so if England's attitude were as National Socialist as he desired, I replied, but in point of fact her attitude was simply English. Napoleon, who almost dominated the Continent of Europe, was thrown back by England aided by the Holy Alliance of Prussia, Austria and Russia. England would employ a similar alliance to fight the Greater Germanic Reich. What came after that would resemble what had happened after the fall of Napoleon, which facilitated a renewal of English policy in Europe. Any nation that considered coming to an understanding with England had first of all to take into account her traditional policy and her peculiar attitude. One ought not to think of her as one would like her to be, but as she really was. Otherwise it was not surprising if there were misunderstandings and cross-purposes, nor if the supposed future partner were swiftly to reject all offers made to her. Himmler made no reply.

20th February, 1942

Himmler said today that English policy was very short-sighted. England had allowed her population to grow too big without possessing the means of feeding it, instead of settling twenty million in the dominions, where they had perfect living conditions and would put the white races in a very strong position. If for example there were now twenty million Englishmen in Australia, it would mean a great deal both to England and to the white races in general. "The British Empire has a very narrow basis. How much we could do if all that territory were at our disposal! We would send men streaming into it. That is the only possible way to control the destiny of the world. But in the long run it can only be done with men, not with money. There always comes a day when men revolt against money and their revolution is successful. England is urbanized, without a peasantry, and crammed with fifty million human beings. Famine threatens the island once it loses its possessions overseas. I have no doubt that one day this will happen."

3rd November, 1943

In view of the generally tense situation, said Himmler, it was beyond his comprehension that the English ruling class failed to see what a mistake it was making in supporting Russia. A Russian victory would certainly lead to England's downfall. At the same time America would so dominate England that nothing would be left of her status as a great power. An understanding with National Socialist Germany would alter the situation for England at a stroke; there would be no further danger from Asia and England would have her rear securely guarded by Germany when she came to fight against America. I reminded Himmler of the Stalingrad catastrophe, after which England was less inclined than ever to the move his fancy prompted.

Finally I asked Brandt whether Himmler was not yet cured of his illusions about England, whether he still could not see that England was simply concerned with destroying the National Socialist Reich. "Not in the least," Brandt told me. "Himmler is convinced that a better outlook will prevail in England one of these days, and when he intensifies the war against England it is with the idea of forcing this outlook upon her. In private he is constantly trying to find out the state of opinion in England and leaves those who serve him in no doubt about his own views."

10th December, 1944

Himmler informed me during the treatment that it was now unhappily evident that this battle between brothers had to be fought to the bitter end. The Jews in England had triumphed; England had thrown her own people and Asia into the general revolt against Europe's Germanic federation. Where would Europe be today if there was no Waffen SS, which acted as a breakwater against the East? This battle would be viewed in a hundred years' time just like that of the German Emperor Henry I, who had stemmed the hordes from the steppes of Asia.

I reminded him of our first talks about England's traditional policy. "You were right, Herr Kersten, we did not judge the facts of the situation correctly. We were looking further ahead and for the moment we were wrong. Time alone will show whether we were also wrong about the future. I don't think so. But if it is the aim of English policy to allow the formation of no great power on the Continent, England must already realize that, in conjunction with America, she is on the way to giving Russia this predominance, and every day that passes must bring her closer to agreement with us. Every day English Continental policy will increasingly envisage Germany as the natural partner in its balance of power."

It was obvious to me what Himmler was trying to do; he was linking up traditional English policy on the Continent with his old idea of an agreement between England and Germany. I replied that, though his assumption might be right in principle, fighting was still going on and such changes were not made in a moment. The other partner, America, would also have something to say.

Himmler said that all propaganda, particularly by way of neutral channels, would concentrate on bringing home to the English how much they had to gain from an agreement of this kind. He would talk to Goebbels and Ribbentrop about this very important matter of policy. It would not fail to make an impression in England that such a suggestion should emanate from him, who represented with his SS the factor which contributed most to order in Europe. It was generally known that his SS could not only fight, but obey. Nor would there be any psychological obstacles in the way of such a change.

Himmler looked at me, expecting an answer. It was obvious to me that he was still swayed by ideology and was quite unaware that his reputation abroad was not that of a factor making for order, but rather that of a hangman, a murderer on a vast scale and above all else the man responsible for the abominable campaign against the Jews. No government would dare to treat with him, even if it wanted to. I hesitated a moment before telling him the brutal truth, then let him have it, holding nothing back.

It was with something more than astonishment that I heard Himmler assert that these 'calumnies' spread about by enemy propaganda would have to be rectified. "The West has accepted a man like Stalin as an ally, and worse things could be said against him." Himmler put an end to the conversation, because he did not like to hear things which would not fit in with his theory, one which has been almost an obsession with him recently—understandably, in view of the increasingly desperate situation.

*   *   *   *   *

This was the last time I talked to Himmler about England. He never gave up his attempts to get England to listen to him. It quite accorded with his attitude that later, when faced with the Dönitz government and the German collapse, he continued to regard himself as the one man whom the West would recognize as a factor making for order—and therefore the proper man with whom to negotiate.

XXXVI

HIMMLER AND THE WAFFEN SS

NEXT to discussing the Germanic ancestors, Himmler's favourite theme was the Waffen SS. This was for him a living example of the possibility of realizing all his ideas about re-educating the German people and rearing a new breed of men. He would sometimes suddenly refer to the Waffen SS while in the midst of discussing Germanic ideals with the words: "You see, this is what I have arranged for my Waffen SS."

When I expressed a doubt as to whether he would succeed in his efforts to persuade his men that it is a detestable crime to seize other people's property, he told me: "No cupboards are locked in the Waffen SS. None of them would dare even to take a cigarette belonging to his comrade. You see, it works."

We discussed plundering and I remarked that many regarded this as 'a gentlemanly crime'. I quoted the case of old Blücher, who, invited to London by the English after the war of liberation, remarked, "What a fine town to plunder," as he rode through it with his adjutant.

"Plunder is certainly not a gentlemanly crime in our eyes," Himmler emphatically replied. "I have had a special 'Notice on the Confiscation of Enemy Property' published, which every member of the Waffen SS has to carry in his pay-book." He gave me a copy and read in a loud voice:

"To take the goods and chattels of the unarmed civilian population is unchivalrous and unworthy of the SS. The Reichsführer SS's orders on the 'sanctity of private property' also apply in time of war even to the enemy."

A soldier might requisition food, clothing, blankets, fuel and medical supplies—that was obvious, he explained to me—but this must be done only in accordance with 'the temporary and personal needs of the individual soldier'. Men were made fully aware of this. They were absolutely forbidden to take table silver, civilian clothes, stuffs,

silk stockings, etc.—that is to say anything intended for the use of the
men's dependants at home. That was looting and was punishable by
death. The death penalty also applied in case of rape. I read the notice
through in detail. Here were all Himmler's orders on the 'sanctity of
private property' and their application in time of war.

Himmler loved the Waffen SS as if it were his very own child,
although he had no say in the operational employment of this force. He
was simply their supreme director; the arming of them and their
political training also came under his control. He was proud that
Hitler, in his Reichstag speech after the French campaign, had praised
him as the organizer of 'The Waffen SS formations'. But as Himmler
was no soldier he failed to realize that he had placed a frightful burden
on the fighting troops of the Waffen SS, and one that had many consequences, by linking them administratively with the Gestapo, the
concentration camp guards, the extermination squads and other such
units. As fighting troops they passed out of his control, yet remained
without a proper Leader of their own.

Thus their situation became tragic; on the one hand they sacrificed
themselves willingly and fought most fiercely against an enemy as
barbaric as the Russians, while on the other there always clung about
them an atmosphere of blood guilt and apocalyptic crime.

I found it all the more difficult to understand Himmler's blindness
to reality and its effects, since I have often seen him sitting over
reports from the front about the deeds of the Waffen SS, his eyes
shining with enthusiasm. Despite his grief over the Waffen SS's losses,
he recited with pride the telegram captured from the Russian higher
command which read: "The German Wehrmacht is streaming back
on all fronts. Only the Waffen SS is standing like a rock in the sea."

I had dozens of talks with Himmler about the Waffen SS; to
publish all my notes on it would require a separate volume. Here I
only include a few which seem to be typical of Himmler's attitude to
the Waffen SS.

I had to have a talk with Gottlob Berger, General of the Waffen SS
and chief of the SS Head Office, in order to get a clear picture of the
Waffen SS and of its European volunteers. For it was Berger who had
brought the European volunteers into being and who was responsible
for the commitment of the Waffen SS. It also seemed to me that
Himmler's imagination sometimes ran away with him and led him to
exaggerate some of Hitler's remarks—for instance concerning the
territory to be given to the soldier-peasants and the new map of
Europe which was also connected with the European volunteers. As

he had direct access to Hitler, even unaccompanied by Himmler, I also expected that Berger would be able to enlighten me on these matters.

It was Himmler's wish that I should give Berger treatment, which offered me the opening I wanted. Berger had an excellent constitution and nerves of iron, although he had been severely wounded in the First World War. My treatment was therefore more of a prophylactic nature, but it enabled me to make contact with him. I came to see more of him, not, as was the case with Himmler, because he needed me but because Berger had similar ideas to my own on humanitarian questions and on their solution in accordance with justice.

Berger had a powerful physique and a head which rather recalled that of an ancient Roman commander—with the features Germanized. An iron self-control showed in his bearing and movements, very different from Himmler's nervous gestures. As he came from Suabia and was so devoted to it, he was known as 'the Duke of Suabia'. From my talks with him I derived a deeper insight both into the European volunteers and into the future planned for Europe under National Socialism. For this reason I include some of Berger's remarks in my notes on Himmler's.

1. *PRINCIPLES GOVERNING THE SELECTION OF RECRUITS*

Field Headquarters
2nd August, 1941

Himmler spoke enthusiastically today about the heroic struggle of an SS division in the Yelna bulge; it held its position for sixteen days against greatly superior forces; it smashed thirteen Russian divisions and defeated the attempt of two or three Soviet armies to break out of the Smolensk pocket.

"This one division of the Waffen SS has played the essential part in deciding the important battle against the Russians caught in the Smolensk pocket. Would you like to hear details of the action? I have the reports in front of me. Here is one Group [platoon] which the Wehrmacht has singled out for mention in dispatches. By throwing grenades the group had marked out a semi-circle of enemy dead in front of its position. The Group-leader, his hand on the pin of his last grenade, his three section commanders, his runner and his driver, were all found dead in the trench. The first section-leader still held his rifle to his shoulder, the runner still had his hand on the case which contained the last dispatch. That's how they were when they were found."

Himmler was silent a few moments, then went on: "That's the way my Waffen SS fights. Here you see the effect of a knowledge of what we are fighting for joined to the finest military tradition. The Commander of the Wehrmacht and the soldiers of the army, who have fought side by side with these units, speak with the greatest respect of the heroism which these men display. Those are the sort of men who will provide the *élite* that we need. Even in peace-time we must so arrange matters that bravery and courage of this kind guide us in the selection of men."

Himmler told me in the course of the treatment that he had decided that in peace-time any man who wanted to become an SS officer would be obliged to make a parachute jump. "Otherwise the reputation that these young men have won for us by shedding their blood and the fine uniform that we wear in peace-time will bring into the ranks of the SS young men about town and intellectuals who will only join because it helps them in their career." The heat of battle showed who were the right men for the SS. Special methods of selection would have to be adopted in peace-time. One way would be to make any man who wanted to become an SS officer prove his practical abilities for at least a year before he was appointed, and that in some really strenuous and dangerous calling, such as a mountaineer's or a sailor's. Future SS officers would only acquire the right attitude to the men under them and their own self-respect by working among other workers. Then there would never again be N.C.O.s and officers of the old sort.

17th August, 1941

Himmler told me yesterday that officers in the SS had to take a special oath to ensure that SS principles would govern the choice of future recruits, and to avoid any kind of corruption. They had to swear not to favour their own sons, nor those of friends or relatives; they had to be incorruptible, uninfluenced by ties of blood or friendship. Only character, achievement and the decisions of the racial examiner should guide the choice of recruits.

I replied that his officers were only men and could not escape from their own limitations. Since he so emphasized the importance that the closest ties of blood and kinship had in other fields, he could hardly view the introduction of a man's own family connections with such abhorrence here.

"Families sacrifice their sons and relatives for the good of the

Reich," Himmler answered, "so they can make this much smaller sacrifice for the good of the SS, which will one day have to shoulder the Reich's burdens. I'm referring here to the toughness within a man and to the categorical imperative of duty. In times of war selection is relatively easy. Merits are obvious now; the Iron Cross and other decorations guide one's decision. Only in times of peace will selection be a matter of conscience. Then it will depend on the moral character of the man responsible for choosing, and he must decide on grounds of race, achievement and character, and must be free of all other considerations."

18th September, 1941

"The leadership of the SS," Himmler declared, "must be subject to very careful selection; its basis is unwavering courage; there can be no more cowards. With this as a basis, we can proceed to the second principle governing our choice—training in knowledge and ability. The first quality, courage, must be equally great in all the men; the second is an individual matter, but one that must be developed to the maximum."

29th October, 1941

Today Himmler discussed the significance of poverty and said this: "My ideal for all members of the SS is the poverty proper to dedicated men. The SS will give them security, for it must be rich enough to give them house and home and to provide for their old age. Every member of the SS, besides carrying out his duty, should be able to follow his own inclinations in the way of sport, scholarship and art. Senseless private wealth and capitalistic activities are unworthy of an SS man. Wealth of knowledge is the best thing, that and real ability —with plenty of children, a few acres of ground and some trees. To die poor is the ideal I have set before myself. I regard the SS as a tree which I have planted, which has roots deep enough to defy all weathers."

I expressed a hope to Himmler that he would succeed in bringing his ideal of 'dedicated poverty' to the notice of certain high officials in the Party, who clearly showed no signs of sharing it.

14th November, 1941

I was talking a few days ago with a high Leader in the SS who told me that he had been an officer in the First World War, had joined

the SS in 1933 and had then transferred to the Waffen SS. I asked him
his reasons. He told me that after the Nazis had seized power, Himmler
had invited a number of senior officers from the World War, scholars,
men of property and industrialists to Munich and addressed them on
these lines:

Every state required an *élite*. The SS was to provide the *élite*, the
constructive political force in the National Socialist state. That could
only come about if its members brought to the social requirements
of the present day the genuine military tradition, the distinctive
outlook, bearing and breeding of the German nobility, the knowledge,
ability and creative efficiency of the industrialists and the profundity
of German scholarship, on a basis of racial selection. In the course of
time these qualities had manifested certain weaknesses. The soldier
had tended to become a mere automaton without opinions of his
own; the scholar quickly degenerated into the intellectual; an un-
restrained and monopolistic capitalism was the caricature of the
industrialist, while the society papers gave a clear enough picture of
what the degenerate form of the nobility was like.

In their struggle against the former order and its representatives,
it was easy to understand how speakers and writers in the National
Socialist press came to emphasize only the negative side; thus, for
instance, they had strongly attacked the intellect in its degenerate and
'high-brow' form. Such attacks still continued at present, but they
would die down in time. His own idea was to make use of the positive
values which all these types of men embodied and to direct them into
the channel of the SS while this was still in its formative period.

It was a matter of linking up the National Socialist revolution
with tradition and effecting the union of everything genuine which
had survived from the past and shown itself capable of confronting the
future. Then the SS would have a properly established basis and be
all the better adapted to fulfilling its tasks.

This explanation made a great deal clear to me that I had never
understood before. I am going to meet my informant again this evening
and will learn more from him.

15th November, 1941

As a sequel to our last talk I heard this yesterday:

Himmler's address evoked general astonishment, for it had been
assumed that Himmler had called this circle together in order to explain
to them all the wrongs of which they had been guilty in the past.

Himmler had further declared that this union of the various

traditions required a long and organic process. This process could be shortened if the representatives of the different groups assembled there would place themselves at his disposal. The officer class and the nobility should contribute the finest elements of their tradition, industrialists their knowledge and experience, in particular of affairs in other countries; scholars should place at his disposal, in practical outline and pregnant formulas, the products of their knowledge. Everybody should bring something to the formation of the Reich's new *élite*; every person could find an opportunity to apply his knowledge and abilities. The formation of a responsible *élite* as a basis for the state was the best way of preventing the abuses which had accompanied the French Revolution from manifesting themselves in their own revolution.

The psychology of Himmler's address was very skilful. In talking to members of this class, Goebbels in particular constantly adopted a bullying attitude; instead of that, Himmler had accorded them full recognition and dwelt on the significance of their previous achievements. At the same time the invitation to take part in forming this *élite* was regarded as an honour. Under the influence of this speech the majority of those present had decided to join the SS and their example had been followed by more representatives from these same classes, especially as membership of the Party was not a prerequisite of entry into the SS.

The man who told me this had himself joined the ordinary SS and since he had previously been an officer he had soon become an SS Obersturmbannführer. In consequence of Himmler's attitude the SS secured a considerable number of men who helped, advised or trained, playing a part, either directly or indirectly, in the formation of this *élite*. They felt that co-operation offered the best means of counteracting the chaotic forces within the Party; and their black uniform seemed to them a sure protection against pressure from the Party. A number transferred to the Security and Intelligence Services. My man had preferred a purely military *rôle*. When the creation of combat formations of SS troops began, he had decided to join them.

2. SERVICE UNDER HIMMLER

Himmler was strict with his SS men, but always considerate, at least indirectly, for he wished each of them to share in the responsibility for the SS principles which he proclaimed. He was very polite, friendly and likable in his behaviour towards his SS Leaders, on whom he made great demands. This seemed to be his natural manner, not one he had taught himself. He constantly took great trouble over their worries and needs, helped them when they were in difficulties, sent flowers when their wives had a child, writing personally to express his good wishes.

When a young and highly decorated SS Leader reported to him, he privately gave orders for a call to be put through to the man's old mother in a Württemberg village. He beamed when the orderly reported that the woman was on the 'phone and handed the instrument to her son.

When he visited the Hirschberg military academy, where young staff officers were assembled for two years' advanced training, his first question was whether these officers were all married. When he was told that a large proportion of them were married, but were not allowed to have their wives with them owing to service regulations, he declared that this ban should at once be lifted. Who could know whether these wives would ever see their husbands again? They would look back with deep emotion on the two years they had been able to spend together. He promised to raise the matter of accommodation with the Ministry of the Interior. Soon the young officers were joined by their wives.

3. THE WEHRMACHT AND THE WAFFEN SS

Friedenau, Berlin
28th June, 1940

I asked Himmler whether the Waffen SS was to become an independent army. He said that this was not intended and that the SS formations were relatively small in numbers compared with the Wehrmacht as a whole. They had developed out of the first SS troops, which in turn had developed from a few hundred men who formed Adolf Hitler's bodyguard. Considering how recent this development was, these young troops already had a great reputation. He would do everything to raise their status and provide them with the best arms and equipment.

I asked why it was necessary to have special SS troops apart from the Wehrmacht. Here follows a summary of Himmler's remarks in reply to this:

"Every revolution tries to control the army and infuse the men with its own spirit. Only when that has been achieved is a revolution finally triumphant. The French Revolution made a success of this, to which it owed the rapidity with which it spread and the power which brought it victory. The Weimar Republic failed in this, never solving the problem of the army. One anguished question hung over every decision it made: 'What is the Reichswehr going to do?' There are two ways of forming a Wehrmacht which would meet the demands of National Socialism. The Führer could have scrapped the old officer corps entirely; for it's the officers who create morale. It would have been possible to rebuild a Wehrmacht in which the officers were reliable National Socialists, men who not only had technical ability but were also entirely acceptable in their general attitude and bearing. That would have been the proper way, the organic one, but it would have taken far too long. The Führer could not endanger the Reich's security by renouncing the older officers' experience and technical ability. Yet he took into account the fact that these men were largely out of sympathy with National Socialism. This was why he recruited troops for special duties and then in the Waffen SS created an armed force to embody the views which National Socialism had to introduce into the Wehrmacht.

"The Waffen SS is the protagonist of the National Socialist revolution in the military field. To our basic requirements it adds the old military tradition and a high degree of military efficiency. These men know what they are fighting for—the Waffen SS is not simply a mindless force obeying orders. Merit is the only way to promotion in it. Comradeship and the recognition of merit rather than social status govern relations between officers and men. These dedicated comrades-in-arms have quite a different attitude to life, and to fighting, from the old army's. That is already apparent and this attitude is constantly being reinforced. I shall take great pains to turn Waffen SS officers into men with firm convictions and views. Then we will have the cadres we need for a new-model army."

This all seemed to me very confused and wholly ideological. So I asked Himmler what he imagined would be the effect of the Waffen SS on the Wehrmacht; would Waffen SS officers be posted to the Wehrmacht and given important commands, in order to influence the Wehrmacht's morale? How otherwise would the two branches of the army grow together?

"At the moment there can be no question of organic growth between them," Himmler replied. "The Waffen SS must first develop according to its own laws. The Polish and French campaigns have already earned it a great reputation. This is very significant, for an army's respect is not gained by lectures on an attitude to life, only by success in the field—the same field on which the Wehrmacht also fights. The reformer has to be efficient and master the existing system down to the last detail; otherwise he loses any right to demand reform.

"In future the Wehrmacht and the Waffen SS will fight side by side, shoulder to shoulder. The whole Waffen SS must win the reputation already achieved by the 'Leibstandarte' and 'Reich' divisions. Wherever the Waffen SS appears, success will attend our arms. Then the question of why victory follows its flag will naturally arise. People will soon be ready to accept the answer: 'Because these are dedicated men who know what they are fighting for, who show by their example that the conviction in the justice of their cause doubles their fighting strength, giving them a force that nothing can resist, making them capable of these great deeds.' It will become the desire of every true young German to serve in this corps *d'élite*; it will be regarded as a very great honour to be a Waffen SS officer, as is already the case in the 'Leibstandarte'. Then the Wehrmacht will adopt Waffen SS principles and mutual organic development will follow. It would be a mistake to foster this artificially."

"I thought we stood on the threshold of peace," I said. "But despite this you are busy creating first- and second-class troops, splitting and weakening the unity and spirit of the armed forces as a whole. That is shown by the reproaches of responsible Wehrmacht officers, that your Waffen SS is robbing the army of thousands and thousands of the best N.C.O.s."

"I'm well aware of that," Himmler replied, "but we've got to take the men we need from somewhere."

4. *THE GESTAPO AND THE WAFFEN SS*

Shitomir
9th August, 1942

I saw yesterday a member of the Gestapo whom I had met previously at Field Headquarters when he was reporting to Himmler; this time he was wearing the uniform of an Untersturmführer in the Waffen SS. I asked Himmler whether he was now planning to incorporate the Gestapo in the Waffen SS.

"How could you have such an idea?" Himmler replied. "The Waffen SS has absolutely no connection with the Gestapo; their work is quite distinct. The Gestapo is fighting against the enemy at home;

the Waffen SS is directed against the enemy beyond the frontier. The Gestapo is the national charwoman who does the dirty work which must be done. But it's only natural that Gestapo officials should do their military service in the Waffen SS. They only serve their time in the Waffen SS. They do their military service there instead of in the Wehrmacht.

"I attach the greatest importance to the complete separation of these two branches. It's entirely forbidden for members of the Gestapo to tell their comrades, when they are serving in the Waffen SS, about the tasks they have to perform, which are often unpleasant. This is also forbidden by the terms of their oath and by the Führer's orders that each man may only be told what is absolutely necessary for his work. I don't want to burden men and officers of the Waffen SS with matters which they are unable to judge or understand. On the other hand it's a relief for men in the Gestapo to breathe the fresh air of the Waffen SS and to feel that it's a job worth doing to protect the rear of their fighting comrades."

In that case, I replied, I was unable to grasp why he had concentration camps guarded by men of the Waffen SS.

"That never happens," Himmler replied. "Concentration camp guards have nothing to do with the Waffen SS. They are a quite separate formation; they wear SS uniform but they have distinctive badges. These young men have only been taken into the Waffen SS because they have to belong to some establishment."

I drew Himmler's attention to the fact that my friends generally assumed that the Waffen SS, the Gestapo and the concentration camp guards were one and the same, and that it was very difficult to tell the difference.

He replied that I should get the details from Pohl; he would tell him when he saw him in a few days' time. He added that he had the further intention of uniting the police, the security service, the administration and the SS into a single corps for the defence of the realm, but that this could only take place after the war; and even then he was by no means certain that he would include the Waffen SS. It depended on future relations between the Waffen SS and the Wehrmacht.

I told Himmler that this odd mixture was bound to be destructive in its effects, instead of constructive, and was really a caricature of the arrangements usually adopted in these matters. As a Finnish Army officer I had realized that a simple system of organization was the best, instead of this complicated system which could only end by confusing every man's identity.

Shitomir
22nd August, 1942

A few days ago I spoke to Pohl, who confirmed what Himmler had told me. I also learnt that the majority of concentration camp guards came from Volksdeutschen and volunteers from outside the Reich, who had joined the Waffen SS, but been rejected as unfit for active service. Pohl told me of the advantages which these guards gained from sharing a common establishment with the Waffen SS. They were all of an economic nature. It had fallen to him to draw Himmler's attention to the possibilities of this. It saved a great deal of money and trouble, satisfied the men themselves and gave them a recognized position when confronted with the authorities. It also put them beyond the reach of the Wehrmacht. The Security Service (Sicherheitsdienst) was now adopting this system. The majority of their men had a Waffen SS pay-book.

I told Pohl that he was arousing opposition, confusion and insecurity with this procedure and that one day the Waffen SS would reproach him bitterly for it.

5. *THE EUROPEAN VOLUNTEER FORMATIONS AND EUROPE*

The European volunteer SS formations played a significant part inside the Waffen SS according to Himmler's way of thinking. He saw in them the protagonists of a Greater Germanic Reich directed against the East, to become, when the war was over, Europe's defence against the hordes of Asia. The names of these formations, regiments and divisions were chosen to emphasize the tradition of which they had to be made aware.

There was the 'Viking' division (volunteers from all the Germanic countries), the 'Netherland' (Dutch), 'Northland' (chiefly Norwegians and Danes from the 'Norway' and 'Denmark' corps of volunteers). Then came the 'Flanders' and 'Wallonia' (Flemings and Walloons) divisions. Charles, 'the Slayer of the Saxons', had to alter his name —how times change—to Charlemagne as a symbol of European unity. An SS division of Frenchmen was named 'Charlemagne' in his honour. The Volksdeutschen of south-eastern Europe (in Transylvania alone twelve per cent of the population were recruited) fought in all the SS divisions and also composed the 'Prince Eugene' division. The Eastern European peoples provided an Esthonian division, two

Latvian, one Cossack and a 'Galician' (Ukrainians). The Moslems were called up and fought in the 'Handschar' (Croats, Bosnians and Herzegovinians) and 'Skanderbeg' (Serbs and Albanians) divisions, also in the East Turkmenistan Waffen SS formation under Kajum Khan, a descendant of Ghengis Khan. Finally there were the Caucasian and Georgian Waffen SS formations. Here are some extracts from our many talks about the European SS formations.[1]

Berlin
20th March, 1941

From a narrowly patriotic point of view, Himmler declared, he could only have a detestation for Charlemagne, because he had been responsible for the brutal and bloody slaughter of the Saxons, who were the most pure-blooded, the toughest and the boldest of all German stocks. "But an imperial unity, which since then has repeatedly saved Europe from the hordes of Asia, demanded these measures to break the resistance of these proud and thick-skulled Germanic tribes. If severity is ever justifiable, it was then. Let us hope that the day will never come when we will have to regret the sin of being too merciful to Asia, when it is a question of Europe's essential unity. But first of all the Waffen SS must restore Europe's position in the struggle with Asia."

23rd April, 1941

Himmler aired his views on a European Reich: "The old 'Holy Roman Empire of the German Nation' comprised three concentric circles: the first circle was an idea which embraced the whole of Europe, that the West was a unity with its own attitude to life. The circle nearest the centre was the idea that the strongest element in this unity was the German people and their Reich, who were therefore called upon to take the lead. Between these two circles was one composed of countries and states under German suzerainty. Then again between this circle and the one outside were the other states who were opposed not in the least to the Western idea of unity, but to the German leadership."

---

[1] All volunteer formations wore the Wehrmacht's field-grey coat, with the SS rune and shoulder-flashes with their country's arms and the name of their division. They carried their own colours and their country's flag. With the Finns Himmler wanted to continue the tradition of the 27th Rifle Regiment; they had the Finnish flag with a lion 'or' on a dark red ground. Himmler wished the Danes to have their traditional symbol always before their eyes, so they had the 'Danebrog', the Danish volunteers' flag, which legend said had been conferred on them by Heaven when they were fighting against the Slavs.

The situation changed with the discovery of America and the growth of colonies. If Europe was to survive, the idea of an empire in the West would have to be resurrected. As Germany was by far the strongest power, she had to restore this empire. Apparently this could only be done by the use of force, for other countries imagined that they could safely make a life of their own with their colonies. But if Europe failed to unite she would only be taken over by Russia or the U.S.A. The Waffen SS and the European SS volunteers were giving their blood for the security of the West, so that it might once more assume its true form, and no longer be split up into groups with conflicting interests.

I pointed out to Himmler that the political condition of Europe was essentially different from the days when peoples had not yet developed a national consciousness. Then the various princes had formed a sort of nation and naturally had to be knit together by the authority of an overlord. Today, however, unity in Europe could only rest on the basis of equal rights for independent peoples and on democracy, not on autocratic power.

Shitomir
20th July, 1942

Himmler told me while we were at table that Quisling had announced that Norwegian SS formations now bore the name 'Germanic SS Norwegians'. Quisling had also declared that the only means to assure Norway's existence as a free and independent nation in the present World War was by entry into the Greater Germanic community. The Führer was very delighted about this and had also expressed great pleasure over his, Himmler's, news that already nearly 50,000 Dutch and a constantly increasing number of Flemings, Walloons, French, Danes, Swedes, Spaniards and Swiss were serving in the Waffen SS. This proved that the idea of a united Germanic Europe was prevailing. This must be presented to the European peoples as a lighthouse, an empire beneath whose revolving beam all might find their appointed place. This idea would attract the most tenacious forces in Germanic Europe and absorb them into the empire.

I asked Himmler whether this empire was to be ruled from Berlin; if so, the peoples of Europe might refuse the invitation. "That is very far from being the Führer's intention," he replied. "He is a true Austrian and knows what holds an empire together. He is already reacting against the Berlin system of making regulations for everything." Organic growth could alone evolve the right methods of administering an empire. He had in mind the way in which England held together her empire. A strong central organ was needed for that; the Germanic people's Waffen SS could form an organ of this kind.

I replied that the inclusion of foreign nationals in the Waffen SS might take people in for a time, but it was quite out of the question to assert that a decisive majority of the population in these countries accepted his view; many more were against it.

Field Headquarters
10th September, 1942

I still had in mind Himmler's threatening attitude towards Finland in his talks with Witting and Ryti in August and September 1942 (see Ch. XIX), when I spoke to Berger about Himmler's designs on Sweden and his plans to extend colonies of soldier-peasants up to the Urals, while at the same time keeping the native populations in an inferior status (see page 138). I reminded Berger of plans to resettle whole national groups in south-eastern Europe or in other areas. In all these matters I wanted to know how much was simply imagination and how much was seriously intended. And were they really clear about the effects which would follow the wholesale destruction of human rights and culture, which must lead in the end to the destruction of Europe herself?

"Only a man whose mind has never developed beyond the age of heroic legends and primitive myth could talk like that," Berger replied. "It's as if he were sitting in front of a mediaeval map and dividing countries up guided only by his wishful thinking, quite ignoring any changes in the world that have taken place since. For at least five hundred years only two things counted in Europe: the temporal power of the princes and the spiritual power of Church and Pope. Between them they decided every country's wars and policies, without consulting their peoples about them. But a new factor has since emerged: those peoples themselves, enjoying a life of their own.

"Industrialism has replaced handicrafts, world trade has superseded national economies. The reason why power passed out of the hands of its former possessors was because they never realized this. The last man who wanted to unite Europe, Napoleon, only half grasped it and that's why he failed. If we fail to grasp it and to act on it, we too are doomed. I am afraid that Himmler has never grasped it, despite his wide historical reading."

Field Headquarters
11th September, 1942

Berger declared that only a voluntary movement could create a new Europe; and only events which were quite out of the ordinary, affecting all peoples whether they liked it or not, would be able to bring such a movement into being. One event of this sort would be the defence of Europe against ideas, influences and conceptions which ran counter to her own way of life. Constructive ideas would be bound to emerge in a defence of this kind. Ours was an age which demanded this defence, against Bolshevism, against the pressure of this old Asiatic spirit which had been threatening Europe since 1917. Germany ought not to be alone in bearing the burden of this struggle; the youth of Europe had to fight with her. The German Wehrmacht was the army of German territories and could only accept European volunteers to a limited extent.

"But the Waffen SS," Berger continued, "is not only a defence force, but the advance guard of an idea. The Waffen SS is therefore able to make room for volunteers from every country. This is the beginning of the new Europe."

"Himmler told me something of the kind," I replied, "but it affected me rather as a lecture by a professor."

"I'm an old soldier," said Berger, "and I can't put up much of a show in that way. But as a front-line soldier in two world wars I say to myself: if a man from one country has seen service with a man from another, they often develop a lifelong friendship, which makes for a better understanding between the two peoples."

These reflections led him in 1940 to suggest to Hitler the founding of a European volunteer formation inside the Waffen SS. He received permission to start and the 'Germanic Controlling Office' was developed as a headquarters for the organization. Berger appointed a Swiss chief of staff, in order to avoid any political intrigues. The different countries were always represented in this office by fellow nationals. Now they included Dutch, Flemings, Walloons, French, Norwegians, Danes, Esthonians, Latvians, Swiss, Swedes. For the European volunteers were to have no resemblance whatever to any kind of Foreign Legion. A Foreign Legion would mean the death of the European ideal.

I expressed a doubt whether in the end the Foreign Legion aspect would not prevail, however much goodwill was shown.

Berger's reply was: "Recognition of the fact that they are fighting for Europe should supply them with a moral purpose and an honourable status." They had their own chaplains, Catholic, Evangelical,

Greek Orthodox; and the Moslems had Mohammedan ones. The volunteers also had obligations towards their families, which was exactly the opposite of what happened in a Foreign Legion. They were also promised that the uniting of Europe would not affect the language, religion, culture or customs of the country in question. Europe would not be forced into the mould of a single state, but would be far more a federal unity, even looser than the constitution that Bismarck had given to the German states in 1871. European defence and police organization would have to be centralized. In stipulating this to Berger, Hitler had also put foreign policy in the same category. Berger showed me a regulation, drawn up in the various languages, which declared that in no circumstances would the volunteers be called upon to fight against their own countries; so that in the event of an unsuccessful outcome to the war, the volunteers could not incur the reproach of betraying their own land.

"But that is just what will happen," I replied, "for the world regards this matter differently. You have yourself admitted that Himmler is a theorist. Now I am making the acquaintance of another theorist, on his own admission—and his name is Berger."

Berger went on: "As a soldier, my feelings are with the soldiers of Europe. French volunteers wear the Iron Cross side by side with the Legion of Honour, even when they have won the latter in fighting against Germany. Two service ribbons from two different countries proudly borne on *one* chest—that's what you get in the new Europe! The theories of the diplomats will perhaps ruin the achievements of the soldiers. That's my only approach to the domain of theory. These gentry will possibly arrange matters in such a way that Europe may still remain as divided afterwards as she was before."

"First get rid of these fearful theorists who ruin everything," I replied, "including theorists in the SS, then you may get some sense. Then the conception of European volunteers will have a sound basis. Then you would be able to appeal to the outside world in the name of Europe."

Berger made no reply. It seemed to me that I had touched on his own secret thoughts.

Field Headquarters
18th December, 1942

"Our measures are not really so original," Himmler declared. "All great nations have used some degree of force or waged war in acquiring their status as a great power, in much the same way as ourselves: the

French, the Spanish, the Italians, the Poles, to a great extent too the English and the Americans. Centuries ago Charlemagne set us the example of resettling an entire people by his action with the Saxons and the Franks, the English with the Irish, the Spaniards with the Moors; and the American method of dealing with their Indians was to evacuate whole races. Concentration camps were first started by the English. In this at least we are different from the English, for we only shut up enemies of the community, its criminal or political enemies, while the English had left women and children to perish in concentration camps when they were fighting against the Boers, the women and children of a legally constituted state. But we are certainly original in one important point: our measures are the expression of an idea, not the search for any personal advantage or ambition: we desire only the realization on a Germanic basis of a social ideal and the unity of the West. We will clarify the situation at whatever cost. It may take as many as three generations before the West gives its approval to this new order, for which the Waffen SS was created."

Hartzwalde
15th January, 1943

Today I discussed with Berger Himmler's remarks about Sweden, Holland and the boundless territories to be assigned to the soldier-peasants, in order to establish how much of what Himmler had said was to be taken seriously.

Berger's conclusions were: "I am a soldier. I can answer for military matters; for instance, those affecting the Waffen SS and the volunteers who are paving the way for the new Europe. But as to the political organization of Europe, I can only quote various pronouncements of the Führer's which came out during discussions over the European volunteers."

Berger mentioned a number of statements on these lines: Europe's weaknesses were, too many customs barriers and too many tariffs, too many different currencies, exaggerated nationalism and emphasis on national sovereignty. These causes of hatred and inefficiency had to disappear. Europe's population, including the North African territories, was three times that of the U.S.A. and she could achieve a corresponding prosperity; nor need her position be any more open to attack than that of the U.S.A.

The European empire would form a confederation of free states, among which would be Greater Germany, Hungary, Croatia, Slovakia, Holland, Flanders, Wallonia, Luxemburg, Norway, Denmark,

Esthonia, Latvia, Lithuania. These countries were to govern themselves. They would have in common a European currency, certain areas of the administration including the police, foreign policy and the army in which the various nations would be represented by national formations. Trade relations would be governed by special treaties, a sphere in which Germany as the economically strongest country would hold back in order to favour the development of the weaker ones. Free towns were also envisaged, having special functions of their own, among them the task of representing a nation's culture.

A nation's culture was also manifested in the courage of her soldiers. For this reason no steps would be taken after the final victory against European soldiers and officers who had fought openly against Germany, for they had only obeyed orders and done their duty. To behave otherwise would be to frustrate any co-operation in the future.

If other states wanted to join this empire, they would be very welcome, but union would only follow a favourable and secret vote of more than three-quarters of the population. Finland however was to remain a completely independent state, honoured with special treaties and economic aid, for Hitler regarded the Finns as the bravest nation he knew.

When Bolshevism had been extirpated in Russia, the Western Territories would come under German administration modelled on the Marches which Charlemagne had instituted in the east of his empire; the methods followed would be those by which England had evolved her colonies into dominions. When peace and economic health were fully restored, these territories would be handed back to the Russian people, who would live there in complete freedom, and a twenty-five-year peace and commercial treaty would be concluded with the new government.

The Poles and the Czechs would be united with their fellow Slavs, the Russians. But a part of the Eastern Territories would be built up into a defence area, peopled by soldier-peasants (see Ch. XVIII). The approved model for this would be the military frontiers held from the sixteenth to the nineteenth century by Austro-Hungary against the Osmanli Turks. It was quite out of the question that this area would stretch as far as the Urals. "You can add Himmler's illusions about the Urals to those he had about Sweden," said Berger.

Field Headquarters
8th February, 1943

"Europe never gets something for nothing. Great achievements can only be brought about by sacrifices on a vast scale and often they have to be repeated. Blood is the strongest sort of cement. The new Europe is being built on the battlefields of the East. The finest Europeans, those who are carrying out this task, are bearing the banner of the new Europe—and they're the men of the Waffen SS," said Himmler.

I asked him whether this was not a case of men, to be encountered in every nation, who undertook military service from a love of adventure and were now being given a halo as the champions of a new Europe. Himmler strongly denied this. "Far from it. I am having reliable statistics compiled showing the origins of these men. The intellectual cream of Europe is joining the volunteer formations of the Waffen SS."

Field Headquarters
25th February, 1944

I saw Waffen SS General Berger today when two officers were reporting to him; they had field-grey fezes with German badges of high rank. Meeting Berger in the evening I asked him about the Moslems.

Berger told me that SS General Phleps, first commander of the Volksdeutschen 'Prince Eugene' division, which was engaged in the confused and very bloody fighting in Yugoslavia, had described to him a year ago the terrible situation of the Mohammedan population in Croatia, Bosnia and the Herzegovina. They were oppressed, robbed and violated by partisans of every political colour. As the country was inhabited by mixed groups of Catholics, Greek Orthodox and Mohammedans, there had been the most fearful bloodshed, even among members of the same family. To protect the Moslems who were suffering worst, Hitler had agreed to Berger's proposal to recruit a Croat and a Bosnia-Herzegovina division composed only of Mohammedans, to which was later added an organization for Mohammedan self-defence. The Moslems realized that these divisions gave them protection and a new life for the religious and cultural expression of their individuality, which had been suppressed.

"It was evident both to them and to us that this required the blessing of Islam's highest priests. On my suggestion contact was made with the Grand Mufti of Jerusalem, and our ideas corresponded with his. Recruiting of the volunteers is entirely in the hands of the Moslem priests, who are far closer to realities than the Christian ones. Now every company has its aman and every regiment its mullah, both of them priests with the rank of officers. The Grand Mufti has inspected them himself. These visits have had an immense effect, because fighting against Tito and the Communists thus becomes for the Moslems a holy war. They are very different from the West European gentry who have prayers said for a Russian victory and themselves offer their necks to the hangman."

When I asked whether the Moslems were good fighters, Berger replied: "First class; they are as tough as the best German divisions were at the beginning of the war. They regard their weapons as sacred. It never happens, for instance, that a machine-gun is lost, unless the whole section has been wiped out. It never happens that a wounded man comes to a field hospital without his rifle, even if he has to drag it along behind him. His rifle has to be at his side, even when he is on the operating table. The Moslems cling to their flag with the same passionate courage, the Prophet's ancient green flag with a white half-moon, stained with the blood of ancient battles, its staff splintered with bullets."

Berger described the Grand Mufti's influence over these Mohammedan volunteers as tremendous. The Grand Mufti was a man of medium build with a fine head, small; he had blue eyes and his hair was red, turning to grey. The reason for this was that for generations his family had taken Caucasian wives. He was widely educated and could discuss mathematics or ballistics as readily as German literature.

Triberg
6th December, 1944

Himmler showed me pictures of the SS volunteer brigade 'Wallonia', after the fighting round the Cherkassy pocket, under their Leader, Degrelle, who had won the Knights' Cross; they were returning on special leave to their homes in the Walloon provinces of Belgium.

"The enemy Press declares that the local population gave the Waffen SS an icy reception on its return. In these pictures you can see the rejoicings of men, women and children. And why are they rejoicing?" Himmler continued. "They regard these men as *their* soldiers, *their* officers. Put yourself in the place of these people. Their own troops were utterly crushed in 1940. They were overwhelmed by their defeat. You only needed to talk with Belgian, Dutch and French officers in those days. And now defeat is forgotten, for we have given them a new aim, Europe's struggle against Bolshevism. We hold out a hand to the enemy of yesterday and give him a place among our picked troops. His sons become officers and are entrusted with commands, our own sons serve under them. In the Waffen SS volunteer divisions you can hear French and Norwegian and other words of command. Not one of my men would take it amiss to fight beneath the white banner of the 'Wallonia' brigade with its device *'Dur et pur'* (firm and true). These are no Foreign Legions, but European divisions in which we are proud to see our own sons serve. Have you considered what it means that we Germans let our own sons serve under the enemy we recently conquered? This is a sure pledge of European unity."

"You're placing on this," I replied, "an interpretation which it simply will not bear. If these men are really received with rejoicings on their return home, it's because they are fighting against Bolshevism, not because they're fighting for your Greater Germanic Reich."

6. A THIRTY YEARS' WAR AGAINST RUSSIA

Hochwald
18th December, 1942

When I came upon Himmler today, he was pacing up and down, very upset, apparently overwhelmed by some great event. I waited patiently. At last he said that the Führer had spoken to him very seriously and assured him that the war against Russia would not be over in a year or two; it would last at least ten years, possibly thirty.

Hitler had declared: "Behind Russia stand the numberless hordes of Asia. Russia is training and arming them, to send wave after wave of them against Europe and conquer the whole vast area between the Atlantic and the Pacific. Germany is only the advance guard of the West in the struggle against Bolshevism. America and England will have to take part in this struggle, if they do not want to be destroyed themselves. I have put the whole resources of the German people into armaments. The whole weight of them and all our man-power has been staked in the war against Russia. If German equipment is exhausted, then America and England will have to replace it, for the German people cannot produce another supply. America and England have not yet grasped this, but the time is coming when they will."

Himmler told me that he had asked Hitler why he let it be generally announced that the war would soon be over. Hitler had replied that if the Russians had allowed us to wait another ten years before making war, then he would have dared to talk openly about a long war, because the German people would have been so much stronger by then. But at the moment their nerves were not strong enough to endure such news. So he had to behave like a doctor who keeps on telling his patient that he will soon be better, though he knows that it will take time to save the man if he is to avoid a nervous collapse. It was hard, but there it was. And the Waffen SS were the spearhead in the fight.

7. CRITICISM OF CORRUPTION AND MEGALOMANIA

Hartzwalde
1st July, 1944

I drew Berger's attention today to the situation at home, which was constantly getting worse, to the gradual changes and signs of corruption, to the behaviour of Koch, Reich Commissioner for the Ukraine; the way he and others were trying to carve out a little kingdom for themselves must surely cause much heart-searching among the European volunteers. I also enquired whether Himmler was not going to do anything about it.

"Do you really think that I would be the man to make the mistake that was made in the First World War," said Berger with emphasis, "when thrones were provided for every other German princeling? Our young men in the Waffen SS, let alone the European volunteers, have not shed their blood for the sake of the Gauleiters of Flanders, Wallonia, Holland, nor of any other territories in the West or the North or the East. We are not covering up any misdeeds or corruption, not even in high places, nor some which pass under the name of police regulations. Wait until the Waffen SS comes home again after the war, then things will begin to hum. I brought this to the Führer's notice and he did not turn it down. Until then unfortunately we have to leave things as they are."

"It's a pity that this too must remain only a theory," I said. "But I'll speak my thoughts out loud: why aren't you the Reichsführer SS?"

"I did not hear you say that," Berger replied, becoming very military.

8. DECLINE OF THE WAFFEN SS

Hartzwalde
19th March, 1945

Himmler was very gloomy today, discussing the losses suffered by the Waffen SS. Considerably over a quarter of a million dead and

100,000 severely wounded, an unheard-of percentage; no army has
made such sacrifices in the whole history of war. I asked whether
this figure included the European volunteers. Himmler replied:
"Their sacrifices are equally great. A similar proportion have fallen
of the 6,000 Danes, 10,000 Norwegians, 75,000 Dutch, 25,000 Flemings, 15,000 Walloons, 22,000 French and the dauntless Mohammedans;
every third man among them is dead. And the figure is relatively high
for the men from the Baltic provinces, the Ukrainians, the Cossacks
and the Galicians. Blood has certainly not been spared—and every day
more flows. Wherever fighting rages, the best blood of the Waffen SS
is shed.

"I'm horrified when I think of still more dead. Does the rest of
Europe refuse to recognize that we are saving them from the most
fearful assault that Asia has ever made? But the Western powers attack
us in our rear and dispatch their weapons to Asia to be used against us,
refusing to see that they are also being used against them."

I pointed out to Himmler that the outcome of the struggle could
no longer be in doubt. "Don't say that," he replied. "We still have to
throw in our new weapons. Although the outlook is dark at the
moment, everything may yet turn out well. But if another fate awaits
us, then in this collapse of an entire world the Waffen SS will fight to
the last man, as the Ostrogoths fought at Vesuvius. For what should
these men do in a world abandoned to despair?"

Impressed by this fearful and shattering event, I pointed out to
the Reichsführer SS what his own final *rôle* would be: "I take it that as
chief of the Waffen SS you will fall at the head of your men, as Teias,
the last king of the Ostrogoths, fell in the battle you mentioned."

XXXVII

HOLLAND AND THE SAVING OF
THE HAGUE

The Hague
1st February, 1944

No w I am in Holland once more, with Heinrich Himmler, it is true,
and Obergruppenführer Berger. I am living in the SS hotel behind the
Palace of Peace. It is good to be here again after so many years' absence.
I have met dear friends again who are good Dutch patriots. For years
they have kept me informed of events in the kingdom of Holland.
Some have had to disguise themselves to escape the Gestapo. Infor-
mants are prevalent even among the Dutch; there are those who will
betray anybody for a bite of food. A few weeks ago Himmler said to
me with pride: "To rule Holland I only need 3,000 police and some
extra rations—then the police know everything." Himmler declares
that he has contacts with every underground movement. I do not
know about that, but one thing I do know—he has no idea of the
people who keep me informed.

This evening Himmler is invited to dine with Mussert in his new
house, which belonged to my dear friend F. T., who was simply
turned out. Himmler asked me whether I would come. I replied that I
was not invited by the owner of the house. "Of course you are," said
Himmler. "Mussert has naturally invited you too."

I replied: "Mussert is not the rightful owner of the hotel, which
belongs to my friend T., who has been turned out."

"Really?" said Himmler. "I was not aware of that. Then you have
some reason for your refusal."

Himmler is living with Seyss-Inquart at Clingendael, where I give
him treatment. After it, Seyss-Inquart appeared, rubbing his hands;
he made a slight bow and said he would make his report on the spot.
He gave Himmler details about the evening and who would be at the

dinner. Suddenly Himmler said: "By the way, my friend, who really owns Mussert's guest-house? Does it belong to the Party?"

"No, not yet," Seyss-Inquart replied. "It belongs to a very doubtful character, one T. There have been such a pile of unfavourable reports about him that we are obliged to send for him tomorrow. He also has a very valuable collection of old masters which we are thinking of putting in a safe place for the SS. Besides T., and F. van V. of Utrecht, we are sending for eight other gentlemen tomorrow." Seyss-Inquart smiled ironically as he spoke. "We want to send them at once to Dachau, for there they will be a little further away from Holland."

"Good, good," said Himmler, "and who are the others?"

"It's a matter of eight prominent men in Rotterdam," Seyss-Inquart replied, "one B. and van der V., who also have very valuable collections of pictures, which we will look after for the SS at the same time. Both also have large estates, where the underground movement holds meetings."

Himmler said it was a splendid idea to remove the people at the top; he would like to have details, so that the same method could be used again in the future. At this Himmler went with Seyss-Inquart to the next room, turning at the door to say to me: "Kersten, are you coming to the dinner?"

I thanked him very much for the invitation, regretting that I could not accept, as I was expected that evening by an old patient whom it was impossible to refuse.

Himmler said: "That is all right; do as you like."

The Hague
2nd February, 1944

This was an exciting affair! But with luck I have managed it! I was at T.'s last night. They are now living at Wassenaar in a very pretty house called 'The Three Parrots'. I was delighted to meet these good friends again. But they are suffering horribly under German oppression. The thought weighed heavily on me that in a few hours T. would be sent for by the Gestapo. Also present was M. de B. with his beautiful and charming wife; he too is involved. I had met him before. I told them how glad I was to be out of Germany and living in Sweden; and that I had the same outlook as all decent Dutchmen. T. said that this was only what he had expected of me.

I left T. at half past eleven and suddenly I had an idea—I must go to Himmler and save these ten men! My plan was already prepared as I drove over the viaduct. I made my way to Clingendael—in a few minutes I was there. I reached the first police outpost, showed my pass, was allowed through, and the same with the second. There was yet another at the door. I asked whether the Reichsführer had yet returned. "Yes, ten minutes ago," came the answer. When the man had checked my pass he called another policeman, who took me to Himmler's room. Himmler was sitting in his bedroom, his shoes already off. He was quite astonished at my appearing like that and said: "Are you also a thought-reader, Kersten? You've arrived just at the right moment. I've an attack of stomach-cramps coming on."

"I suspected as much," I replied; "that's why I came in such a hurry." Five minutes later Himmler was in bed and I started to give him treatment. The pains stopped almost at once and he was very pleased. Suddenly I said: "Herr Reichsführer, I have a great favour to ask. You're the only person who can help me."

"I'm quite willing," Himmler said, "what is the matter?"

I told him that I had overheard his conversation with Seyss-Inquart that morning and learnt that my friend T. and others were to be arrested the next day. I begged and urged him to prevent this, out of kindness to me. T. and D. were among my closest friends. Any steps taken against them affected me personally.

"But, my dear Kersten," Himmler replied, "what will you ask next? These men are traitors to the Greater Germanic ideal. Besides, I can't cancel the order. It would put my men here in such an awkward position. We have got to protect the rear of our fighting troops."

I was a quarter of an hour contending with Himmler. Finally he gave way and said: "Very well, I'll talk to Rauther about it tomorrow."

"That will be too late," I replied. "These gentlemen are going to be sent for in a few hours' time." He would have to call Rauther immediately.

"But perhaps he is already asleep," said Himmler.

"Then he must be woken up," I replied.

"You always must have the last word, Kersten."

"But I help you too," I said. "What would your health be like today without my treatment?"

"There's no need to talk of that, I am quite aware of it," Himmler answered.

"Can I call Rauther?" I enquired.

"Very well," Himmler replied in a tired voice. "Put the call through."

I gladly did this and Himmler ordered Rauther not to proceed with the arrest of the ten men in question. He would come to a decision about them when he was back in Berlin. Anyhow he did not want the matter to be pursued at the moment no matter what the circumstances.

As Himmler laid down the receiver, I said to him: "I thank you, Herr Reichsführer, in the name of Holland's history."

After a brief pause, Himmler said: "It does not matter whether we let one or two go free or not. For they are all traitors here, even Mussert. But I promise you that the day is coming when I'll have that rascal strung up, too. He imagines that he is going to be head of the government under the Queen of the Netherlands."

I started to laugh and said: "Then perhaps I have a chance of becoming Dutch court physician once more."

Himmler laughed and said: "That would just suit you. No, no, my friend, you are staying with me. For I will need my full strength after our final victory to complete the gigantic task of building up the Greater Germanic Reich, for my Führer. Then there will no longer be any Dutchmen in Holland, only my fine Waffen SS, who have won the soil in honest fight. It's a thousand pities that the Dutch were not re-settled in 1941. Then many things would have been very different today."

"It wasn't possible," I replied; "you were too ill. Your health would never have stood it."

"Possibly," said Himmler, "and possibly not. I suspect, Kersten, that you were a little too cautious with me. Would you have been the same if I had been going to resettle Mongolians and Mohammedans?"

I looked at him quite calmly and said: "It was for your own good. Your health has never been so bad as it was in March and April 1941. And you must admit that you have never had such acute pain since. Why now do you distrust me?"

"Yes, yes, I agree," said Himmler, "you're quite right, it's true enough. I feel much better now and I am very grateful to you."

This seemed to me the right moment to take my departure. Himmler called me back as I was going and said I should take some apples with me. Seyss-Inquart had made him a present of them. I put half a dozen apples in the pocket of my coat; Himmler also gave me two packets of chocolate. He added that I need not worry, nothing would happen to my friends.

ARNHEM

Triberg, in the Black Forest
19th December, 1944

While I was giving him treatment, Himmler told me that the pick of the English troops had lost their lives at Arnhem. The English had planned a large-scale attack with their best parachute units. There had been very severe fighting. In the end the Waffen SS had triumphed. "We had known for a long time that the English were planning something, but we didn't know where. Then, six days before the English attack on Arnhem, we got reliable information about it. So I was able to bring my Waffen SS quietly into position round Arnhem and give the English a warm welcome. This time we were more wily than they were."

I admired Himmler's sagacity and said that if he had not got wind of it at the right moment, it would certainly have been a severe setback for Germany. "I suppose there were no German troops stationed at Arnhem?"

"None," Himmler replied, "it was practically denuded of troops. The English would have had things all their own way. But, you see, there are decent Germanic people, who have a feeling for Greater Germany; and one of them was on the Dutch staff and he warned us. I will be eternally grateful to that fine Dutch officer for this."

I asked Himmler: "But how is it possible to get a warning through the front line?"

"You must let that be my secret," Himmler answered, laughing. "I can tell you nothing about the details."

Hartzwalde
8th March, 1945

Dr. Brandt showed me a secret order of Hitler's this morning, telling the Reichsführer SS, in the event of withdrawal from Holland, to arrange for the blowing up of the fortress of Clingendael, the city of The Hague, with all important buildings and the Zuyder Zee dam. Brandt was as horrified by this order as I was. I said at once: "That must not happen." Brandt doubted whether I would succeed in preventing it. Hitler had sent Fegelein to give the order to Himmler in person.

Himmler was in a very nervous state during the treatment and I was unable to bring the conversation round to Holland; perhaps I will be more successful tomorrow. Our only discussion today concerned the handing over of concentration camps with white flags on the Allies' arrival. Himmler began to give way on this.

Hartzwalde
10th March, 1945

I broached the subject of Holland today and enquired whether the old city in The Hague would be defended, in the event of an Allied advance on the town. Himmler at once answered sharply: "Defended? No. I have orders to blow the town up." Himmler answered my protest that the town's civil population were all there by saying: "The Führer has given me the order to destroy The Hague and I have got to do it. The Dutch have betrayed the Germanic mission for which our best men have given their lives. There can be no pity for these low-down Dutchmen. We have enough V2s to do it."

I told Himmler, in reply to this, that we had no common ground for discussion. I regarded The Hague as my second home. Quite apart from that, its destruction would be an immense blow to the whole civilized world. He could never answer to history for it. At a moment when the war was obviously lost, it was an act of complete madness which could only have issued from an unbalanced mind. He should consider whether he was to go down to history as the man who had carried out such an order without a moment's reflection. My words did not fail to have effect. But Himmler came to no decision.

Hartzwalde
14th March, 1945

I had another long talk this morning with Himmler on the fate of The Hague, Clingendael and the Dam. I put my point of view to him again and appealed to him in the name of humanity not to carry out Hitler's secret order. Then I went straight to the point and asked Himmler whether it was not possible to give a direct order to the responsible authorities that nothing be blown up.

Himmler replied that Germany's military position had so deterio-rated that first place had to be given to military considerations. I pointed out to him that military considerations did not arise here. The blowing up of Clingendael would not affect the course of the war one way or another. But it could not be a matter of indifference whether thousands and thousands of innocent men, women and children were destroyed; he could not answer to history for such a crime. Such an order would be viewed as the ravings of a madman, which he had only obeyed because he had himself lost the use of his reason.

It was obvious to me that Himmler was hesitating; he seemed to be wondering whether he dared to countermand Hitler's direct order. Therefore I started on him again and showed him once more how the order could have no effect on the military issue. I urged him to consult his conscience and heed his own humanitarian feelings. I would have been able to understand his attitude if such measures could have the slightest effect on the course of events, but as it was it was incomprehensible. I saw that I was slowly gaining ground.

Himmler took his pencil, wrote a few lines on a piece of paper, then called Brandt and in my presence gave the order that, if the situation arose, The Hague, Clingendael and the Dam were to be handed over undamaged. Then he turned to me and said: "Then The Hague will not be destroyed. But the Dutch certainly don't deserve it. They have done everything to undermine our victory over Bolshevism."

I thanked Himmler warmly. "Once we had good intentions towards Holland," he replied. "We regarded them as our Germanic brothers. For us, Germanic peoples are not enemies to be destroyed; they have to be won over. Harshness has to be used on those who seek to turn us from this purpose; and those who are deluded enough to offer resistance are traitors. The Dutch have learnt nothing from history since the English robbed them of command of the sea. They will lose their colonial empire and then Holland, as it is over-populated, will sink into poverty. They could have helped us and we could have helped them."

XXXVIII

WAR IN SCANDINAVIA AVERTED

1. *A FATEFUL ORDER*

Stockholm
25th February, 1945

YESTERDAY and again today I was with Foreign Minister Günther, who drew my attention to this danger: the Allies expected Sweden to go to war with the Germans, if the remnants of the German Army and the Party were to continue the war in Norway—according to his information—after the collapse of the German front and the occupation of Northern Germany. I promised to fly to Himmler to prevent this; the whole of Scandinavia was menaced.

Field Headquarters
4th March, 1945

During the flight I went over the arguments which I might muster to Himmler. Today I put them before him: when the greater part of Germany had been occupied, the Allies would no longer recognize the existence of a German Government and German troops would be regarded as *francs-tireurs*. In that event it would no longer be possible for Sweden to remain neutral. The Soviets were already exercising strong pressure on Sweden and they would march through the country into Norway. The Swedes had to come to a decision, however much they protested against this; they had to choose between openly entering the war on the Allied side or being overwhelmed by Soviet troops. The second choice could only lead to the strengthening of Soviet power in Scandinavia. Where would Europe be then?

Hartzwalde
16th March, 1945

Today I put my arguments to Himmler for the fifth time and concluded: Moscow was openly counting on a return to Isolationism

271

in the U.S.A. after the war, which would leave Europe to England and Russia. But England would be busy with troubles in her Commonwealth, India, Burma and the Middle East, so that the Soviets would remain the chief factor in Europe. They could only be kept away from the Atlantic if the Germans avoided fighting in Norway.

Then Himmler decided to put this point of view to Hitler.

Hartzwalde
20th March, 1945

Himmler told me about his conversation with Hitler, who had been extremely irritated and had concluded with these words: "If we lose the war, the enemy will only enter Norway when it's in utter ruins. I owe that to the German soldiers who have fallen there."

My heart sank at these words, for I saw the whole of Scandinavia going up in flames. Himmler paced up and down in agitation. Then he said: "You've convinced me. Europe must never fall into the hands of the Soviets; that's what matters. War in the North must be averted, even if we have to make the sacrifice. I will order the SS formations to avoid opening a new theatre of war in the North and I will make preparations for a surrender in Norway, should that become necessary. I hope to bring the Führer round to agree to this in the next few days."

Stockholm
25th March, 1945

On the 23rd of March I let Günther know of the results achieved by my talks with Himmler. Today Brandt called me up to say that Himmler's orders to the SS had gone through and to add that Himmler said I could rest assured that there would be no fighting in Scandinavia. The former Dutch ambassador in Stockholm, Baron E. van Nagell, heard this conversation on an auxiliary line. Today I reported it to Günther.

2. *HIMMLER'S PEACE OFFER TO EISENHOWER*

Hartzwalde
21st April, 1945

In the course of talks between ourselves over the negotiations with Masur (see pages 286 ff.) Himmler suddenly asked me: "Have you any access to General Eisenhower or the Western Allies?" When I answered 'no', he further enquired: "Would you undertake to fly from Sweden to Eisenhower's headquarters and open discussions with him about the immediate cessation of hostilities?" Without waiting for my answer, he went on: "The SS and the Wehrmacht are ready to continue the battle against Russia, if the Anglo-Americans will agree to an armistice with us. It is impossible for us to conclude peace with Bolshevist Russia; any agreement we reach with her is worthless, as Russia respects no engagements. So we must fight on to save Europe from the horrors which await her unless Bolshevism is driven back. Make every effort to convince Eisenhower that the real enemy of mankind is Soviet Russia and that only we Germans are in a position to fight against her." After a brief pause he added: "I will concede victory to the Western Allies. They have only to give me time to throw back Russia. If they let me have the equipment, I can still do it."

I answered Himmler that unfortunately I was not the right man for this job, as I had no contacts with Eisenhower. I had never concerned myself with politics, but I was quite prepared to discuss the matter with Günther and to enquire of him as to the right person to make the desired contact. Then suddenly it occurred to me that there might be a quicker way. I proposed that he should get into touch with Count Folke Bernadotte, who was already in Germany in charge of the Red Cross transport columns which were removing men from the concentration camps released under the terms of the agreement between Himmler and myself. I imagined that Count Bernadotte would have direct access to Eisenhower. Himmler accepted this suggestion; he was seeing Bernadotte in Hohenlychen anyhow and would discuss the matter with him.

3. SURRENDER OF GERMAN TROOPS IN NORWAY, DENMARK AND HOLLAND

Hartzwalde
21st April, 1945

I spoke to Himmler today on the necessity of arranging a surrender of the German troops in Norway, Denmark and Holland. I repeated and emphasized my previous arguments: that there was the possibility of Swedish intervention in Norway and that further bloodshed offered no prospect of success to the German troops. Himmler asked me whether there was any chance of Sweden's allowing the German Army in Norway free passage through Sweden. From my general knowledge of how matters stood I at once replied that this was out of the question, but I expressed my firm conviction that Sweden would be prepared to intern this army. Obviously unnerved, Himmler replied that, not possessing full authority, he could not decide this question without consulting the Führer. But in view of the Führer's state of health it was impossible to bring the matter to his attention at the moment.

Himmler was very agitated as he added: "I care nothing about saving the Swedes, these fanatical neutrals; they have not waged war for more than two centuries and have simply prospered on the disasters of other people. The Führer was right when he said that the worst mistake of his life was not occupying Sweden at the same time as Norway; then there would have been no Scandinavian problem today." He quickly concluded the talk with these words: "For myself I am quite ready to evacuate Norway, Denmark and Holland at once, but I know how much the Führer is against it."

When I asked Himmler for a definite answer on this matter, he said that he was seeing Hitler in Berlin the same day and would try to convince him that evacuation was necessary. A month ago he had already sent a warning order to the SS formations in Norway for this eventuality.

Stockholm
24th April, 1945

Yesterday and again today I had talks with Günther: I reported on my renewed negotiations with Himmler which had the aim of averting war from Scandinavia and arranging for the surrender of German formations in Norway. I put this into writing at Günther's request.

I also told him of Himmler's desire to initiate talks with the West, while continuing to fight the Russians. Günther said that it would not be possible for Bernadotte to visit headquarters; contact would have to be made by way of the Swedish Foreign Office.

Later I learnt that the orders Himmler gave on my request had laid down the essentials of an agreement which others were able to bring to fruition in subsequent discussions on technical points. The danger of war in Scandinavia was thus averted.

XXXIX

A TRIUMPH FOR HUMANITY

1. *KERSTEN'S PLAN AND THE WORLD JEWISH CONGRESS*

Stockholm
2nd March, 1945

ON THE 25th of February, 1945, I was introduced in Stockholm by Ottokar von Knieriem, of the Dresden Scandinavian Bank, to Hilel Storch, one of the leading men in the World Jewish Congress of New York. The World Jewish Congress had received reliable information that Jews under arrest in Germany, hoping soon to be freed by the arrival of the Allies, were in the greatest peril. Orders from the Führer had decreed that, on the Allies' arrival, concentration camps should be blown up, with all their occupants including the guards.

Every previous effort to intervene, whether by way of the International Red Cross or through various influential individuals, with the purpose of securing the removal abroad of Jews from the concentration camps, had, with one or two minor exceptions, proved a failure. The situation had so deteriorated since this last order of Hitler's that, according to Storch, it was now desperate. Storch asked me whether I was prepared to make a direct approach to Himmler to stop the carrying out of the concentration camp order. I agreed.

In the course of the next day we both decided that this intervention with Himmler should also be made the occasion of a major effort on behalf of Jews under arrest in Germany, the aim being to help them directly with food and medicines, while also securing the removal of as many as possible to neutral territory. We drew up the following proposals:

1. Dispatch of food and medicine to the Jewish prisoners.
2. Assembling of all Jews in special camps where they would be under the care and control of the International Red Cross.

Storch considered that the World Jewish Congress might gradually be able to take over the provisioning of these camps.

3. Release of individuals on special lists.

4. Release of Jews under arrest and their removal abroad, chiefly to Sweden and Switzerland. For Sweden a figure of between five and ten thousand was envisaged.

The Swedish Government is behind this attempt and shares the opinion of the World Jewish Congress opinion that the blowing up of the concentration camps will be carried out as a gesture of desperation, with the result that hundreds of thousands more people will meet their death at the very end of the war. I fly to Himmler tomorrow and shall discuss these questions with him.

I received a communication from the World Jewish Congress with a memorandum of Storch's on these same questions, which concludes with these words: "We are aware of your deep humanitarian feelings and thank you for everything you have achieved in this direction; and we hope that you will be as successful now in aiding us in this very desperate situation."

2. CONTENDING WITH PLAGUE AMONG THE JEWISH PRISONERS

Hartzwalde
11th March, 1945

During the preliminary discussions there occurred, most unfortunately, an outbreak of typhus in the Bergen-Belsen camp, for whose occupants the World Jewish Congress was so concerned, and this was not reported to Himmler. At once I remonstrated with him and pointed out that he could not in any circumstances permit this camp to become a plague centre which would imperil all Germany; he had to take action quite apart from his feelings towards the camp's occupants. I had the satisfaction of obtaining Himmler's agreement to immediate action. In his order, a copy of which I had from Brandt today, he made use of the terms I had chosen in urging measures against the plague.

3. IN THE NAME OF HUMANITY

Hartzwalde
12th March, 1945

Discussions with Himmler began on the 5th of March. He was in a highly nervous condition; negotiations were difficult and stormy. He put forward the following argument: "If National Socialist Germany is going to be destroyed, then her enemies and the criminals in concentration camps shall not have the satisfaction of emerging from our ruin as triumphant conquerors. They shall share in the downfall. Those are the Führer's direct orders and I must see to it that they are carried out down to the last detail."

After discussions which were very exhausting, as they lasted for days and had their dramatic moments, I succeeded in convincing Himmler that this final outburst of large-scale slaughter was quite senseless, and, in the name of humanity, persuaded him that he should fail to carry out the order in question. Today I reached the following agreement with Himmler:

1. Himmler will not pass on Hitler's order to blow up concentration camps on the Allies' approach; none is to be blown up and no prisoners killed.

2. On the Allies' approach concentration camps are to show a white flag and be handed over in an orderly manner.

3. Further killing of Jews is suspended and prohibited. Jews are to receive the same treatment as other prisoners.

4. Concentration camps will not be evacuated. Prisoners are to be left where they are at present and may receive food parcels.

Himmler signed this agreement 'Heinrich Himmler, Reichsführer SS'. I countersigned 'In the name of humanity, Felix Kersten'.

That was the first decisive step which averted danger from the Jewish prisoners and at the same time saved the lives of thousands of prisoners of various nationalities. Never in my life have I been so sublimely happy as at the moment when I put my name to this document below Himmler's. I felt as though I were the representative of an invisible power, above all the powers of the earth. When I took up the pen to sign, I was still unaware of the form of words I was going to use. But as I watched Himmler's slow and stilted writing appear on the document, it became evident to me that in negotiating with Himmler I was representing a great power—humanity itself. I expressed this by signing 'in the name of humanity'. Himmler stared at me thunderstruck, nodded, folded the paper, and gave me my copy without adding a word. I pocketed it and got up to take my leave.

I had not the time to set down in detail the phases of these negotiations with Himmler which preceded the signing, as I had done in earlier talks with him. New problems and difficulties were constantly cropping up; I sat for hours at the telephone and made use of every contact available to me. Brandt helped me, sounded Himmler and prepared the ground for the next deal. Though it is obvious to any outsider that the end is near, Himmler, in a way that is quite inexplicable to me, still lives in constant fear of Hitler and those around him, especially Goebbels and Bormann. I noticed it again and again when I broached other points agreed between myself and Storch. Left to himself Himmler would make far-reaching concessions, if only he was not possessed by this constant fear. Obviously there is always on his mind the possibility that at the very last moment the situation may radically alter—and then how would he stand with his Führer?

It is quite evident to me now how powerful is the hypnotic influence which Hitler has exercised over Himmler. He is still subject to this hypnotic power, even though it is obvious that the end is at hand. He is constantly swearing me to the strictest secrecy; his worst worry is that the document will fall into the hands of 'the jackals of the Press'. I must promise him on my word of honour not to show the document to a living soul; no copies must be made; it may not be photographed. I took this memorable document with me to Sweden.

4. THE QUESTION OF·RELEASING THE PRISONERS

Hartzwalde
13th March, 1945

I asked Himmler today for the release of the French women in the Ravensbrück camp, which he had already promised me in December 1944. I pointed out to him that there was no reason for holding them any longer, as France was no longer under German occupation; the purpose of their arrest had lost all meaning. I thought that this request of mine would be a comparatively easy one, but to my astonishment I found that Himmler was not inclined to accede to it. Apparently some of the prisoners were held on higher orders and Himmler was fearful of complications. After much delay and some stormy discussions, Himmler finally agreed to the release of 800 French women and their removal to Sweden. At the same time he declared that he wanted to keep some in order to have a hold over France. It seems that he will select women whose release involves no danger. I am to get in touch with Brandt at once as to measures to secure the women's immediate liberation.

5. THE TREATMENT OF JEWISH PRISONERS

Hartzwalde
14th March, 1945

I went with Himmler today into the question of releasing Jews in the Bergen-Belsen camp. They are all to receive South American passports and permission to enter Sweden. I asked Himmler to consent to the removal of these Jews. I observed that the World Jewish Congress attached great importance to the release of these Jews and gave him Storch's memorandum, which he read through very carefully. He gave it back to me without defining his attitude.

On another point I had more success. Himmler showed himself well disposed towards the dispatch of food and medicines to concentration camps; these were to be addressed to individuals in the first instance, whether Jews, Dutch, Norwegians, Danes, French, English, Belgians or North Americans. If the individuals could not be found, they were to be shared out equally among other occupants of the camp, so that in any event the prisoners would benefit.

15th March, 1945

Himmler told me during today's treatment that he would go fully into the question of releasing definite categories of Jewish prisoners to Sweden and Switzerland; and would let me have further information on the matter. He also promised to discuss it with Count Bernadotte.

At the same time Himmler raised the question of half-Jews. A few days previously I had told Brandt that there was no sense in sending any more half-Jews into the concentration camps at a time when the question of releasing a number of full-blooded Jews was under consideration. Apparently Brandt had brought this to Himmler's attention. He was remarkably reluctant to yield on this point. I showed him how unreasonable this attitude was and how persistence in it would be bound to affect civilized opinion in Europe towards Germany. My arguments clearly impressed Himmler, with the result that, in my presence, he gave Brandt the order to put a stop to proceedings against half-Jews and those of mixed blood.

I took this opportunity to propose to Himmler the assembling of all Jews in special camps under the control of the Red Cross, which would also be responsible for looking after and feeding them. Himmler was very well disposed towards this suggestion. He showed considerable appreciation. I was very pleased to have made progress on all the matters discussed with Storch.

Hartzwalde
16th March, 1945

I again discussed with Himmler today the release of certain categories of Jews to go to Sweden and Switzerland; I had gone through with him the lists given me which concerned the release of various individuals. Himmler was very open with me and promised to go thoroughly into the question of releases. I had the impression that he was prepared to make more concessions. He raised the matter of transport himself and remarked that Sweden or Switzerland would have to be responsible for this.

I took advantage of this favourable moment to talk to Himmler again about the treatment of Jews in concentration camps. He drew up a special order in my presence which forbade any sort of cruelty to Jewish prisoners and prohibited the killing of Jews. Later, on the 24th of March, he sent detailed instructions to all camp commandants ordering humane treatment of Jews. From that date every camp commandant would be held responsible for every Jewish prisoner's death and would be obliged to make an exact report on the circumstances.

Himmler emphasized that all these concessions would be withdrawn if they became the subject of comment in the world Press and were interpreted as a sign of weakness on Germany's part.

6. RELEASE OF JEWISH AND SCANDINAVIAN PRISONERS

Hartzwalde
17th March, 1945

Having once more raised the question of releasing certain categories of Jewish prisoners with Himmler, I got from him today the assurance that he would let 5,000 of them go; they could be removed either to Sweden or Switzerland. Some urgent telephone calls interrupted our discussions. I took the opportunity to tell Brandt how far I had got and to ask him whether it was not possible, once the principle had been accepted, to raise the figure of those to be released. Brandt agreed and said that with time and discretion it should not be difficult at least to double it.

When I was summoned to Himmler again, I tackled the problem of releasing Scandinavian prisoners and all those for whose release I had asked Himmler at an earlier date. I had ready a comprehensive list for this purpose. Himmler promised greater concessions, but postponed his final decision until he had examined the matter.

7. *PLAN FOR NEGOTIATIONS BETWEEN HIMMLER AND THE WORLD JEWISH CONGRESS*

17th March, 1945

I took advantage of the favourable prospects to put before Himmler a plan which had occurred to me today as I was considering the best way of securing more releases. The idea came to me of arranging a meeting between Himmler and the representative of the World Jewish Congress. It was an attractive proposition. If it succeeded Himmler would have accepted an atmosphere of agreement in which he might be ready to make very great concessions; it would also serve as a test for the sincerity of all his promises. It would moreover be a great historic event, the day when Himmler and the representative of the World Jewish Congress sat down at the same table to discuss matters with each other. I was very curious to see Himmler's reaction to the proposal. At first he promptly refused. "I can never receive a Jew. If the Führer were to hear of it, he would have me shot dead on the spot." I had expected that—always this fear of the Führer; yet it was an encouraging sign, for he said nothing about refusing on his own account.

I seized hold of this, therefore, and acted as though he had himself already agreed to it; and I asserted that his position as head of the German police responsible for frontier control gave him every facility for preserving complete secrecy about flights into and out of the country. If he gave the proper instructions, neither Goebbels, nor Bormann, nor Hitler would hear a thing about it.

This was apparent to Himmler. I proposed that the talks should take place at Hartzwalde. It would be for him to decide who was to take part in them. Himmler said that only Brandt and Schellenberg could be considered. I replied that I was entirely agreeable to this and asked whether I might inform Herr Storch, the representative of the World Jewish Congress, that he was prepared to discuss things personally. Himmler waited a moment before giving his answer, then said: "Yes, Herr Kersten, you may."

Hartzwalde
18*th March,* 1945

When I was with Himmler today I returned to the question of a meeting between him and the representative of the World Jewish Congress. At first I tried to find out whether Himmler had gone back on his decision at all, but that was not the case. Next I informed him that on the other side the question of a safe conduct would surely arise, and I asked whether he could give me assurances on this point. Himmler replied: "Nothing will happen to Herr Storch; I pledge my honour and my life on that." This was enough for me. I was intensely curious as to how this affair would develop.

On the 22nd of March I am to fly to Sweden to report. Before going I shall write a letter to Himmler detailing our agreement, which I shall give to Brandt as a safeguard against anything that might happen. I shall also give Brandt an exact account of all those points on which Himmler has shown himself well disposed, but has not yet given a final decision. Brandt is really an extraordinary help to me as well as a friend.

8. GOODWILL?

21*st March,* 1945

Dr. Brandt wrote to me in reply saying that Himmler had shown his goodwill in granting the requests made to him. At the same time Brandt informed me that Himmler had meanwhile also granted some extra requests on which he had been unable to come to an immediate decison before.

I also received by special messenger a personal letter from Himmler which gave me very great pleasure and satisfaction. Himmler informed me that the release of 2,700 Jews had now taken place, those for whom I had interceded on the occasion of the Swiss initiative to rescue Jewish prisoners in August 1944. I can also take with me to Sweden the reassuring news that effective measures were being taken to combat the outbreak of spotted typhus in the Bergen-Belsen camp.

It is good that I can take this letter and the assurance that other requests will be granted with me to Sweden. The letter came before Himmler had received mine in which I summarized our agreements, so that he wrote of his own accord to express his reactions to all the negotiations I had conducted with him in recent weeks 'in the name of humanity'.

Does Himmler realize that all is lost? So that he no longer feels himself obliged to carry out his fearful task of annihilating the Jews and feels that he can now revert to his original ideas? For he had often before said that he had other ideas for solving the Jewish problem in Germany.

9. NEGOTIATIONS IN STOCKHOLM

Stockholm
22nd March, 1945

I arrived safely in Stockholm and went at once to Günther to report to him on the results of my trip. He was very satisfied with the agreement obtained. The concentration camp rescues particularly impressed him—he called this 'a political event of global importance'. Günther wanted to know the approximate number of prisoners to be transported to Sweden. I said there would be between twenty and twenty-five thousand: between a thousand and fifteen hundred Dutch and the same number of French, between five and six hundred Belgians, five hundred Poles, seven thousand Norwegians, five thousand Danes and between five and six thousand Jews. The figures to which Himmler had agreed were somewhat lower than this, but Dr. Brandt and Schellenberg had given me a firm promise that they would be exceeded when the transport arrived.

Günther thanked me and said: "These people will all be heartily welcome in Sweden." Sweden would spare no efforts and no expense in fetching them. Finally he asked me whether I was prepared, if it should prove necessary, to fly to Germany again to help in case of still greater difficulties arose. I agreed. Günther thought that it would be a great step if Himmler and Storch should meet. But he did not think that it would come off, as there had been repeated efforts to make similar arrangements in recent years, but always without success.

I replied: "I am convinced that it will come off. I hope to be able to fly with Storch to Berlin next week." I am expecting Storch tomorrow morning.

Stockholm
23rd March, 1945

Today I had a letter from Himmler telling me that my intervention on behalf of the former Austrian Chancellor Seitz had met with success and that he had been released.

Storch came to see me this morning at eleven o'clock. He said that he was quite willing to treat with Himmler personally, provided that I would accompany him. I said that I was ready to do so. I informed Himmler by telephone of Storch's agreement. Storch was highly delighted at the results of my negotiations with Himmler. I have an impression that he is not quite convinced of all that I have told him and is afraid that I am mistaking my own wishes for concrete facts. At the end of the interview Storch said to me: "Jews all over the world will be eternally grateful to you."

Stockholm
13th April, 1945

In the last few days Storch has kept me constantly informed of further needs and requests which had reached him through agreed channels. As I am in a position to telephone directly to my secretary and to Brandt, this enables me to continue the discussions initiated with Himmler and members of his Stockholm staff and to have these special requests carried out. Storch was most concerned about further confirmation of the assurance given me by Himmler about stopping the killing and evacuation of Jews in concentration camps and the orderly handing over of the camps with white flags to the Allies. I got this confirmation from Himmler by telephone.

I also had a letter from Dr. Brandt, written on the 8th of April, which Count Bernadotte brought from Berlin for me on the 10th. In this Dr. Brandt confirmed that the search for individual prisoners was being pursued, that a new commandant had been appointed to the Bergen-Belsen camp and that the Red Cross were being allowed to visit Theresienstadt. I immediately communicated this news to Storch. All this prepared the way for the coming journey and a meeting between Himmler and Storch.

10. *THE SECRET FLIGHT TO HIMMLER*

Stockholm
17th April, 1945

Himmler has now fixed a date on which he would receive Storch. But Storch has said he is unable to go. Norbert Masur, director of the Swedish section in the World Jewish Congress, New York, is to take his place. He has no entry visa, but will travel incognito under the promise of a safe conduct in my company. Himmler expressly demands that the German Embassy should not be informed. He is afraid that Ribbentrop would intervene and make trouble with Hitler.

Gut Hartzwalde
7 *a.m.*, 21st *April*, 1945

I flew with Masur from Stockholm at two o'clock in the afternoon of the 19th of April and was driven on here in an SS service car. Masur and I were the only passengers on the aircraft, one of the normal service between Stockholm and Berlin, which was full of Swedish Red Cross parcels for the Red Cross in Berlin. The flight took four hours, during which time we saw no Allied nor German planes in the sky. As the aircraft came down on the Tempelhof airport, we were greeted by a group of police, half a dozen smartly-turned-out men, with the words: "Heil Hitler." Masur took off his hat and politely said, "Good evening." On the airfield I received Masur's safe conduct from the Reichsführer SS, signed by SS Brigadeführer Schellenberg.

11. *PRELIMINARY TALKS WITH SCHELLENBERG AND HIMMLER*

Gut Hartzwalde
21st *April*, 1945

Schellenberg reached Hartzwalde at two o'clock in the morning of the 20th of April. We had a thorough discussion of the Swedish Government's wishes and of the need to release as many Jews as possible for Masur as a proof of goodwill.

Schellenberg was depressed because the Party leadership, in the person of Bormann, had been exercising such strong pressure on Himmler that he was not in a mood to make further concessions. The Party leadership demanded that Himmler should carry out the Führer's instructions: if the *régime* fell, as many of its enemies as possible should be liquidated. We talked for hours, considering the best way of getting round Himmler. Schellenberg agreed with me that swift relief was essential.

At nine in the morning I introduced Schellenberg to Masur, who thus had an opportunity of expressing his wishes. I got from Schellenberg a firm promise to support Masur's demands with Himmler.

At two in the morning of the 21st of April the Reichsführer SS came to Hartzwalde accompanied by Schellenberg and Dr. Brandt. I had a private talk with Himmler outside the house.

I asked Himmler to be not only amiable but magnanimous towards Masur. Not the least important factor in considering Masur's requests was the chance to show the world, which had been so disgusted by the harsh treatment accorded to the Third Reich's political enemies, that this had been reversed and humanitarian measures undertaken. It was of the first importance to produce such evidence, otherwise history would make a one-sided judgment on the German people. Various earlier talks had shown me how receptive Himmler was to this type of argument.

Himmler promised me to do all he could towards granting Masur's requests. His actual words were: "I want to bury the hatchet between us and the Jews. If I had had my own way, many things would have been done differently. But I have already explained to you how things developed with us and also what the attitude was of the Jews and of people abroad."

12. TALKS AND AGREEMENT BETWEEN HIMMLER AND THE REPRESENTATIVE OF THE WORLD JEWISH CONGRESS

After this preliminary talk outside we went into the house and made the introductions; Dr. Brandt joined us a little later. Himmler said "Good day" to Masur in a friendly manner and expressed satisfaction at his arrival. Then we sat down at the table and I had the tea and coffee served which I had brought with me from Sweden. Here round the table of my Hartzwalde house were peacefully seated the representatives of two races who had been at daggers drawn, each regarding the other as its mortal enemy. And this attitude had demanded the sacrifice of millions; the shades of these dead hovered in the background. It was a shattering reflection.

Himmler started the conversation by saying that his generation had never known any peace. He then came at once to the Jews and said that they had played a leading part in the German civil war especially during the Spartacus disturbances. The Jews were an alien element in Germany; earlier ages had failed to drive them out of the country. "When we took power we wanted to solve the Jewish question once and for all. With this in view I set up an emigration organization which would have been very advantageous to the Jews. But not one of the countries which pretended to be so friendly towards the Jews would accept them." The English had demanded that every Jew should take at least a thousand pounds out of the country with him.

Masur, who was outwardly very calm and conducted the conversation with Himmler very cleverly and with expert knowledge, objected that it had never been in accordance with international law to drive men from a country in which they and their ancestors had lived for generations.

Himmler made no answer but began to talk about the problem of Eastern Jewry. "These Eastern Jews aid the partisans and help the underground movements; they also fire on us from their ghettos and are the carriers of epidemics such as typhus. In order to control these epidemics, crematoriums were built for the countless corpses of the victims. And now we are threatened with hanging for that!" Masur kept silent.

Himmler at once went on to speak of the ferocity of the war with Russia. Among other things he said: "The Russians are no ordinary enemies. Their mentality is impossible for us Europeans to understand. We must conquer or perish. The war in the East is subjecting our soldiers to the most brutal test. If the Jewish people have also suffered from the ferocity of war, it must not be forgotten that the German people have not been spared anything either."

Himmler went on to defend the concentration camps: "They should have been called training camps, for criminal elements were lodged there besides Jews and political prisoners. Thanks to their erection, Germany, in 1941, had the lowest criminal rate for many years. The prisoners had to work hard, but all Germans had to do that. The treatment was always just."

Masur, who was now obviously upset, interrupted him here to say that it was impossible to deny that crimes had been committed in the camps.

"I concede that it has happened occasionally," Himmler replied, "but I have also punished the persons responsible." He had in mind SS Standartenführer Koch, commandant of the Buchenwald camp, whom he had had shot for corruption and ill-treatment of prisoners.

The conversation seemed now to have taken a dangerous turn. I intervened therefore and said: "We don't want to discuss the past; we can't alter that and we'll only create the wrong atmosphere. We're far more concerned in discussing how much can still be saved."

Thereupon Masur said: "At least all Jews who still remain in Germany must be assured of their lives, if we want to build a bridge between our peoples for the future." Then he asked for the release of all Jews.

Himmler again made no answer, but began to talk about the handing over of the camps on the Allies' arrival. He had arranged for the Bergen-Belsen camp to be handed over as agreed, the same as with Buchenwald. But he had been very poorly repaid for this. In Bergen-Belsen one of the guards had been tied up and photographed with some prisoners who were already dead. These pictures had received publicity all over the world. Similar things had occurred at Buchenwald. "The advancing American tanks suddenly opened fire and set the camp hospital aflame. As this was made of wood it was soon in full blaze. The corpses were then photographed and more material for atrocity propaganda against us provided."

Himmler went on: "When I let 2,700 Jews go into Switzerland, this was made the subject of a personal campaign against me in the Press, asserting that I had only released these men in order to construct an alibi for myself. But I have no need of an alibi! I have always done only what I considered just, what was essential for my people. I will also answer for that. Nobody has had so much mud slung at him in the last ten years as I have. I have never bothered myself about that. Even in Germany any man can say about me what he pleases. Newspapers abroad have started a campaign against me which is no encouragement to me to continue handing over the camps."

Masur protested that it was impossible to tell newspapers throughout the world what they should write; the Jews had not been responsible for the articles he quoted. The release of the Theresienstadt Jews had received a good Press and that was a reason for extending the same process. Not only the Jews themselves but other countries were interested in the rescuing of those Jews who survived and it would have a good effect even on the Allies.

Talking of the Theresienstadt camp, Himmler said that it was one of a special type set up by himself and Heydrich. "It was a kind of town inhabited exclusively by Jews, who also administered it themselves and managed all the work. We had hoped that one day all the camps would be like that."

Then we went thoroughly into the subject of releasing occupants of the Ravensbrück camp, which Himmler had promised, and their transport to Sweden. Masur pressed for detailed agreements. Himmler hesitated. When I realized that the talks were coming to a standstill, I asked Himmler to go with me through the lists which I had received from the Swedish Foreign Office indicating the names of those to whose release special importance was attached. Masur and Schellenberg left the room, as Himmler did not want to go through the lists in Masur's presence.

When I was alone with Himmler and Brandt, I impressed upon Himmler that he had to be absolutely definite in his attitude. He had to stand by our March agreement; it would not do for him to be less magnanimous than he had always been with me at the very moment when he was confronted for the first time with a representative of the World Jewish Congress. Himmler replied: "Then I will fix the figure at a thousand. But there will be more." Then he granted me the release of the persons designated on the Swedish Foreign Office lists.

When Masur re-entered the room with Schellenberg, Himmler kept his word and released the thousand Jewish women from Ravensbrück. But he stipulated that they should be described as Polish women, not Jewesses, in order to get round Hitler's express orders against the release of Jewish prisoners. To Masur Himmler emphasized: "Even the arrival of these Jewesses in Sweden must be kept secret."[1]

Himmler then discussed general political questions. He turned to the German occupation of France and declared that the country had been well administered; unemployment had been almost abolished; everybody had had enough to eat. Himmler laid strong emphasis on Germany's struggle against Bolshevism in these words: "With the National Socialist state Hitler has revealed the only conceivable form of political organization capable of calling a halt to Bolshevism. If this bulwark should fall, then American and English soldiers will be contaminated with Bolshevism and their countries given over to social unrest. The German masses, forced to look to the Left, will hail the Russians as brothers and the chaos in the world will be indescribable. But the Americans wanted it like that; they have won the war now and got rid of German competition for ten years. But they have only achieved this by aiding the victory of Bolshevism and digging their own graves."

The talks lasted for two and a half hours, ending at five in the morning. Himmler made no demands concerning his personal future, a thing which at one time had seemed probable.

I negotiated, in Masur's presence, partly with Schellenberg, partly with Dr. Brandt. Convinced as I was of Himmler's agreement in principle to the release of a number of Jews, I succeeded in these talks in securing Schellenberg's and Brandt's firm support for these two points:

1. The number of Jews to be released.

2. The strict observance of the agreements already achieved to relieve the lot of the Jews.

[1] Masur commented on this: "It was typical of Himmler, his fear of letting the Jewesses go free under their correct designation. Although power at this time was certainly in Himmler's hands, he still did not want to have any trouble on the Jews' account."

The important aspect of this second point was to prevent the passing on of orders which ran counter to the agreements and might be turned against the Jews in a moment of panic or confusion. As we had obtained Himmler's consent to the release of the Jews, Brandt and Schellenberg promised me that they would raise the number considerably; they would also prevent the circulation of any final desperate orders, such as the indiscriminate shooting of Jews and political prisoners at the approach of the Allies. The extent of the damage done to German communications over the whole telephone and telegraph network was some guarantee that this promise could be kept, as it facilitated the holding back of orders. Since both these men had previously shown themselves reliable in respecting my wishes, I had even stronger grounds for trusting them.

·In the course of the day I drove to Berlin with Masur. Dr. Brandt stayed at Hartzwalde to take the necessary measures which would give effect to our agreement. At our departure Brandt gave me the special pass from the Reichsführer SS for Masur to leave the country.

XL

PARTING FROM HIMMLER

Gut Hartzwalde
7 a.m., 21st April, 1945

AFTER the talks with the representative of the World Jewish Congress, Norbert Masur, had ended at five this morning, Himmler said good-bye to Masur and left the room with me. Outside the house I had my last talk with Himmler.

It was a constant preoccupation of mine to secure further confirmation from him that the city of The Hague, Clingendael and the Dam there should not be destroyed. I had been in Sweden for a month and could not be certain whether Himmler might not have countermanded his order of the 14th of March, nor whether Holland might not at the last moment be menaced with irremediable disaster. I asked Himmler whether I could count on it that The Hague and Clingendael would not be blown up, and that he would keep to the agreement of the 14th of March.

Himmler replied: "I give you my word of honour that I have stopped the demolitions from taking place. We have lost the war. The Hague is a Germanic city; it will not be destroyed. Certainly the Dutch have not deserved this favour, for they have done everything possible to undermine our victory over Bolshevism. As a Finn you certainly never had faith in our victory. Now I realize that you were right on many points."

"How should I have believed in a German victory?" I replied. "You yourself gave me an insight into the way in which you were unleashing a vast conflict against the whole rest of the world. It was an unequal conflict for Germany."

Himmler said: "Ach, Herr Kersten, we have made serious mistakes. If I could have a fresh start, I would do many things differently now.

But it is too late. We wanted greatness and security for Germany and we are leaving behind us a pile of ruins, a falling world. Yet it remains true that Europe must rally to a new standard, else all is lost. I always wanted what was best, but very often I had to act against my real convictions. Believe me, Kersten, that went very much against the grain and it was bitter to me. But the Führer decreed that it should be so, and Goebbels and Bormann were a bad influence on him. As a loyal soldier I had to obey, for no state can survive without obedience and discipline. It rests for me alone to decide how long I have still to live, since my life has now become meaningless. And what will history say of me? Petty minds, bent on revenge, will hand down to posterity a false and perverted account of the great and good things which I, looking further ahead, have accomplished for Germany. The blame for many things which others have done will be heaped on me. The finest elements of the German people perish with the National Socialists; that is the real tragedy. Those who are left, those who will govern Germany, hold no interest for us. The Allies can do what they like with Germany."

We went to Himmler's car. He got in, sat down and stretched out his hand to me, saying: "Kersten, I thank you from the bottom of my heart for the years in which you have given me the benefit of your medical skill. My last thoughts are for my poor family. Farewell!"

Himmler had tears in his eyes as he spoke.

The car drove off. . . .

XLI

BACK IN STOCKHOLM

1. *REPORT TO THE SWEDISH FOREIGN MINISTER*

Stockholm
23rd April, 1945

WITH the Russian guns thundering about us we flew from the Tempelhof airport yesterday afternoon to Copenhagen; thence we returned to Stockholm by train.

At Stockholm I went the same evening to make my report to Foreign Minister Günther. Today I handed him my full report and a summary of the negotiations with Himmler.

2. *HIMMLER'S WORD DOUBTED*

Stockholm
27th April, 1945

Storch is still unable to grasp what we managed to achieve with Himmler. He is specially dubious whether Himmler will keep to the agreement and will not at the last moment give a contrary order which will lead to the destruction of the Jews in the concentration camps. Relying on my knowledge of Himmler's mentality, I have assured him that this will not happen. I had also specially provided against this eventuality in my talks with SS Brigadeführer Schellenberg and Dr. Brandt, who were to prevent any such order being passed on. But Himmler kept to his agreement, as I had expected. I also informed Storch why the released Jews had to be described as Poles.

XLII

HEINRICH HIMMLER

1. *THE DOGMATIST AND THE ROMANTIC*

When I was summoned to Himmler for the first time in 1939 I found myself face to face with a man whose appearance corresponded not at all with the image one usually formed of a Reichsführer SS and head of the 'Secret Police'. It was a little man who gave me an alert glance from under his pince-nez; one would almost say that there was something oriental in his broad cheekbones and round face. He was far from being an athletic type, cramped, instead of being loose and elastic.

His health was in a very bad way. He was very worried about the severe pains he had in the region of the stomach, which sometimes lasted as long as five days and left him so exhausted that he felt afterwards as if he were convalescing after a severe illness. It took him a long time to recover from these attacks. He was afraid that these cramps meant some severe and incurable disease; he had a terror of cancer (his father had had cancer of the saliva glands in the stomach). As a child Himmler had twice suffered from paratyphus, and twice from dysentery; apart from that his stomach had never been sound. When he asked for my help he was also only just recovering from acute fish poisoning and had great difficulty in getting over it. In the course of a fortnight I was able to get rid of his cramps and I went back to Holland.

When my friends enquired how Himmler had struck me, I said that if I had met him in the street or in a public house without knowing who he was, I would have taken him for some respectable city clerk or a schoolteacher, or even a headmaster.

Soon I got to know Himmler better and learnt that there really had been teachers in his family; I noticed too that his real character was

that of a teacher. His position and the tasks assigned him forced him
to explain his Führer's ideas and their detailed development—but he
also had to teach them. This encouraged his natural disposition to
instruct, which also received a fresh stimulus in many other directions.
If we discussed politics, then he developed his views into a body of
doctrine; if we talked on some historical subject, he at once deduced
the consequences and applied them to the present day, laying down
what ought and what ought not to be done. If we approached some
medical topic, then here again it was Himmler who had his own
opinion and wanted to give a lecture on it. He had studied and obtained
a degree in agricultural economy, and he never tired of turning the
knowledge thus acquired to good account in advising others.

Yet he was not at all overbearing in these lectures of his, but quite
amiable and not without a touch of humour. A deadly seriousness
showed, however, behind this humour whenever it came to a question
of what Himmler considered beneficial or dangerous to the German
people and the Germanic race. He was always trying to extend his
knowledge by studying the latest literature. One could not imagine
him without a book or a document in his hand. However tired he was,
he always took a book with him to bed.

That brings me to the second essential trait in Himmler's character.
His whole attitude of mind was governed by an image of human
nature which rested on historical models. Himmler had drawn from
his study of history an idea of the achievements and behaviour of
Germanic man; and it was this Germanic man whom he offered first of
all to the SS as their absolute ideal; he outlined this Germanic man in
all his pronouncements and wanted one day to set the whole German
people on the same track.

This cult for his Germanic ancestors was an obsession with him.
There were no exceptions to the rule that whatever these ancestors had
done was right and proper. He looked for historical examples in every
difficulty he encountered, instead of using a sure instinct to meet
present requirements. For him history was the only means of dealing
with the present. The right solution to any immediate problem had
been found once he had a model drawn from Germanic history; to
reject this was to sin against the spirit of his ancestors. How often I
have heard him say: "In these circumstances Frederick the Great [or
some other ruler] would have done such and such a thing. . . ."

It was always a question of education with him, a question of
directing Germanic life into the proper channels. This tendency
showed itself inside the framework of the SS, when he directed that
every SS man before his marriage should receive permission from the

SS Racial and Settlement Head Office; it showed no less in his general attitude towards the marriage sacrament. Officer cadets at the military academies had to write essay after essay and make a thorough study of characters whom Himmler regarded as specially important, such as Henry the First, Frederick the Great or even Ghenghis Khan. He lived so much in the world of his imagination that he even regarded himself as a great Germanic leader, to whom Providence had assigned the task of developing new Germanic institutions at the side of his Führer. His belief in reincarnation led him to see himself as the re-embodiment of Duke Henry the Lion, while Hitler was the return of a brilliant Aryan figure such as is only granted to a people once in a thousand years. When Himmler stood before Henry the First's grave in Quedlinburg Cathedral he must have congratulated himself on finally accomplishing that mission in the East which this king had begun and which Henry the Lion had taken a stage further. He did whatever he could to promote research into the lives of both these rulers; he had all the material at his finger-tips. Henry the First was his silent counsellor; when he made the effort he even believed that he could hear his voice deep within himself. Symbols exercised a strong influence on him. His large round dining-table in Berlin was celebrated. Twelve was the maximum number allowed to sit round it, as was the case with the legendary King Arthur.

But it was not enough for the Germanic ideal to dominate the German people's mind and soul once more; Himmler wanted it to appear in their physical traits and revert to the original Germanic type with blonde hair and blue eyes, according to the Mendelian law. The whole SS was to be of this blond type; he wanted to have only tall, blonde and blue-eyed people about him. Secretaries in SS offices were selected from this standpoint, with the further object of encouraging marriage with suitable partners. After the final victory, he intended to have only blonde people in all important posts; then too his SS men would only get permission to marry if they had chosen a blonde and blue-eyed wife. He told me that he had calculated, on the basis of the Mendelian law, that this policy pursued for 120 years would result in the German people once more becoming authentically Germanic in appearance; history would be grateful to him and in a thousand years his life's work would be regarded in the same way as King Henry the First's was now. In Himmler's view the Greater Germanic Reich could only last for ever if all lesser elements had been purged from its blood. To him dark eyes and hair were simply the outward signs of inferiority; blue eyes on the other hand were always to be trusted. Himmler viewed the history of Europe as the eternal struggle between the inferior dark races and the light-haired Germanic Herrenvolk.

This theory encountered great difficulties with the dark eyes and hair of the Bavarians. Himmler got over this by saying that they had shown themselves so wholeheartedly on the side of Hitler in his struggle for power that they had given proof of their Germanic feelings and attitude of mind. Besides, the best of the Bavarians were all in the SS and intermarried with blonde women. In another generation perhaps the Bavarians would look as Germanic as the rest.

Himmler sometimes quite seriously asserted that a blonde and blue-eyed person could never behave as badly as one with dark hair and eyes; he was never able to punish the blond and blue-eyed members of his SS so severely as the dark ones. In such cases he always had a photo of the man concerned brought to him; it was the same when the question of showing mercy to prisoners arose. If it was a matter of deciding which prisoner to release, you could always be sure that he would select a blond and blue-eyed type. Blond and blue-eyed rascals showed great skill in exploiting this weakness of his.

This attitude and the consequences springing from it involved Himmler in constant battles with himself. He championed the Germanic racial type, yet his own round skull was very far from being nordic. He was all for sport and athletic accomplishments, but in person he was stiff and inflexible. It was really funny to see him try to adapt himself to the rules he had himself invented. Brandt laughed as he told me what efforts Himmler had made to get through the Sports-badge trials for the mile race, his attempts to swim and the figure he cut when skiing, which he tried hard to learn in later years. Himmler further maintained that Germanic man was always healthy and consequently he suffered all the more when his stomach-cramps were so severe that they almost reduced him to unconsciousness. He demanded that every SS man should exercise the greatest severity towards himself, but he could not prevent himself from being thoroughly upset by a boil on the neck or from being driven out of his headquarters to recover at Hohenlychen from an influenza germ.

Although a Bavarian, he was an enthusiastic admirer of the Prussian kings, especially Frederick the Great and Frederick William I, the Soldier King, who wanted to have his own son shot because he did not obey him as a soldier should. He constantly referred in his speeches to this Prussian austerity as an example to be followed. However ready he was to overlook mistakes in everday matters, the punishments he gave were always ruthless when definite orders were in question. He made Koch, commandant of the Buchenwald camp, suffer the death penalty for corruption and mistreatment of prisoners, although the man was an SS Standartenführer and held the gold badge of the Party. "Anybody who puts himself outside the community by causing unnecessary suffering has to be ruthlessly punished." He even had his own nephew shot, after he had been repeatedly and urgently warned and finally punished, yet still reverted to homosexual offences which, according to Himmler's outlook, undermined the country's morality.

He maintained that a Waffen SS officer should combine in his person iron discipline and the greatest degree of military efficiency with comprehensive education and exclusive racial qualities; and his achievements should surpass those of an officer in the Wehrmacht. He would have liked to be supreme commander of the Waffen SS, but in fact he indoctrinated them and was their ordnance chief, an excellent supervisor of their arms, equipment and supplies. Himmler was not without military ambitions of his own: why should not he manage to do on a smaller scale the things which his Führer accomplished? Friends who had been at school with him said that he had always had two hobbies, warfare and crime. Although he disputed this, he was really delighted when he was appointed supreme commander of the Reserve Army after the attempt on Hitler's life. He was given command of the Vistula army group, no doubt following an intrigue by Bormann and his set in order to show up his incompetence and bring him into disgrace with Hitler; but he would certainly never have undertaken this if his military dreams had not unconsciously worked on him.

2. HIMMLER AND HIS FÜHRER

Hitler's word was law to Himmler, supreme above all the ideals and directives he issued himself; when Hitler had spoken, his own convictions were at once laid aside. He regarded Hitler's orders as the binding decisions of the Germanic race's Führer, pronouncements from a world transcending this one. They even possessed a divine power. It was obvious to him that Hitler was on intimate terms with that other world, being directed by it and having a special gift for interpreting its messages. The phrase 'The Führer is always right' had a mystical significance for Himmler. Himmler would have had his own brother shot, or even shot himself without hesitation, if the Führer had ordered it. For Hitler, being the Führer of the Greater Germanic Reich, had to know why he made the decisions he did, even if Himmler could not understand them or thought they were wrong—in this case it could only be put down to Himmler's own lack of vision. Himmler was the mystical instrument of a higher authority which issued the Führer's orders.

The belts of the SS had these words on them: 'My Honour is my Loyalty'. This expressed his followers' absolute loyalty to their Führer, Adolf Hitler, for the Guard formation (SS) regarded themselves as his personal bodyguard. This oath which had originated in his bodyguard during the struggle for power became the motto of the SS. But this loyalty was simply loyalty to a man. Himmler had no conception of a loyalty which involved both parties, that trust between master and man which had been the very essence of the old Germanic feudal states whose history has left us such striking examples of it. Once Hitler had spoken and decided against one of the Leaders under Himmler, then Himmler yielded and lacked the strength of character to put the whole matter before the SS Leader whose boss he was, even though he clearly saw that he was doing the man an injustice. Brandt was able to relate to me many shattering cases of this. He called this the principle of 'Dictatorship modified by discipleship'. The capacity to resist was quite lacking in Himmler, even in technical discussions involving important questions of home policy.

Himmler had asserted that it was never his idea to solve the Jewish problem in Germany by actually annihilating the Jews. But when the opposite idea gained currency, Himmler toed the line, applied the policy in spite of all the harshness it involved and did what was really repugnant to him in order to furnish proof that he was no 'backslider' —also of course in order to take the wind out of the sails of Goebbels and Bormann, who always kept a close eye on Himmler's actions.

The same thing happened over the treatment of foreign peoples in the Eastern territories. How Himmler would have enjoyed training them in his own doctrine; if he could not manage it at once, he would have diverted the next generation into the proper nordic channels. What possibilities opened before him in the conquered territories! His scheme to pick out the best and bravest of these peoples, mix them with nordic blood and then transplant them to the old Reich was already worked out and ready to go into action when contrary orders came through from Hitler. These orders scrapped any idea of education: the foreign peoples were to be left to vegetate in a primitive way of life. Himmler once again submitted without a struggle and buried his dream, even though his heart was heavy. He once more drove the men serving under him into actions whose accomplishment could bring him nothing except responsibility for suffering.

Himmler soon saw how catastrophic was Hitler's policy when he had before his eyes their devastating effects as carried out by Erich Koch, Reich Commissioner for the Ukraine. The reports of his security service gave Himmler an opportunity to inform Hitler of these effects and he should have staked everything on altering the course prescribed by going thoroughly into the matter with Hitler. But he did this only in the rarest cases, and even then with the greatest caution and reserve. He never wanted to put himself in the position with Hitler where he would be making use of his reports to criticize orders which emanated from the Führer. I so often found Brandt in despair because Himmler was filing away the Security Service's reports, which he read most attentively, instead of taking them with him to discuss with Hitler.

I have often asked myself the reason for Himmler's behaviour. Why did he never dare to speak his mind freely to Hitler, when he himself was quite ready to be contradicted and indeed despised those of the Leaders under him who did not dare to open their mouths? He knew how to listen patiently when a man enlarged on his own opinions, provided the proper forms were observed. First of all I thought that he was not very sure of his own position and avoided putting himself forward more for tactical reasons. But matters were no different when Himmler stood at the height of his power. My next idea was that he was deliberately letting events take their course in order to take advantage of them and assume Hitler's mantle when the right moment came. I was confirmed in this idea when Himmler made no move, though he had read the report on Hitler's illness. It was conceivable that Himmler was waiting for striking proofs of the illness in its political effects. But I soon learnt to think differently when I answered the telephone during one of the treatments and Himmler turned to me with his eyes shining and said: "You know who that was? You have been listening to the voice of the Führer—you're a very lucky man."

When one has witnessed such an incident as this with one's own eyes, it is quite possible to realize Himmler's complete subservience to Hitler. An unfavourable comment by Hitler on one of his measures was enough to upset him thoroughly and produce violent reactions which took the form of severe stomach-pains. Simply an indication that Hitler might have a different opinion sufficed to make Himmler hesitate and postpone a decision until he had been able to make sure of Hitler's attitude. However much Himmler disliked a man, once he heard that the man was *persona grata* with Hitler he tried to get on the right side of him, took him into his SS and had him promoted. Nobody who had not witnessed it would believe that a man with as much power at his disposal as Himmler had would be in such a state of fear when he was summoned to Hitler; nor would anybody believe how Himmler rejoiced if he came out of the interview successfully or, better still, received a word of praise. But in the light of this one may realize how afraid he was of bringing anything disagreeable to Hitler's notice and how a frown would make him draw back in panic. Himmler had nothing in him to counterbalance the effect of Hitler's personality. Reliable observers have informed me that a word or gesture from Hitler could brush him aside or so finish him that he no longer dared to make a remark.

This weakness of his made Himmler suffer indescribably. He tried to strengthen his position by making the most detailed preparations; he thought over any possible objections that Hitler might make beforehand and went very thoroughly into everything before facing the ordeal of an interview. It was his specialized knowledge which saved him, for in that he did not have to use his personality in order to convince. In these circumstances it is understandable that he was by no means anxious to report to Hitler and was glad when he was not summoned, though it would have been his duty as a member of the government to see Hitler as often as possible and to put before him views which were often in complete conflict with his and grounded on the fullest information. In this state of affairs important matters did not get reported; the 'Führer's file' grew larger and larger, and when Himmler at last came to make his report he was at a loss to know how to begin.

He tried to conceal from himself and others this most unforunate relation to Hitler by a theory of the soldier's obedience to his supreme commander—although he himself was no soldier, nor were his tasks of a military nature. Rather had fate placed him in a key political office where such standards did not apply. He also referred to himself as 'Foremost paladin of the Führer', whose greatest ambition was to give the Führer the feeling that he could rely on him absolutely, as his loyalty was unreserved. In this Himmler was confusing the position of a man in command of a bodyguard with that of a statesman or politician. Both the organizing of measures on the home front and the consequences of the war led to a constant increase in Himmler's power. But his attitude to the man whose policy inside the country it thus became his task to administer or oppose always remained that of Leader in a guard formation (SS) dating from days when they were engaged in their struggle for power.

3. HIMMLER THE MAN

Perhaps his ancestry, of which he was conscious, may help to throw light on the various elements which went to make up his character. Himmler's great-grandfather was a guardsman in the service of Prince Otto of Bavaria, who in 1830 was chosen as King of Greece. After his return this Himmler became a police official at Lindau on the Lake of Constance. Himmler's father was tutor to Prince Henry of Bavaria, who was killed in 1916 while commanding a regiment in Roumania. The name 'Henry' was chosen in honour of him. Himmler's father then became a private schoolteacher in Munich. Heinrich Himmler, as he grew up, was surrounded by an atmosphere of officialdom, police-work and teaching; and he also received the impact of old Germanic ideals and gods which were being revived round about 1900. In his blood there were not only teaching and the meticulous exactitude of officials, but also the love of police and military affairs. From these officials came something of the subservience towards his superiors, which was so marked in him, but which showed most clearly in his relations with Hitler.

Himmler was extremely industrious in trying to do justice to his many different tasks. To the horror of his staff he worked almost every day up to two or three in the morning. A number of his interviews with members of his staff took place at night. He declared: "History will not enquire how well Heinrich Himmler slept, but how much he achieved. It will be time enough to sleep when the war has been won. There is always too much talk and not enough action with us in Germany. The Führer must have at least one man on whom he can implicitly rely, and I want to be that man."

From this arose the impression that he was concerned far too much with the details of his work, was far too apt to consider that he had to go painfully through every line of his orders and enactments, instead of limiting himself to controlling them in broad outline. He was drowned in a sea of documents. Brandt tried to organize matters in such a way that he was able to deal with lesser affairs himself, but he got into serious trouble if among them was something that Himmler regarded as important. In his colleagues' opinion Himmler lacked a proper administrative routine. When Brandt had repeatedly urged me to make his boss realize that, in the interests of his health, he should cease to concern himself with matters of secondary importance, Himmler's reply was to ask me whether I had never read how thoroughly Frederick the Great had examined matters which appeared to us as trivial nowadays. The secret of his success had resided in the trouble he took with the least affair of state. Surely I was not going to tell him that he had as much to do as Frederick the Great. He had to give his personal attention to any papers which were addressed to him; what would happen if widows, orphans and those who sought help were refused by his adjutant?

Himmler was personally incorruptible; he despised riches and luxury, and declared that his greatest ambition was to die poor. He received a relatively small salary in the region of twenty-four thousand marks[1] a year, which he managed economically. When I brought him a watch with me from Sweden and told him that the price was 160 marks he was concerned, took out his purse and paid me fifty marks, all that he had at his disposal, and asked whether I could let the rest remain outstanding until the first of the month, on which day he punctually paid the sum. In the SS he punished any sort of peculating with public money or expense accounts no less severely than theft. He would have liked best to follow the old Germanic custom and cut off the offender's hands. He never used SS property to enrich himself, but employed the profits from their woods, forests and industrial undertakings to extend the powers of the SS, to finance research, to increase the SS capital and to aid the *Lebensborn*, to support the widows and orphans of his SS men and to build up his intelligence service. Himmler despised Göring for the luxury in which he lived and was harsh in his condemnation of those who diverted public money to personal ends. Any sort of display was repugnant to him and he set against it the motto of the SS: 'Be more than you appear'. He was never tired of saying that the whole texture of a state could be determined by those two phrases: 'Honour is Loyalty' and 'Be more than you appear'.

This plainness and simplicity were reflected in his own manner of life. He was extremely moderate in matters of eating and drinking. His midday meal consisted of soup, then a fish or meat dish, with apple or lemon juice; he smoked a cigar with his coffee. After lunch, which was not allowed to last more than threequarters of an hour, he carried on with his conferences until his evening meal at eight o'clock. This consisted either of a hot meat dish or a pea soup followed by cheese and salted rolls. Himmler drank a glass of red wine with his supper, after which he lit his second cigar of the day. Then he went straight back to work. During meals service matters were not discussed, but nor was there any small talk. Himmler liked to discuss historical subjects on these occasions—the kingdoms of the Goths, the Vandals,

[1] Approximately £2,000.

the Vikings, the Vorangians and the Normans; the transformation of
Europe by the three great movements of Germanic tribes; the settlement policy of King Henry the First; Ghenghis Khan and his methods
of government; the great founders of states, etc. It was not at all the
case with him that he liked to keep all the talking to himself; on
the contrary, he liked his colleagues or guests to contribute to the
discussion. But he reserved to himself the deducing of a practical
application from such discussions. When he had guests, the food put
on the table was very much the same as at other times. They had to be
aware that there was a war on and that the table set before them was
very much superior to anything that came the way of the fighting
troops.

During the war the greater part of Himmler's life was passed at
what was known as Field Headquarters, far from his own headquarters,
which had the code name of 'Hochwald'. It was close to the village of
Possesserm in the Angerburg district of East Prussia. Himmler lived
in a barracks two hundred feet long, where he possessed an office
eighteen by twenty-five with four windows. The furnishing showed
taste but it was simple and suited to its purpose.

I was able to observe Himmler very closely in his personal dealings
with various groups of people. Unless he had special reasons for being
angry, he was always polite and formal, yet very often friendly.

Himmler was a married man. His wife, a nurse who had looked
after him in hospital, was older than he. The marriage did not appear
to be a specially happy one, but he always spoke of her in the most
respectful way. He had a daughter whose photograph stood on his
desk. Himmler was always extremely respectful towards women and
he detested any sort of double meanings or obscenity, seeing in this an
insult to his own mother. He was very fond of children. Widows and
orphans, especially victims of the war, received his whole attention,
and when they wanted to talk to him it was strictly forbidden to turn
them away with the excuse that the Reichsführer had too much work
or could not spare the time.

"Compared with their sacrifice," he liked to say, "the half hour
which I sacrifice to them is such a small matter that I would be ashamed
if I failed to listen to them or to give them the feeling that there was
somebody to whom they could turn." He went out of his way to
become extremely unpleasant if some official took too long to carry
out their proposals or desires. He always got the official responsible on
the telephone and made his own position clear to the man with some
severity.

Himmler detested any sort of pettiness. He thought that in the SS he had an organization of men who were decent and honest, with whom he hoped to regenerate both the state and the Party. He hated the little Party bosses. Those round Himmler made no secret of calling them 'village soviets'. He trusted the word of his SS Leaders without any qualification. Here too he remained a theorist and accepted it as obvious that every man in the SS was honest and unself-seeking, living plainly and simply. For all that, he did possess influence as a man who taught them something, though his SS Leaders saw his weaknesses very clearly. They laughed about his military efforts and were amused —especially if they were officers in the Waffen SS—by his utterly unmilitary appearance and the unfortunate figure he cut at Hitler's parades. But on the other hand they respected his simple way of living and valued him as their best advocate against the bureaucrats.

They usually appeared to have no inkling of what went on inside the concentration camps and regarded them as a political matter which was no concern of theirs. They regarded themselves as soldiers, a picked corps definitely military in character, the 'Reich's fire-brigade'. They had a great respect for Himmler's excursions into history and considered him an authority on the subject. His discourses had a striking and enduring effect on them.

His political colleagues were completely acquainted with his personal manner of life and forgave him his Germanic mysticism. But they did not regard his plans for the Eastern territories as at all romantic. They suffered greatly from his deficiencies with regard to Hitler and his hesitations and refusals to act when faced with unresolved problems at home which had been aggravated by the war; and the war itself posed many problems for a man in his position and with his power.

Brandt once summed up the whole situation for me in these words: "The Reichsführer SS has very able colleagues; he knows exactly what he has to do; the proposals which have been put before him to reform the existing situation have been thought out in detail and would have the greatest significance. But what is the use of all that if, at the very moment when the word should be given, nothing happens? We all talk about far-reaching plans, but when we get down to tackling a practical problem we work without any plan and simply tinker with things which at any rate have got to be patched up somehow. The Reichsführer has comprehensive ideas and plans for the future. But the really decisive question is how we are going to get through the next year."

As the bailiff of an estate, as the mayor of a small town, even in some higher position in the Ministry of Public Worship and Instruction,

Himmler, with his interest in scientific research, would perhaps have done valuable work. Fate gave him a position which he was not able to manage. There was something spasmodic in everything he did. I have already drawn attention to the division in his nature; it was fundamental; his own character was weak and he preached toughness; he carried out actions which were quite foreign to his nature simply because his Führer ordered them—even the actual annihilation of human beings.

This Himmler who had the mind of an ordinary civilian was dominated by another Himmler whose imagination was controlled by such phrases as 'The preservation of the Germanic race justifies cruelty', or 'Unqualified obedience to the Führer'. This other Himmler entered realms which transcended the merely human and ventured into another world. Thus it was possible for such things as this to happen: Himmler, towards the end of the war, explained to one of his officials in my presence that he should make it clear to the wife of a man who had been executed that this was indeed a severe blow that fate had dealt her—it was only natural for her to be upset—but that the needs of the state transcended any human destiny.

His severe stomach-convulsions were not, as he supposed, simply due to a poor constitution or to overwork; they were rather the expression of this psychic division which extended over his whole life. I soon realized that while I could bring him momentary relief and even help over longer periods, I could never achieve a fundamental cure. The basic cause of these convulsions was not removed, was indeed constantly being aggravated. It was inevitable that in times of psychic stress his physical pains should also increase.

Thus the reader who has some acquaintance with psychology is already in a position to answer the question which is constantly being put me: how was it possible that I was repeatedly able to influence Himmler in directions which were flagrantly opposed to the orders of his Führer, beginning with the release of individual Jews and going on to the reception of the World Jewish Congress representative and the great campaigns to release prisoners in the years 1944 and 1945? Strange though it may sound, this was essentially a medical problem. I might almost say that it was Himmler's stomach-cramps which enabled me to rescue my *protégés*—but not in the superficial sense that the release of prisoners was my price for treating Himmler; it was far more that when he was ill I first came into contact with the human side of Himmler's character. When he was in good health, this was so overlaid with the rules and regulations which he invented or which were imposed upon him that nobody, not even his closest relations, could have got anything out of him which ran counter to them. In the event of any conflict arising he would have behaved, even to his own relations, exactly as the law demanded. His blind obedience was rooted in a part of his character which was quite inaccessible to other emotions.

As this obedience to law and order was, however, really based on something quite different, namely on Himmler's ordinary middle-class feelings, it was possible for anybody who knew how to penetrate to these feelings to come to an understanding with him—even to the point of negotiating agreements with him which ran counter to the Führer's orders. Because he was utterly cut off from his natural roots and needed somebody on whom to lean, he was happy to have a man beside him who had no connection with the Party hierarchy, somebody who was simply a human being. At such moments I was able to appeal to him successfully.

It is also evident that disasters could only ensue when a character of this stamp achieved a position of supreme power. His was a vacillating figure; he had something in him of a Wallenstein, something of a Robespierre. He was accorded both the respect which controls armies and the terror inspired by overwhelming power. His head contained both the plans of a Faust and the schemes of a Mephistopheles; it was the head of a Janus, for one side showed traits of loyalty, while the other revealed nothing but a skull.

To give a complete picture of Himmler or reveal his innumerable rules and regulations is beyond the scope of this book. My notebooks, a considerable part of which is reproduced here, are only a contribution to a full presentation of Himmler. I know what consequences can be drawn from these notes and what is beyond their power. Whatever is taken into account, no absolution of Himmler can overlook the fact that for countless human beings his sole significance was death and destruction.

PHYSIO-NEURAL THERAPY

THE therapy I have evolved after years of intensive study is quite distinct from any other; it is a method which I have formed and tested myself in the course of twenty-eight years devoted to the scientific treatment of patients. Over this period of time practice has again and again confirmed that my physio-neural therapy, which is the name I give to my method of treatment, is successful in diagnosing and treating certain types of illness.

The essential element in my physio-neural therapy is not the ordinary sort of massage which aims at calming or stimulating the patient by manual pressure or the use of vibrations; its essence resides rather in its characteristic effect on the nerves. A practical term for it is a therapy of the nerves. Its special effects take place beneath the surface, for it relaxes the sub-cutaneous and muscular tissues and vessels no less than those of the skin. My therapy can then be described as a process for relaxing the nerves.

A very highly developed sense of touch is the first essential in a treatment which aims at penetrating beneath the skin and relaxing the nerves. Observations made at the beginning of my training in Finland as a specialist in massage had already convinced me that my finger-tips possessed an extreme sensitivity, enabling them to detect points where resistance was lowered or vital force diminished, as well as regions in the organism which are peculiarly susceptible to disease.

I made use of this special gift on the majority of patients who came to me at the outset of my career to be cured of their pains, first of all by seeking to locate the point at which the pain was most acute. Soon I was able to locate these points simply by my sense of touch, without needing to hear anything that the patient might say. But treatment was also attended by another result: in each case I was able to discover a thickening of the tissues in other parts of the body and also remove an unsuspected source of pain.

I had myself noticed in the course of practice that when I exerted pressure on one of the sensitive points I had discovered, my patients very often admitted that the pain travelled from here to another point, sometimes in quite a different part of the body. Usually I found a further thickening of the tissues which was sensitive to pressure.

It was much later that my own observations were confirmed when I became acquainted with the work of Cornelius on the treatment of nerve-centres and that of the Swiss doctor Otto Naegeli.

At the present time the great significance of my phsyio-neural therapy has been recognized and acknowledged by outstanding representatives of medical science. It rests on a scientific basis and makes no claim to be a remedy for everything. But it shows results which were not anticipated with certain forms of suffering and is based on the objective condition of the tissues before and after treatment.

As to the patho-physiological basis of my therapy I will briefly note that from a biological standpoint there is a very close connection between the circulation of the blood and the nervous system, mutually compulsive in its effects. Disturbance in the circulation can produce headaches; it can also be characterized by migraines. There may also be peripheral pains: neuralgia and other nervous disturbances in the functioning of the internal organs, such as heart trouble, digestive ailments, etc.; and finally there may also be psychic disturbances even to the point of fully developed neuroses. The contrary is also true: psychic occurrences, such as excitement, fright, worry, overwork and depression exercise a constant and often fatal effect on the vaso-motor function of the vessels and therefore on the circulation of the blood, also on assimilation, as in a narrower sense on the digestion and finally on internal secretion. This interconnection between the physical and the psychic has led to a whole host of these disturbances being designated as 'nervous' complaints. This term is acceptable so long as it is only meant to imply that these disturbances manifest themselves in the nerves. But the possibility of a cure in such cases exists, once it is realized that what the nerves require is oxygen, nourishment and the dispersal of unwanted blood; the strengthening of shattered nerves can be achieved by the mechanical stimulus of nervous relaxation and a basic treatment on the lines of my physio-neural therapy.

The fundamental effect of this physio-neural therapy, which is often really astonishing, rests on an intensive treatment of the tissues, based on anatomy and physiology. The essential point is its ability to penetrate, in a way that is quite beyond the scope of ordinary manipulation. Blood and lymphatic fluids in the vessels treated are pressed towards the heart while unwanted blood is correspondingly sucked back. In brief the circulation in the blood and the lymphatic vessels is strengthened and accelerated. The consequence of this is a more rapid renewal of the blood and a more effective nourishment of the tissues and muscles treated. Ordinary massage cannot include this specialized procedure, as this demands a fundamental and specialized insight into the anatomy and physiology of the human body and a technical training which is no less fundamental.

The practice of my physio-neural therapy is dependent on a preliminary examination of the patient which usually tells me almost at once whether I am able to help him or not. I undertake no treatment until I have made quite certain of this beforehand. My highly developed sense of touch, of which I became aware even as a child, and which has become intensified with the years, enables me to perceive differences in the thickening of the tissues in the various layers of the body. Ceaseless practice in the course of the years has brought this gift to a higher stage of development. Once I have confirmed that I can be of help to a patient, I never limit myself to one or two treatments but always a series, usually spaced out, with a fortnight's interval, over a period of a month or six weeks.

The use of physio-neural therapy is specially indicated in disturbances due to defective circulation, manifesting themselves in constricting pains, no less than in inadequate nourishment of the nerves and other tissues, or interruptions in the working of one or another organ dependent on them. I have treated a number of illnesses successfully: neuralgia, gout, migraine, rheumatism, menopause; intestinal, stomach and heart troubles; and the whole complex of occupational disease. Among the ailments that I treat are also exhaustion and chronic fatigue, weakness and fainting fits, insomnia, skin irritations, convulsions, nervous over-excitement, restlessness and worry—always provided that these arise from nervous disturbances and not from some organic trouble. A diagnosis according to the rules of academic medicine is often quite impossible with a patient requiring physio-neural therapy. But in the majority of cases I could proceed from my own diagnosis and confirm a localized disturbance in the supply of nourishment to the tissues, which in my experience indicated nervous trouble; and often I was able to bring considerable relief or even achieve a complete cure. Pains and sensations of ill-health were removed, the joy of living and pleasure in work restored.

The majority of my patients who were subject to pains of one sort or another had already passed through the hands of other doctors. The prevailing neglect of complaints which are only subjective had led many of these doctors to be suspicious, when a preliminary examination failed to show any objective symptoms of illness on which they could put their finger; they were inclined to dismiss such complaints as figments of the imagination. Today anybody who is acquainted with the scientific researches of modern psychiatry should surely be aware that the images in our minds and our imaginations possess an extraordinary effect on health and sickness. But this knowledge is not sufficiently widespread even among doctors. As long as this state of affairs persists, the reproach of being a *malade imaginaire* or even hysterical remains a very heavy burden on the patient and a great obstacle in the way of his restoration to health. It is tantamount to accusing him of only pretending to be ill. I am constantly experiencing the gratitude of patients whom I am able to free from the imputation of this stigma by means of my examination and treatment. To secure this release not only inspires confidence, but facilitates a real cure.

Anybody today who holds some very responsible position—political, administrative, industrial or in any other sphere of public life—is constantly obliged to impose on himself physical and psychic stresses which are not only unaccustomed, but may even be described as unnatural. Men and women of this sort are, however, for the sake of the community as a whole, least able to abandon their tasks. They can hardly ever escape the effects of civilization and city life, which are so harmful to health. The result is to be seen in the frightening increase of illnesses in these classes due to the wear and tear of civilization: today the term 'occupational disease' has been coined, and this is a 'managerial' disease. Illnesses of this type do not affect the elderly in the first place, but strike directly at those engaged in responsible work when they are still at an age which used to be described as 'the height of one's powers'. This sort of illness cannot be effectively treated with medicine alone; far more important is a complete alteration in the habits and way of life.

It is no chance, therefore, that has led to my gift of healing being directed, for many years now, particularly to these classes of the population. A practice extending over many years has convinced me that men who are obliged to make such inroads on their physical and psychic powers can nevertheless be maintained in health and happiness through a regular course of my physio-neural therapy, so that they can be equal to the heavy tasks constantly imposed upon them. It was always my sincerest wish to be at hand, unremitting in helping and relieving pain.

Today the discovery of vital nerves is in the forefront of interest among recent achievements of medical research. It reveals a nervous system in which every cell of the body is joined to another, which can affect the course of health and illness. The work and teaching of the German Professor Ricker and the Russian Professor Speransky have contributed to extend our knowledge of the nerves, which was formerly so limited. New therapies are coming into being. When appeal is made to Speransky and his assertion that the nervous system can cause illnesses and that a doctor can effect the cure of an illness by treating an impaired nervous system, I can only signify my assent.

I already knew that some thirty years ago, when I was an assistant in Berlin to my Chinese Professor, Dr. Ko; and in the years since then I have further developed the art of this treatment by means of my physio-neural therapy. In any case I have never given injections with novocain, impletol or other remedies to affect centres of disturbance, which were capable of causing pains and illness in parts of the body quite removed from them. From the very beginning of my practice I only made use of natural therapy, and my hands, with their gift of healing, have made it possible for me to turn this to the benefit of a great number of patients. The modern recognition of vital nerves enables one to visualize the further development on a scientific basis of an art of healing, which had already been known in Asia for thousands of years, though today it is almost forgotten there; a kindly fate granted me unusual gifts and an intuition in this matter which has enabled me to practise the art.

In his *Roman Elegies* Goethe uses a phrase which expresses the very essence of my art: "See with a feeling eye, feel with a seeing hand."

FELIX KERSTEN

INDEX

Made in the USA
Lexington, KY
22 February 2015